Strategy and Politics

This book examines the subject of strategy and its relationship with politics.

Despite the fact that strategy is always the product of political process, the relationship between the two concepts and their ancillary activities has scarcely been touched by scholars. This book corrects that serious deficiency, and explains the high relevance of political factors for matters of general defence. Each chapter aims to show how and why strategy and politics interact and how this interaction has had significant consequences historically. Neither strategy nor politics can make sense if considered alone. Strategy requires direction that can only be provided by political process, while politics cannot be implemented without strategy.

In summary, this volume will explain:

- what strategy is (and is not);
- why strategy is essential;
- what strategy does and how it does it; and
- how strategy is made and executed.

Written by a leading scholar and former practitioner, this book will be essential reading for all students of military strategy, strategic studies, security studies and war and conflict studies.

Colin S. Gray is Professor Emeritus of Strategic Studies at the University of Reading, UK. He has published twenty-eight books and innumerable journal articles. Recent books include *Strategy and Defence Planning* (2014), *Airpower for Strategic Effect* (2012), *War, Peace and International Relations*, 2nd edn (2011) and *The Strategy Bridge* (2010).

Strategy and Politics

Colin S. Gray

LONDON AND NEW YORK

First published 2016
by Routledge
2 Park Square, Milton Park, Abingdon, Oxon OX14 4RN

and by Routledge
711 Third Avenue, New York, NY 10017

Routledge is an imprint of the Taylor & Francis Group, an informa business

© 2016 Colin S. Gray

The right of Colin S. Gray to be identified as author of this work has been asserted by him in accordance with sections 77 and 78 of the Copyright, Designs and Patents Act 1988.

All rights reserved. No part of this book may be reprinted or reproduced or utilised in any form or by any electronic, mechanical, or other means, now known or hereafter invented, including photocopying and recording, or in any information storage or retrieval system, without permission in writing from the publishers.

Trademark notice: Product or corporate names may be trademarks or registered trademarks, and are used only for identification and explanation without intent to infringe.

British Library Cataloguing in Publication Data
A catalogue record for this book is available from the British Library

Library of Congress Cataloging in Publication Data
Names: Gray, Colin S., author.
Title: Strategy and politics / Colin S. Gray.
Description: New York, NY : Routledge, 2016. | Includes bibliographical references and index.
Identifiers: LCCN 2015034706| ISBN 9780415714761 (hardback) | ISBN 9780415714778 (pbk.)
Subjects: LCSH: Strategic culture. | Strategy--Political aspects. | National security--Political aspects.
Classification: LCC U21.2 .G6727 2016 | DDC 355.02--dc23
LC record available at http://lccn.loc.gov/2015034706

ISBN: 978-0-415-71476-1 (hbk)
ISBN: 978-0-415-71477-8 (pbk)
ISBN: 978-1-315-88241-3 (ebk)

Typeset in Times New Roman
by Taylor & Francis Books

Contents

Preface		vi
Introduction: the argument		1
1	Politics, power, and security	10
2	Peace and war: politics at home and abroad	23
3	War and warfare	36
4	Theory for practice	50
5	Making strategy	64
6	History and geography	79
7	Culture and circumstance	95
8	Civil–military relations	111
9	Politics and defence planning	126
10	Morality and its ethics in politics and strategy	141
11	Strategic future	156
	Key terms	162
	Bibliography	165
	Index	171

Preface

The idea of writing a book keyed to a serious probe of the several mutual dependencies between strategy and politics is hardly a very original one. However, to my surprise when I looked closely at the existing literature, I discovered that really very little attention has been paid to this most critical of relationships. Everyone, seemingly, agrees with Carl von Clausewitz that war, indeed military behaviour more widely, is by strict definition political in nature. This perspective on strategic matters is not at all controversial. Indeed, it is so far beyond sensible dispute that scholars would appear to have decided to pass over it in a consensual silence. In fact I came to realize fairly rapidly that many elements in the relationship between strategy and politics were not at all well treated analytically or, in some cases, even understood properly. In this work I have attempted to throw some needed light on the connections between the two clusters of ideas. I can only speculate as to the reason for the acute shortage of books on these subjects.

One reason may well be the complication that is anticipated and discerned in the relationship. Unifocal scholarship tends to be content with careful treatment of strategy, or of politics, but not with the need to relate each to the other. It is clear enough to this author that most, if not necessarily all, strategic efforts are foredoomed to disappoint their political parents if they are not founded and then sustained on deep enough understanding of the societies they are intended to influence. In point of fact I have been more than mildly surprised to discover how modest have been the official efforts to decide, settle upon, and then sustain, the political architecture of state and alliance policies. We should have been reminded by our very disappointing protracted experiences in Afghanistan and Iraq that war and its warfare always must be about politics. If the political rationale for international intervention is confused and therefore confusing to most local participants in the consequent action, sensibly purposive results should not be anticipated – and so it has proved in both Afghanistan and Iraq. One either works as a partner with the local cultural grain of a society, or one is near certain to fail. This dictum ought to be recognized as a truism, but a decade-plus of substantial misadventure in exotic places proved unduly challenging of American, British and other allied efforts. It seems obvious enough to this author that a permissive political context should be regarded as an essential enabler for any foreign intervention that aspires to prove other than a 'forlorn hope'.

This book may aid public understanding by/with its focus upon the persisting importance of political factors for the quality of performance of the strategic and military ones. I must admit that I was tempted to call this book *Politics and Strategy*, rather than *Strategy and Politics*, but I convinced myself that the theory and attempted

Preface vii

practice of strategy could encompass political process well enough, provided it treated the *ends*, in ends, ways, and means, with due respect. Should some readers choose to regard politics as the superior concept of the two, I would not be unduly surprised or disappointed.

Recognition of the high importance of the political is a feature of this whole book. This is not a history book, rather is it a sustained effort to probe and examine the influence of political considerations upon the course chosen for strategy. As a supportive companion to this work, readers should find my study of strategic history very helpful (Gray, 2012). At times it may appear that strategy and its military consequences can seem to occupy much of the space available here; by and large, I hope, that appearance will be more than superficial. There have been and continue to be conflicts wherein either strategy or politics are inappropriately hegemonic in their influence. Notwithstanding the neatly briefable distinctions that differentiate political phenomena from strategic ones, real-world experience commonly may more resemble chaos than it does good order. In this work I seek to explore the nature of the phenomena of interest, whether or not the picture thus painted is expediently well ordered for our disciplined attention.

This work rests upon the evidential base that I have accumulated over the course of nearly fifty years, living and working in Britain, Canada, and the United States. I have taken much by way of understanding from these three very different political and strategic cultures. In particular, I am heavily indebted to friends, colleagues, and of course my students. My list for scholarly gratitude is challenging to confine, but I must mention the following scholars with my appreciation for the quality of their efforts to let some needed extra light shine on the subject of this work: Carl von Clausewitz, Michael Howard, Richard Neustadt, Ernest May, Harold Lasswell, Jeremy Black, Patrick Porter, and Raymond Aron. These eight scholars, from six countries, contributed vitally to my conceptual armoury, and I am most grateful.

As much and most sincerely also, I must thank my professional computing helper, Mrs Barbara Watts for her devotion to what proved to be a heavy challenge. My ever tolerant family needs to be thanked beyond standard praise. I am, I hope sincerely, suitably grateful for their support and love.

Introduction

The argument

Reader's guide: The mutual dependence of strategy and politics.

Politics provides strategy with its purpose, while strategy provides politics with the way in which that purpose may be realized in practice. The relationship between these two vital concepts thus is one of complete mutual dependence. That essential truth duly said, this book explains why relations are never perfect, and may even appear to be absent altogether, in the real world of statecraft and military power. Indeed, some disharmony between politics and strategy is entirely commonplace. Although this author is a strategist by scholarly, and sometime also administrative, profession, he is not writing here in any sense as an advocate of strategic thought and behaviour. The main purpose of this work, its principal argument certainly, is as the substantive title to the Introduction asserts: to explain fully just why and how politics has to be the senior partner in its relationship with strategy. The seniority, indeed effectively the sovereign authority, of politics is rarely challenged in theory, though assuredly it has been much neglected historically in practice. These chapters explain that the relationship between politics and strategy frequently is misunderstood, often with dire consequences for those who were confused.

Before moving at full throttle into the argument necessary here, it is important to note significant general sources of harassment that typically lower the quality of political and strategic performances. Specifically, both individually and collectively it is all too human to make mistakes. The key to success is not an all but magical ability to avoid error, but rather an ability to adapt to unexpected challenges, including those produced by one's own previous misjudgements. The relevant standard to reach politically and strategically is best characterized as the 'good enough' rule. For recent historical examples, whether or not America and Britain were wise in choosing to intervene on the ground in Afghanistan and Iraq in the 2000s, did they manage to perform well enough to provide a sensibly defensible record of achievement in their protracted efforts? Mistakes in politics – and the resulting policy – are near certain to ensure that context for strategic performance will turn out to be different from the one anticipated. For very grand historical examples of the repeated recurrence of unanticipated strategic contexts, it is worth considering the heroic scale of faulty anticipation of future political and strategic context demonstrated by all the greater powers in the twentieth century, repeatedly. None of the three general wars of the period (the First, then the Second, and in addition the Cold War) was expected authoritatively in the leading capitals of global politics.

2   Introduction

Readers are advised that this book takes as a major, though certainly not primary, theme, the historically ubiquitous and even apparently eternal prevalence in significance of assumptions. An assumption simply is a belief that may be right or wrong, but always is made on the basis of a deficiency in evidence. For example, it was assumed in the West, the United States in particular, that the North Korean invasion of South Korea in June 1950 had been planned and then launched by Stalin, employing the Communist North as his agent. We know now that the invasion was principally a home-grown initiative born and bred in Pyongyang, with Stalin (and Mao) very much in supporting roles, at least at first. Given that the future cannot yield direct evidence, it is easy to understand that all forward leaning and looking behaviour cannot help be other than assumption dependent. History, political and strategic, is littered with the wreckage caused by false assumptions not prudently hedged with suitable 'Plan B' preparations. By and large, the greater choices in statecraft and its strategy have not been protected, albeit silently of course, by careful provision for corrective behaviour should unanticipated but possibly dire consequences occur: such situations usually are captured, conceptually at least, in the familiar Churchillian speculative hypothesizing, 'If....' As First Lord of the Admiralty in 1915, Churchill proposed, pushed very far, and then attempted to execute a maritime outflanking of the land-locked Central Powers by means of an amphibious seizure of Constantinople; seizure of the coast of the Dardanelles strait leading into the Sea of Marmora was the vital first step. The Dardanelles expedition failed catastrophically and Churchill was disgraced and compelled to resign from the wartime British government. His rather personal, though nonetheless brilliant history-come-memoir of the Great War (*The World Crisis*) was heavily laden with long retrospective guesses as to the opportunities for victory that simply were lost in and through this adventurous expedition.

This book seeks to explore and explain our political and strategic experience in realistic terms. I am impressed by official political and strategic performance that proves to be 'good enough'. However, it cannot be denied that the 'good enough' standard may prove distressingly tolerant of seriously imperfect behaviour and its consequences. For leading examples, both Britain and America were successful in their conduct of the two world wars in the twentieth century. However, although both chose policies and strategies with which the wars were won, a high price was paid. What was decided and done by London and Washington certainly was good enough for victory to be achieved. But the human cost, particularly to Britain, of a strategy geared to attrition in the First World War was truly massive, while the circumstances of necessary Soviet alliance in the Second World War set the stage for the Cold War of 1946–89. This is not necessarily to be fundamentally critical of Anglo-American statecraft in the two world wars, but certainly it is to claim that sometimes in history extremely high prices are paid in the mortgaging of the future for the purpose of securing necessary contemporary success. Of course it is vital to recognize that costs in the future unavoidably are unknowable, whereas success today is enjoyed in the present or at least the near term future. Somewhat cynically, it needs to be said, the likely high price to be paid in the future for success, even survival, today, usually is judged easier to manage currently because of the immediate afterglow of victory. Because the future is always unknowable, typically it is discounted with respect to awesomely unpleasant possibilities, on the understandable if occasionally seriously regrettable ground that, after all, the worst may well not happen! Government in a democracy unsurprisingly tends not to favour sharing its more serious anxieties with the electorate. That was true of the 1930s, while it has characterized Western domestic political systems throughout the nuclear era.

It is essential that the most important concepts for this book should be defined clearly. Consequently, *grand strategy* is defined as meaning 'the direction and use made of any or all of the assets of a security community for the purposes of policy as decided by politics' (Gray, 2010a: 262). *Military strategy* is defined as the direction and use made of force and the threat of force for the purposes of policy as decided by politics. With respect to *politics*, the book chooses to follow American political scientist Harold D. Lasswell, who advised that '[t]he study of politics is the study of influence and the influential' (Lasswell, 1936: 3). These are not chosen for employment here because they are eternal truths; they may not be, but they are better than all common alternatives and assuredly are good enough to capture what is necessary to be contained and analyzed here. From time to time it is necessary for me to comment on some notably poor uses of the concepts of politics and of strategy. Readers are warned that the language of officialdom, scholarship, and journalism almost habitually chooses to misuse these ideas in order to promote often undeserved claims for the alleged virtues of their thought and behaviour. This rather antagonistic characterization of mine applies particularly to the typically unmerited and inappropriate adjectival use of strategy as allegedly applying to some preferred course of action in the future. My choice of Lasswell's definition is explained by the potency, perhaps the essential truth, in his identification of the constant quest for influence, for whatever purpose, as comprising the core of politics. Examples abound: to cite but two of similar genus, in the US Presidential elections of 1960 and again in 1980, the essentially challenging contender, John F. Kennedy, and then Ronald Reagan, both won by running successfully against a particular idea, and some verified reality, of the Soviet Union. In both historical cases the narrative that gained the necessary popular influence was one that rested upon claims of American vulnerability to growing Soviet military power. The first category in Thucydides' justly renowned summary of motivation for statecraft, fear, is a hardy perennial, a truly stalwart performer in the search for influence with electors (Thucydides, 1996: 43).

Another vital distinction that tends to evade the more casual user is that between strategy and tactics. Although this study is all about strategy, particularly in its many connections with politics, it is necessary never to forget that strategy is made only of tactics. While strategy is all about the consequences of choices, military and other, tactics are all about the actual doing of the actions in those choices. Rephrased, one *has* a strategy, while one *does* tactics. It is a very common error to believe that there are strategic moves as opposed to tactical ones. This is nonsense, notwithstanding the conceptual indiscipline of armed forces around the world who claim in their organization that there are both strategic and tactical troops and equipment. They are wrong because all troops and equipment are tactical in their employment, and also, as a result of their behaviour, strategic in their consequence. The purpose and results of military behaviour are in the realm of strategy, but action 'in the field', on a great or a small scale, is the subject of tactics. The NATO Commander in Afghanistan in 2009–10, US General Stanley McChrystal, has written memoirs that are as excellent as one could wish on tactical and some operational matters, but are notably barren with respect to strategy and high policy.

As strategy and tactics frequently are confused and therefore confusing, so also are the differences in many common uses and misuses of the concepts of policy and politics. The former typically is not sufficiently well appreciated in its relationship to politics. It

4   *Introduction*

may be noticed that the concepts of politics and policy often are employed as if by casual choice of language by commentators in English on defence. While Carl von Clausewitz was only rarely confused in his theorizing about war, he has been found to be confusing when his German *Politik* is translated rather uncertainly as meaning either politics or policy (Strachan, 2007: 102, 165–9). The German authentically is ambiguous to us today, unless, that is, one chooses to see no difference worthy of note between these two ideas. In contemporary English, at least, there are distinctive meanings to politics and policy, and the differences matter greatly. However, the two are not merely linked, rather are they made essentially in a common process of contention about values. For Clausewitz in authoritarian Prussia, *Politik* referred exclusively to the political relations between states, whereas for us today it must carry a far wider meaning, often privileging a domestic focus. As noted already, politics is employed here as the concept that covers all thought and activities that bear upon the need and desire to secure influence. Often it is most appropriate to mean, if not always to refer explicitly to, a process. The idea of continuity is important to this book. My subject is corralled as a duopoly about politics and strategy understood and explained as phenomena that have persisted through all of history. In his *History of the Peloponnesian War*, Thucydides did not write explicitly about strategy as it is understood today, but certainly he wrote with and about strategic argument in language readily recognizable to us as such.

The eternal process of influence seeking and exploitation that we understand as politics enjoys a parental relationship to policy. As used in this work, policy refers to decisions for action or inaction decided as a result of more or less contention in a political process. It would not be wholly wrong to understand policy simply as meaning particular politics. However, in practice it is both more accurate, as well as convenient for clear comprehension, to understand policy as being the product of politics, as contrasted with being merely a reflection of it. There is considerable need for nuance here.

Although a security community will regulate itself and direct its behaviour as matters of policy and by policy, the legitimacy of that effort rests substantially upon the dynamics of often notably unstable political process(es), domestic and international. Although policy will be the authority behind action, politics and its process will, indeed must, be the authority behind that. Whatever we examine by way of episodes of conflict and war itself, we stumble into political controversy and argument. Whether we look at Vietnam in the 1960s, or Afghanistan and Iraq in the 2000s, we find not conclusively determinative policy analysis, let alone calculation, but rather contending political enthusiasms and sometimes sincere beliefs with noteworthy moral content; in other words, the desire to do the right thing and the good thing! And, in order to satisfy one's moral urge as a policymaker, one needs a vital edge in quantity, if not quality, of influence in and over the legitimating political process. Politics is the master in its relationship with strategy, but the policy that it designs and pushes in order to advance its security interests cannot long be dismissive towards strategic constraints. In practice, policy is the somewhat dynamic product of an effectively permanent political process. The reality of significant dynamism, or simply change, can be lost in casual commentary and even scholarship. Just about all policy, everywhere and at all times, in practice will be liable to change. The subjects here, strategy and politics, commonly are manifested in continuities of thought and behaviour, but even radical change is possible, if usually unlikely.

It can be a challenge to explain phenomena ever subject to change, yet which reveal distinctive continuity. One helpful way in which to attempt to understand a dynamic historical reality characterized unmistakeably by both change and continuity is through acknowledging the need to recognize irony rather than paradox. In historical practice one will have to seek long and hard, and ultimately most probably fail, in order to discover true paradox, meaning authentic contradiction. But, by way of significant contrast, history is stuffed, if not littered, with evidence of irony. By irony generally we mean the unintended and usually unanticipated consequences of our actions. An obvious major reason why history is so richly populated with ironic occurrences is because the unforeseeability of the future has to render most of our forward leaning decisions notably problematic. By way of a hypothetical example in contemporary statecraft, in 2014 the NATO Alliance sought to deter further adventurous Russian advance into Ukraine, but ironically, in the context of a considerable depression in global oil prices, and a notable absence of enhanced Western military power, Russia may seek added security by a policy of greater boldness. This unfortunate contrast between NATO's relative weakness in military preparation, and its strength of negative financial impact through economic sanctions, is a classic example of incoherence because of disharmony between instruments in grand strategy.

The all too contemporary example of weakness in strategy serves helpfully to highlight the importance of a vital contributing factor in the making of policy by politics. The system of strategy has a common structure at all times and in all places, regardless of culture and circumstance. The system of strategy is driven by what can be regarded as a political engine, and it generates policy choices, usually expressed antiseptically simply as policy ends. For the strategy system to work well enough in practice, there needs to be a tolerable mutually enabling balance among its vital constituent parts. Strategy works effectively when it is directed by policy and its politics to proceed on a course of forceful effort that makes appropriately effective use of the military assets available. Also, the whole endeavour needs to be founded on good enough assumptions concerning such critically important matters as net tactical effectiveness and enemy competence and willpower.

Although a security community can fail to perform well enough with respect to any of the four elements that comprise the strategy system – (political or policy) ends, (strategic) ways, (military and other) means, and assumptions – there is no doubt that policy weakness tends to be especially deadly in its consequences. Analyses of the politics of policy ends often argue that students of strategy tend to underrate the relative importance of passion; but I am not entirely convinced that 'liberal societies' have been as guilty of relative neglect as charged (Smith, 2014). However, the insistence that passion really matters certainly is an enduring truth about politics and therefore about strategy also.

> [W]e return to the idea of the centrality of moral forces in war: those intangibles, which can be just as important as material combat power and technical proficiency. Moral forces boil down to passions, the motivating spirit that animates war in this realm.
>
> (Smith, 2014: 36)

The politics of policy central to my argument often are better characterized by noting passion, than they are by attribution to the cold and bloodless calculations of defence analysis. The politics that share title here are always being more or less open to penetration and even control by the effects of moral forces usefully summarized as passion. It is more than a little worrying to appreciate that every element in the system

6   *Introduction*

of strategy is open, or should I say vulnerable, to the influence of the moral force(s) of passion. The functioning of the strategy system is likely to impose healthful discipline for prudent restraint upon the urges of passion, but before that general truth is demonstrated by events to be so, a great deal of damage can be caused and effected.

Clausewitz warned as follows of the danger that may lurk in popular passion. The peril of which he wrote was, of course, not a common one in his day, when high policy typically was the active concern of the sovereign and his, or her, principal advisors. Nonetheless, he was certainly right to flag the danger that may reside in popular passion.

> The political object – the original motive for the war – will thus determine both the military objective to be reached and the amount of effort it requires. The political object cannot, however, *in itself* provide the standard of measurement. Since we are dealing with realities, not with abstractions, it can do so only in the context of the two states at war. The same political object can elicit *differing* reactions from different peoples, and even from the same people at different times. We can therefore take the political object as a standard only if we think of *the influence it can exert upon the forces it is meant to move.* The nature of three forces therefore calls for study. Depending on whether their characteristics increase or diminish the drive toward a particular action, the outcome will vary. Between two peoples and two states there can be such tensions, such a mass of inflammable material, that the slightest quarrel can produce a wholly disproportionate effect – a real explosion.
>
> (Clausewitz, 1976: 81)

It is probably ironic to have to note that there can be immense peril in a sudden drop in the moral forces of passion if senior policymakers in effect simply succumb to fatalism. In both 1914 and 1939 policymakers would only strive just so hard to avoid war, beyond that point they all but collapsed and allowed the momentum of events to trigger the shift from crisis to war. This potential for collapse of the will to resist a drift to war remains a danger in the nuclear age. Statesmen can feel trapped and no longer able to exercise the necessary control over events: in other words, they might give up on the possibility of peace (Barrass, 2009).

By privileging politics here, we privilege also, as a logical and empirical consequence, the high importance of the moral forces that tend to motivate high policy choices. Material and other technical factors are undoubtedly of great importance to strategy, but, that granted, still it would be difficult to exaggerate the relative significance of moral forces (Clausewitz, 1976: 91). With reference to the logical architecture of strategy, always and everywhere it has been the case that:

- *Policy ends* are chosen, or even appear to choose themselves, as a result of political contention heavily spiced with passion.
- *Strategic ways* reflect preferences keyed to values and norms, as well as believed capabilities and contextual suitability.
- *Military means* are assessed both materially and, one could say, morally. If a will to fight hard, and possibly effectively, is assumed, even a grossly unfavourable imbalance of forces will not be definitively discouraging.
- *Assumptions* constitute a category in preparation of statecraft and strategy that can be maximally damaging in the ill effects of unsound and unlucky guesses about a truly unforeseeable future.

Introduction 7

Notwithstanding the ample historical evidence that supports scepticism towards efforts to be careful in the making of strategy, in practice states often do not perform anywhere near as poorly as I have just suggested that they might. There are sharks in the global waters of international relations, but fortunately the oversimplified menace outlined grimly by the 'offensive realists' of the recent Chicago School, led by John J. Mearsheimer, contains much exaggeration (Mearsheimer, 2014). Great states do not quest invariably after a superiority in relative power best characterized as hegemonic. However, admittedly such predatory motivation and behaviour has been sufficiently well recorded in all of history for us to be adequately warned. The politics and strategy pursued more or less assiduously and with variable success over the course of centuries, attests to a common familiarity with the perils of unmatched power (Simms, 2013: 530–4).

In the sharpest contrast imaginable to the variability, if not always the suitable adaptability, of the political choices in policy and the judgements (involving both calculations and guesses) about strategy, the essential logic of strategy is a rock-like constant. This text is about the rich variety of strategic challenges which political communities are ever seeking improved security in order to meet, but there is at least one logical structure that is ubiquitous and eternal: the basic logic of strategy. Of course, judgements about what should work well enough are almost infinitely capable of being wrong on some among the grounds that impact the feasibility and effectiveness of particular strategies, but the general theory of strategy should help discipline choice. It would be a serious error to dismiss the austere quadripartite architect that explains and expresses the logic of strategy simply as an unduly familiar and elementary mantra. The four interdependent elements run thematically throughout this book as a fundamental guide to aid good practice in statecraft and strategy. For a book which seeks to explore and explain the relationship between politics and strategy, the merit in the basic logic that connects all but umbilically, ends, ways, means, and assumptions is ever authoritative. Obviously, the values that need to be attached to each of the logical elements must be specific to the particular case. This is why Carl von Clausewitz argued for his theory of war as an important and enduring aid to assist the process required for thinking about specific military challenges. *On War* was conceived and generally intended as a contribution to the education primarily of soldiers, not as a source of 'how to' doctrine. The general theory of strategy does not exist for the training of would-be strategists, but rather for their education. Ends, ways, means, and assumptions may provide the desirable and necessary structure to thought for decision by politicians making policy. But, in the real world of shifting and unanticipated events and imperfect information, policy often, probably usually, is made on the basis of political calculation of a near-term character, and impulsive energy that may have substantial moral force. It tends to be surprising, even shocking, to learn that decisions to fight frequently are not made with noteworthy structural assistance from the logic of the basic theory of strategy. For example, on the evidence of British policy and dubious or absent strategy in the 2000s, it is not at all obvious that the Government or its senior military advisers ever sought rigorously in advance of events to think about its ends, ways, and available means for Afghanistan and Iraq (Elliott, 2015).

The basic four-part logic of strategy holds as a constant even when much else appears to be changing. For example, the Roman Empire performed the strategy function recognizably for centuries, as it needed to find effective ways to deploy and employ its large but limited military means for the purpose of maintaining or restoring security

8 *Introduction*

(Luttwak, 2001). The practical challenge always is to apply the ends, ways, and means formula to the relatively unfamiliar and possibly rapidly changing circumstances of the day. Running through this study is the repeated phenomenon of both politicians and military strategists who fail significantly to take sufficient account of the whole logic of strategy. It is all too commonplace for leaders so to privilege their political desires, their confidence in tried and therefore presumed to be true methods, or simply their faith in the combat quality of their military instrument, that there is no real balance among ends, ways, and means. When the possible errors in reigning assumptions are considered also, it is easy to see why statecraft and strategy are creative arts rather than scientific fields of activity. Belief that politics and strategy can be treated scientifically is one of the many popular errors that I seek to correct here.

Both politicians making and re-making policy and soldiers making and re-making strategy are obliged to cope with circumstances that largely were not their own creation. A near perfect example of a desperate need to cope with an unanticipated strategic context was the situation in which Air Chief Marshal Sir Hugh Dowding and his RAF Fighter Command found themselves placed in summer 1940 (Bungay, 2000). This persisting unalterable great fact about history is important, but should not be permitted to constrain us from indicating what we find to be well evidenced prudent behaviour. Statesmen and strategists, who might be regarded as behaving in a common category of responsibility, aspire to nudge their polity's political and strategic situation along a path of adequate security. This text is closer in the spirit and focus to being a study of grand strategy than of strategy approached narrowly in a strictly military mode. Similarly, and for much the same set of reasons, the 'politics' in this book's title does not refer only to the international politics that commonly bound scholars' analyses.

The military strategy that is core content here is contextualized heavily by matters pertaining to grand strategy. I define this somewhat opaque function as 'the direction and use made of any or all among the assets of a security community in support of its policy goals as decided by politics.' Grand strategy is the theory and practice of statecraft itself (Gray, 2010a: 18). Because of the democratization of opinion formation over foreign policy and the now global ready accessibility of information with strategic content, much of the separation of domestic from international affairs has ceased to be operative. Here I take a notably global view of both strategy and politics, despite the often convincing scepticism well directed by Patrick Porter in his sceptical book, *The Global Village Myth* (2015).

This work has an operationally active title in *Strategy and Politics*, not merely a rather notional decoration on familiar content. The book is driven by my conviction that neither strategy nor politics are as well comprehended as they need to be in relation each to the other. The worlds of politics and military strategy persistently are substantially mutually uncomprehending, despite their interdependence. Politicians as policymakers typically do not ask seriously probing questions about strategic feasibility of their senior military advisers. However, it should be noted that the historical evidence of policy initiatives for war taken in military ignorance is not consistently unfavourable to politicians' behaviour (Cohen, 2002). Sometimes, the realm of politics needs to tell military strategy to adapt and adopt as speedily as possible. Given that the practical needs of warfare can change rapidly under fire in the field, as happened with respect to experience in 1914 and 1915, politicians need to be prepared to challenge soldiers when they prove unwilling to adjust to new circumstances. Each chapter is intended to show how and why strategy and politics interact and have historically significant consequences, some anticipated and others, ironically, not. Notwithstanding the distinctive focus of each chapter, this work provides a unified whole view of its subject. Neither strategy nor politics can make sense if considered alone. Strategy requires direction that can only be provided by political process, while politics is always in need of executive enablement by the endeavour understood as grand strategy, though more usually simply as strategy.

It is well worth noting that Churchill affirmed an essential unity between politics and strategy, as the words quoted immediately below attest. Whether or not he overreached in his argument, I must leave to readers of this book to decide for themselves.

> There are many kinds of manoeuvres in war, some only of which take place upon the battlefield. There are manoeuvres far to the flank or rear. There are manoeuvres in time, in diplomacy, in mechanics, in psychology; all of which are removed from the battlefield, but react decisively upon it, and the object of all is to find easier ways, other than sheer slaughter, of achieving the main purpose. The distinction between politics and strategy diminishes as the point of view is raised. At the summit true politics and strategy are one.
>
> (Churchill, 1938: 464)

Key points

1 Strategy always and everywhere is political in meaning.
2 Although strategy must have political meaning, it is distinctive from politics.
3 Strategy is about the consequences of behaviour, while tactics is about the behaviour itself.
4 Policy is the product of politics and is ever liable to change.
5 Politics, and therefore strategy also, is driven by 'passion', not necessarily by rational calculation.
6 The essential logic of strategy has a practical authority that is ubiquitous and eternal.

1 Politics, power, and security

> *Reader's guide:* The interdependence among politics, power, and strategy. The nature of power and its relationship to the 'moral force of passion'. Security as an incalculable value. The importance of context, both domestic and international uncertain security.

Introduction: the strategy enabler

A great chain of consequences, enabled by strategy, purposefully connects political process with power and, more arguably, with security also. This chapter will explore and explain the meaning of three concepts of central importance to our study: politics, power, and security. Different cultures have exhibited destructive understandings and practices with respect to each of these three concepts. There has, however, been unavoidable continuity in the practical authority of the basic architecture of logical authority in the general theory of strategy. Chapter 1 considers critically just what it is that politics and strategy are about and why they are about it. The focus here is on the consequences desired to flow from legitimate political process and enabling strategy. It will be suggested that political process licenses and substantively directs grand or military strategy to enable chains of events understood as amounting to power and to a condition commonly termed security. This book is about the creation of security as a product, even a commodity, generated as a result of the political generation of power that needs to be navigated by competent strategy. All too obviously, the real world of strategic history has not lent itself very often to so pristine a characterization of cause and desirable effect. This chapter examines realistically how the potent concepts of politics, power, security, and strategy, both work together, but also often work to frustrate what may well have been prudently intended.

Politics, power, and strategy

The title to this section is noteworthy both for the high importance of the three concepts and, ironically, for the imprecision or worse that frequently reduces their value in analyses. Although there are some grounds for legitimate argument about the proper meaning of each of these concepts, the following definitions serve well enough to capture the most essential functions of the activities and behaviours in the terms. We can understand these key concepts in the following functional ways:

> *Politics* is understood to refer to behaviour intended to achieve influence over the thought and activity of others.

Power is understood to refer to the ability to do and act (for whatever purpose).

Strategy is understood to refer to the direction and use made of (any) means by chosen ways in order to achieved desired political ends.

Considered functionally, as here, it must be the case that these functionally conceived concepts will be incomplete if we fail to take a value inclusive view of politics. Political process is the engine that generates the substantive policy goals that strategy must seek to enable in practical terms. With politics providing a more or less dynamic stream or trickle of policy desiderata, state and other power can best be regarded as a generally employable menu of capabilities. This menu of means is available for option(s) selection by statecraft and strategy.

This book endorses a notably interconnected view of the subject. It makes no sense to seek to analyze strategy except with regard both to what it is ordered by political process to endeavour to achieve and also how much, and what kinds of power are judged likely to be accessible and exploitable. The subject of this text cannot be captured and comprehended usefully by attempts to consider each vital element seriatim, because each factor only has meaning in company with the others. All conflicts, hot or merely warm, can be approached for better understanding by use of the principal concepts employed here, especially with particular regard to the necessary relations of dependency among them. The scholarly analyst seeks to know what policy is demanded by politics, and what power should be available for skilful employment by strategy. However, even, honest and competent analysis of the triadic system conceived as comprising ends, ways, and means – or strategy politics, and power – is going to be seriously deficient in understanding should it neglect the inconvenient fact that strategy only makes sense when considered in a politically adversarial context (Simms, 2013). It is a considerable challenge so to manage a security community's assets that policy ends are planned to be used in ways that privilege the more positive qualities believed enjoyed by friendly forces. Nonetheless, it is always necessary to consider the enemy and the conflictual context that his behaviour promotes. Politics and strategy can never legitimately be treated as though they constituted a closed system, meaningful strategically strictly on domestic or allied criteria. This is not to deny that often it is difficult enough to plan and execute a plausible fit among ends, ways, and means, without having to worry about potential foreign complications. Sadly for the practical utility of many defence planners, the standard they need to meet is not only one of tolerable harmony domestically among politics, strategy, and military power. Also, they need to key their well enough balanced armed forces to an ability to exercise and execute national power in violent competition with other polities (Clausewitz, 1976: 75).

The full context for analyzing politics and strategy has to be a conflictual one. Because we humans always seek community for security, the possibility of conflict between these communities is akin to constituting a law of political existence. Conflict is an integral and permanent part of Man's Estate. Our history should be understood as having proved the permanence of a quest after security, a rather imprecise as well as elusive condition. The detail and conceptualization of politics and strategy have altered massively in the past and can be assumed likely to continue so to do in the future. However, the functions that really matter most, security pre-eminently, alter only in character, not in their nature. Considered as a rather intimate set of relations, politics and strategy inevitably are locked into a triangular geometry that must include events, foreign and domestic. We do not expend scarce resources for the tidy administrative purpose of

12   *Politics, power, and security*

maintaining balance between our wealth in assets and our military power. Although the power to do and act is critical for meaning, in vital addition it is necessary to specify just what it is or may be necessary to be able to do, with explicit reference to an external security environment. We emphasize the legitimacy of threat identification looking abroad, but in fact the relevant politics and strategy of a security community may well be directed domestically for good reason. This book is not confined in its content to the analysis only of currently sovereign states. Politics and strategy can be, and often are, transnational as well as national and international. People always and everywhere, individual and collective, are the players in the grand historical narrative that matters most to us both collectively and individually.

The political process that fuels the permanent need for power *ipso facto* necessarily requires the service of strategy. Readers may well wonder just how and why political process, with its focus on the gaining of legitimating authority, settles upon the policy goals that it does. Although politics is best understood as a competition for relative influence, it works by employing and exploiting society's values. The interests that politicians attempt to advance can be regarded as comprising assets with diverse societal value. Political process most typically is about the legitimating of governance. In that most functional of senses, claimed interests are chess pieces in the game of political power. This circular logic has interests of value being advanced by agents of power, which in its turn also is constantly in need of enhancement and burnishment, because… In short, politics and power can be mutually reinforcing or contradictory. Both have eternal necessity for advancement by prudent strategy.

Lawrence Freedman argues that strategy is 'about getting more out of a situation than the starting balance of power would suggest. It is the art of creating power' (Freedman, 2013: xii). This is clever, often is true, but it is perilously obscure. It would be quite a challenge to attempt to argue that all strategists, everywhere and at all times, are engaged ultimately in a contest to create more power. This is one of those definitions that create more difficulties than they resolve, and as a consequence should be rejected, albeit with regret. The structure of the logic of strategy, although sound in principle, historically in practice almost requires oversimplification. The austere Power-Point presentation that is crystal clear on the distinctions between and among ends, ways, and means, is only an idealized representation of the core elements of general theory. In practice, ends, ways, and means penetrate each other across categorical boundaries that are not rigidly fixed. As Commander-in-Chief of the principal Coalition army in the War of Spanish Succession, for example, the Duke of Marlborough needed to be master of contemporary policy, strategy and tactical feasibility. He had to be as attentive to the politics of policy in the anti-French Coalition, as he certainly was more narrowly on the options and allied preferences in military strategy. In addition, when Marlborough's personal participation was necessary for moral force in the fighting power of his troops, he had acute battlefield need of a grasp of tactical combat realities (Hattendorf, Veenendaal, and Westerflier, 2012).

Although the logic in the theory of strategy is both sound and true in core meaning, the realm of practice nearly always shows more evidence of inter-categorical traffic than the triad of ends, ways, and means might lead one to expect. To say this is to risk muddying water in the comprehension of strategy's components and their working. I have written elsewhere of a metaphysical 'strategy bridge' that allows needed traffic to pass between the military bank of the strategist, and the political one of the politician policymaker (Gray, 2010a). Here, I am indicating that there is considerable traffic between and among the fiefdoms of politics-policy, military strategy, and military tactics. As an aid to clarity of understanding, I suggest that a Venn diagram with its intersecting circles allowing some content colonization among politics, strategy, and tactics is close to historical strategic practice.

A challenge here is to know how substantial one needs to allow alien content to be in its function as demandeur of attention at another level of concern. How welcoming should one be to strategic reasoning and conclusions that either or both cast doubt upon politically deeply desired policy ends and feasibility through combat? Once we abandon the simple architecture of categorical integrity regarding political ends, strategic ways, and military means, we risk a perilously fuzzy, perhaps confused, world. Tolerance of inter-categorical understanding, far from vitally enriching the understanding, instead has the unfortunate net effect of reducing discipline concerning needed integrity at other levels of influence and command.

In June 1944, General Dwight D. Eisenhower, recently appointed Supreme Commander, Allied Expeditionary Forces, was obliged by his critical position to confront and cope with choices and dilemmas arising from the actual or credible potential difficulties indicated here immediately above. Political direction as high policy was classically simple: invade continental Europe and defeat Nazi Germany. However, he knew and understood that the British government was not entirely convinced that an invasion would succeed, and looking over his shoulder back to the United States, Eisenhower knew that the American public and electorate was not thoroughly persuaded that it was necessary or even desirable to defeat Germany first, before the Empire of Japan. Eisenhower knew that if the planned invasion either was defeated when attempted, or was aborted or postponed for other reasons, the Soviet army most likely would be the only Allied armed force on the ground in continental Europe. The Allied forces in Italy were effectively contained before the Alps and the Dolomites and were not convincingly poised for war-winning success. All of these matters meant that Eisenhower the military strategist was in command of a planned venture that must have the deepest of political consequences. He did not make policy for the Grand Alliance, that was the prerogative of President Roosevelt and Prime Minister Winston Churchill, sometimes substantially influenced by the Combined Joint Chiefs of Staff Committee. Nonetheless, Eisenhower's largely military judgements had profound political meaning.

Eisenhower rather embarrassingly was bereft of personal command experience of combat; in part as an understandable consequence he was not outstandingly well equipped with tactical or operational military skills. Fortunately, those notable deficiencies were more than counterbalanced by his extraordinarily high quality of political and strategic understanding. Inevitably, planning for D-Day, and then its execution, placed the Supreme Commander in the non-trivially grim situation of needing to make military decisions that were beyond his full professional competence. Also, he needed to influence, and if need be control, military subordinates – some of an Allied persuasion – who were as strong in operational experience as he himself was woefully weak. He was persuaded, for example, that the large-scale airborne operation was a necessity for the confusion and distraction of German coastal defenders. But also he was told that the parachute assault most probably would prove a tactical catastrophe, leading inexorably to an operational disaster, and therefore also inevitably to the strategic failure of the whole D-Day amphibious enterprise. Such failure inevitably would have had dire political consequences for the course of the war. What we are flagging here are the connections among all the levels of command in war: political/policy, strategic, operational, and

14   *Politics, power, and security*

tactical. Also, it is necessary to appreciate that Eisenhower and his principal military subordinates at the operational level of command were hoping to float well enough on a sea of assumptions. Would Eisenhower's invading forces and supporting air and naval power be able to meet the Wehrmacht and succeed in combat on the greatest scale? The American army had shown in Italy that it was becoming tolerably effective in combat, but no better than that. The airborne operation against Axis-held Sicily had been an expensive shambles, while considerable doubt also continued (deriving from the Anglo-French Gallipoli misadventure in 1915) to be felt about all amphibious operations, let alone one as uniquely massive as D-Day.

Admittedly D-Day 6 June 1944 is an extreme example to employ in aid of understanding here. My purpose is to explain that each theoretically distinctive category essential to the theory of strategy in historical practice has been infused by action in and from other categories. An army may fight well, but it will achieve little worthwhile if it is committed politically to a hopeless venture. Or, outstanding operational art in execution to advance brilliant strategy will be of no avail if the troops are not willing to fight and if need be, die. Wise policy deriving from well conducted political process in principle is enabled by skilful strategy, if Clausewitz's 'moral forces' march with us (Clausewitz, 1976: 75).

The challenge to us seeking to make sense of the subject essentially is to secure a clear comprehension of strategy's necessary structure – ends, ways, and means – while being ready to accommodate as necessary the transfusions among conceptual categories indicated diagrammatically by Venn geometry, and empirically by all strategic history. Historical accuracy is far more important than clarity that misleads. The cost is too great in providing a distorting mis-characterization of strategy by theory that is neat at the price of inaccuracy.

Power and passion

The ability to act and do which is the core meaning of power is driven by the motivations underlying political decisions made manifest in and as policy. As M. L. R. Smith argues, the energy necessary to mobilize for war, as well as to behave effectively in it, can be understood as the product that may suitably be characterized as passion (Smith, 2014). Much, indeed probably most, of our contemporary literature on strategy neglects phenomena that can be so labelled. Cool calculation of anticipatable net advantage and disadvantage typically dominate strategic analysis, as scholars and commentators proceed largely in ignoring the motivational fuel of emotion for human conflict. This is not a charge that could be levelled credibly either at Thucydides or Clausewitz. It may be recalled that the Athenian general and author identified 'fear, honor, and interest' in his summary of the primary motivations in and for statecraft and its strategy (Thucydides, 1996: 43). For reasons at present somewhat obscure, the critically important subject of political motivation, its sources of fuel and its often dangerous consequences, commonly is not considered as it merits. It is usual to analyze state interests and even assess their relative weight, non-metrically, of course. But, the emotional energy that is sparked and fuels the will to act and do with variable determination escapes careful notice. In practice, each of Thucydides' three great categories of motivation pertain significantly to the particular subject of this part of our study. Fear and honour obviously are heavily emotion laden, while even the third vital category, interest, cannot sensibly be divorced from consideration of the energy expended in its pursuit. The political process that produces the flow of consensual intention known conveniently as policy is itself unlikely to be innocent of evidence of passion. Given that politics always has to be a process fuelled by arguments about alleged public costs and benefits, those being the most common sources of influence, it is undeniable that human emotions permanently are the targets for attention by those aspiring to be the most influential, otherwise known as politicians. Strategy assuredly is in part a material subject, but in greater part it is one that engages emotions. Furthermore, even when there is material matter in dispute, say the ethnically German Sudetenland in Czechoslovakia in 1938–9, those aspects of the motivation behind contending state policies that are metrically representable are in fact more about politically exploitable emotions than a calculable balance of power. To leap rapidly to the near present, the theorists and practitioners of what they hoped would be effective nuclear deterrence at least appeared to understand that perception of determination is the key to influence. A favourable imbalance of armed forces might be useful, or, ironically, possibly dangerous, but adversary perception of a danger of war was the gold standard for achievement of desired influence (Kahn, 1960: 287).

Thucydides' third category of motivation, interest, is not irrelevant to, or seriously disciplinary for this analysis, because there has to be some engagement of emotion for interest to be decided it is such. Typically, what matters in international politics is not so much the identity of asserted state interests, rather it is the emotional energy mobilized and employed in political process on their behalf. The literature of strategic studies is seriously lacking in judicious analyses of the potency of emotional energy behind and in the working of political process and the determination with which strategy is conducted. These are not minor matters strictly of worth only for specialist attention.

The greatest among the theorists of war, Carl von Clausewitz, wrote eloquently about what he termed the 'moral forces' that can be critically determinative in war. He advised that '[m]ilitary activity is never directed against material force alone; it is always aimed simultaneously at the moral forces which gave it life' (Clausewitz, 1976: 137). He had already observed that '[w]hen we speak of destroying the enemy forces we must emphasize that nothing obliges us to limit this idea to physical forces: the moral element must be considered. The two interact throughout: they are inseparable' (p. 97). This is not to say that the policy ends generated by political process and ordered to be the goals for strategy are only the product of emotion. But, it is to claim that politics energizes strategy and decides which objectives will be selected and which will not. Political process is not necessarily unmoved by, let alone unfriendly toward, intellect and rational method. However, one needs to recognize that the political ends legitimately provided to strategists are by no means only the product of cool calculation of interest and possible opposition. When Britain and its empire went to war both in 1914 and 1939, the reasons for the decision to fight lay as much in the 'moral' realm as in that of rigorously considered material interest. The soundest British argument for war in 1914 was the need to ensure that the balance of power in Europe – and hence the world – was not upset to the advantage of the Central Powers of Germany and Austria–Hungary. But, the balance of power was no more appealing a reason for war in 1914 than it had been early in the eighteenth century. In order to excite and mobilize the moral force of English opinion, evil misdeeds in the light of the reigning norm of good enough behaviour needed to be found and exploited. Moral outrage was felt over the aggressive behaviour of Louis XIV, while it was easy to find and deploy for the influencing of a sufficient popular bellicosity in 1914. Such enthusiasm for a fight was not much in evidence in Britain in 1939, but it did not need to be; the British public overwhelmingly

16 *Politics, power, and security*

had come to believe, albeit reluctantly, that Hitler's Third Reich simply had to be opposed. Certainly there was cold calculation that proved to some of the calculators that the British and French empires would greatly overmatch the resources commanded by the new Germany, but that was not key to the policy choice for war. That decision was founded most essentially upon a classic array of what it is most appropriate to consider moral forces. This rather anachronistic sounding concept was all about prudence, determination, fortitude and resilience; it owed little to ethical notions of right conduct. Overwhelming moral indictment of Hitler's regime was created in notable part by the opportunity for evil created by war when it came.

One does not wish to succumb too easily to unbridled cynicism, but the analysis here might appear to suggest that policy substance often is available for political hire by politicians. They have need to provide, at least encourage, electors or other legislators of authority, with interests they should be willing to endorse at some cost to themselves. Almost invariably, the struggle for policy adoption and then sustainment and adaptation in practice, needs to be effected by the moral forces collectively termed passion. The political leadership necessary to secure agreement in government to costly policy goals typically has serious need of analytical support. Nonetheless, even when there is clearly calculable, certainly guessable, benefit to be gained by a course of action, apparent facts alone are unlikely to carry the day. Scholars have been known to forget that facts always need interpretation, and that propels us rapidly and inevitably into the political terrain where passion both rules and reigns. We humans assign values to many facts, and values can be notoriously reluctant to shed emotionally agreeable, but false, arguments. The passion that energizes political process and outcome typically takes an instrumental view of rational logic.

It is necessary to accept as inescapable reality the working both of political process (of whatever character) fuelled heavily and diversely by the passion of 'moral' force, and of analysis and calculation that seeks reliable knowledge. Political process is a game played universally, though by locally established rules guarded uncertainly by cultural norms, for the purpose of communal governance (Farrell, 2005; Booth, 2007: 441–52). For good or ill the extraordinary power enjoyed by political leaders enables no less extraordinary creativity in the sources that may be exploited in policy in order to enhance largely domestic influence. Political process is a game that always has to be won at home before it can be played abroad. Because politics has the future as its game board, and given that it can reveal none of its secrets ahead of time, the politician policymaker and his chosen strategists are compelled to consider the future through a fog of assumptions (Gray, 2014c). In good enough conscience, political process is conducted and strategy selected and executed, on the basis largely of assumptions that have to consist of guesses. There is much we believe we know about politics and strategy because of our variable access to the historical record of the past two and a half millennia. However, when we dare peer speculatively beyond today, we are confined emphatically to hope and belief. It has to be said that policymaking politicians and their strategists are apt to forget that the future is not foreseeable.

Security: journey's end?

It is necessary to try to avoid being captured by matters that really are essentially only instrumental in their primary function. Politics is about the seeking of influence, while (military) strategy is about the intended consequences of the use of armed force. But, these are distinctly instrumental views of the subject. In practice politics and their people do not seek simply to be influential, or to be able to take action effectively. What is the policy end to be advanced by such behaviour? At some risk of sounding naïve, what is it all about, finally? Ignoring a few possible theological answers to that fundamental question, we are obliged to answer that the ultimate purpose of the strategy and politics in focus here is captured inclusively by the concept of security (Booth, 2007). Unfortunately, security is as useful a core idea as it is notoriously elusive to try and capture for disciplined analysis. Also, the very uncertainty of security's content and quality probably contribute markedly to its persisting popularity. Regardless of the skill and rigour demonstrated in the quest for the achievement of security, there remains vital, if variable, uncertainty about its potentially significant detail (Williams, 2013).

The frustrating truth of the matter is that security is not and can never be assigned objectively correct value. There is no thoroughly plausible answer to the question of security, if it is levelled seriously. A search for certainty of knowledge about security is a quest that must fail. It may come as a surprise to many people to learn that the defence needs of the country, or the NATO alliance, are not calculable. There is no single right answer to the classic question, 'how much is enough'? (Enthoven and Smith, 2005). As explained in a later chapter (Ch. 9), politics, power, and strategy are all sensibly managed in the spirit of a search for sufficiency. Some aspects of strategy certainly lend themselves to, indeed require, careful metric analysis. However, the larger, let alone the truly largest, of questions about politics, strategy, and security do not lend themselves conveniently to demonstrably correct answering. Understanding of past strategic history inevitably is coloured by our knowledge concerning the plausibly presumable consequences of past political and strategic choices. But, at the time, indeed at all time in the past and present, the future is an impenetrable mystery. In this context of literally irreducible ignorance about detail in the future, how can we know reliably what we need to purchase, and how we ought to behave, in order to be tolerably secure? Indeed, what will we find that we are able to tolerate?

Undeniably, consideration of security as the major policy end requires the making of a full allowance for the vagaries of political process. Thucydides and Clausewitz offered essentially the same advice regarding the incalculable requirements of security. Both of them, though in different terms, acknowledged the high salience of 'moral forces', to privilege the great Prussian. Neither was indifferent to quantity of power, but both argued that non-material factors are as important as they are beyond calculable certainty. For example, what was the benefit in political influence achieved by virtue of the strategic skill and reputation of Alexander the Great, Julius Caesar, the Duke of Marlborough, and even, less certainly, Robert E. Lee? How much harder did their men fight, because of confidence in their general? What was their participation in defence, ultimately for security, worth to their polities? Plainly, the soft features termed moral forces in strategic history literally defy ability to calculate strategic need. This might be thought a mere pedantic academic quibble, save for the inconvenient fact that security in its several aspects is the most important charge upon governance we are obliged to make. To summarize the argument thus far:

- Security is a subjective feeling, rather than an objective condition.
- Although the subjective feeling of security is ours alone, it is open to influence by our somewhat chosen reaction to the behaviour of other polities.

18 *Politics, power, and security*

- Through political process we decide how much defence preparation enables us to feel tolerably secure.
- Security makes sense as an idea strictly in relation to menace. That menace, actual or only notional, is essential to the meaning in feelings of security.

In practice, historically viewed, political process resting upon both real and imagined evidence produces an answer that a largely domestic consensus of opinion deems good enough. Because people take comfort from familiarity when confronted by irreducible uncertainty, the defence or national security bite out of national wealth tends to remain steady over the years. In good part because we cannot know the unknowable, ahead of sudden changes in the international strategic context, one cannot know whether national defence provision is, or is not, good enough. There is much to be said in appreciation of the merit in the common saying and caveat that familiarity breeds contempt. Is security/ insecurity a matter of either/or? Perhaps we should approach analysis principally in a spirit of 'more or less'. But how much less secure are we, or rather do we choose to feel, on the basis of our perception and understanding of Others' behaviour? Presumably, at least it is presumed and asserted by politicians, the level of defence preparation, to some imprecise degree, provides a metric indicator as to the state of our security. Although a larger take from our wealth is to be expected when strategic history seems to march ominously in our direction, deep, though not necessarily correct, understanding of the concept and requirements of security may argue for a contrasuggestive policy path. We will be reminded of the ironic truth in the 'security dilemma', which suggests that somewhat mindless effort to enhance security through more military investment is near certain to harm our security, regarded systemically as it needs to be (Booth and Wheeler, 2008).

It is little short of startling to appreciate fully the plausibly possible implications of the argument advanced here. If security is not a calculable need identifiable metrically by honest rigorous analysis, it has to be very much at play in the game of political process, wherein feelings are likely to rule. If there is no objectively right answer, then who decides, and how, what will suffice? If Clausewitz's 'moral forces' are of great importance, how does that significant argument impact security debate? Can we argue that although the numbers in a conflict are against us, our soldiers are more resolute, may be more skilled, and surely are better led than their adversaries? It should be needless to say that the dangers in such forms of argument as this potentially are severe.

Political process is the engine generating the energy that drives policy and therefore, consequentially, strategy. But, much as tactical performance can be so demanding physically, emotionally, and intellectually that it leaves its practitioners with scant resources to spare for operational, let alone strategic, considerations, so political process perpetually can menace the deep reflection that choice of policy objectives and their enabling strategy should receive (Handel, 2001: 353–60). There may not be the time or energy available for thought about prudent strategizing. One of the themes here is the difficulty that attends efforts to maintain integrity for an entire enterprise in strategic endeavour. It is unreasonable and inappropriate to require of soldiers that they focus upon the possible and probable consequences of their tactical action in combat. But, it is necessary that their tactical commanders should constantly be aware of the operational meaning intended for current fighting. At the higher level of operational command authority and responsibility, there is always necessity for strategic sense to be a potentially dominant source of discipline over other, more transient, urges. The real-world problem is that each level of behaviour and distinctive responsibility – tactical, operational, military strategic, grand strategic, and policy-political – has its own troubles and opportunities or temptations, and is apt to function as if in a realm all its own (Luttwak, 2001).

The enduring condition thus described does not stop short of political process at the highest level. That level, where political process is managed and exploited to produce the choices among policy goals authoritative for strategy, is entirely capable of near total absorption in its own rarefied ambitions, beliefs, and jealousies. Debate, if such is permitted, may be framed, shaped, and determined not so much by what strategists understand to be feasible in the light of recent empirical knowledge, but rather by the personal style and possibly the power in argument of particular individuals representing distinctive interests in the whole structure of government. The energy of society and its governance on strategic concerns really is, perhaps one should say ought to be, about security. Strategy must seem stratospherically senior in proper authority to those focused day to day on the non-trivial issue of personal and small unit survival. Nonetheless, it is necessary to remind ourselves that perfection of, even just competence in, strategy is not what the subject here is about. Senior in authority though certainly it should be to operations and tactics, excellence in strategy prudently requires understanding as relating to performance that has strongly desirable consequences. Journey's end for this analysis, however, cannot be superior strategic practice in support of achievable political goals. Instead, alas for simple argumentation, the real goal of political process and its strategy enabler needs to be recognized frankly as being a sufficient security.

The beginning of wisdom on policy and strategy is frank recognition that security is a subjective value that carries no particular inherent metric or other quality. Security is a feeling with no fixed requirements. At particular times in and over particular places, security will appear to enjoy some material empirical referents. If a country's leaders decide that security requires the building of a main battle fleet at least equal to the battle fleets of the two next strongest naval powers, one has a standard that may seem to guarantee security.

The essential indeterminacy of military adequacy necessarily provides ample material for intense political argument. When we review the questions and assertions that invariably fuel security debate, it is not hard to appreciate why this subject can attract heated argument. Consider the questions that follow in the light of what ought to be known about the difficulty of providing prudent and convincing rival arguments.

- How secure are we?
- How do we know how secure we are?
- How can we become more secure?
- How important is security relative to other values for our society?

If a secure condition is considered to be akin to 'journey's end', how will we know when we reach it? The indeterminacy of security, keyed to an unavailability of objective data that might guide us should we so choose, compels us to conclude that this aspect of strategic studies must be judged ever contestable. What matters is our reaction to the realization that insecurity is a feeling that may, or may not, be well founded. In strategic practice, judgement and guesswork about security largely is the product of factors best characterized as contextual.

Strategic historical context

The purpose and meaning of strategy always are the products of historical context, inclusively understood (Gray, 2005: Ch. 2). That context always will be 'given', since yesterday is done and gone, beyond retrieval for trial of choices different from those made yesterday. Because strategy is an adversarial concept and practice, it is necessary to grant that a polity's strategic context, regarded historically, could never lend itself to independent appraisal, because to seek such would be to offend against the meaning and therefore the function of strategy. Enemies may only be adversaries or even merely foreign hostile sceptics concerning one's intentions, but the adversary box always needs to be ticked. This claim rests upon an all too rich historical narrative of inter-communal conflict, not upon a warped view of human behaviour. A world that finds no use for strategy and strategists would be one radically different from that which we occupy today as we did yesterday, and prudently must assume will do also in the future.

The politics and strategy of any particular time and place in history will have context distinctive to their position in the great stream of time (Neustadt and May, 1986). However, the political process that generates the power for strategy to plan and employ must ever be unique in precise historical placement, though also, if possibly confusingly, eternal in major features. The details of political process, mobilizable military power, and strategic choice necessarily are specific to each particular time, place, and circumstance, in other words to context. But, as significant as this uniqueness must be, so also is the empirical actuality of functional kinship across continents or centuries. The inter-dependent trinitarian unity argued here for politics, power, and security, has integrity across the ages and in all geographies. For example, political forms of legitimate governance have varied widely, but we should not be seriously confused about political relations of authority. Rome shifted fairly abruptly in the time of Augustus from a republican to an imperial form, but that does not matter when we seek to understand the political process in its function as generator, organizer, and executive for strategy. This is not to deny that particular forms of political authority may well have preferences in strategy distinctive to themselves. When governed by the Whig political persuasion, Britain in the eighteenth century was strongly committed to continental European strategic effort, whereas Tory Administrations habitually sought to advance Britain's prosperity and security largely through maritime colonial effort.

A society's strategic options tend to be less impressive in their potential diversity than critics like to imagine. A well-known German maxim exaggerates usefully the importance of historical context for this discussion: 'Politics is the daughter of history and history is the daughter of geography' (Simms, 2013: 502). Accident, bad luck, and incompetence are each and all capable of shaping strategic choices in a direction that future history may demonstrate to have been hugely imprudent. Nonetheless, notably contextual and largely enduring factors lend much stability to the succession of strategic choices that political communities are obliged to make. My purpose here primarily is explanation for better understanding, it is not policy or strategy advice. The particular intention in this chapter has been a determination to explain how choice of policy and strategy essentially is limited by little other than deficiencies in capability. However, it should not be imagined that political and strategic contention lack sources of discipline.

Both notionally and even legally, state behaviour is significantly sovereign unto itself. The Peace of Westphalia of 1648 may not have been quite the dramatic pivotal point that nineteenth-century historiography chose to believe, but nonetheless it did substantially

Politics, power, and security 21

unhitch potential state behaviour from external constraint. The persisting reality of strategic history is of a narrative that reveals the disciplinary effects of considerations of relative state power. The modern strategic historical context for, say, Britain, the United States, Germany, and Russia/the Soviet Union that was, has fluctuated in perceived menace and opportunity dramatically from decade to decade through the past hundred years. Nonetheless, the argument here that seeks to explain the multiple dependencies among political process, power, and security, is not vulnerable to assault deriving from recognition of changes in circumstance. Political process, power, security, and strategy demonstrably are permanent functions in the tapestry of strategic history. This enduring feature of world politics is overstated in the contemporary theorizing of so-called political realists, but it is an overstatement of a basically valid argument (Mearsheimer, 2014).

Conclusion: uncertain security

Because both strategy and security are necessary and make sense strictly in a context of challenge, they cannot sensibly be approached save with respect to their anticipated performance when opposed. Although security truly is far more a feeling than it can be some quality admitting of metric representation, nonetheless there is a source of discipline that strategists find greatly useful for guidance in their endeavours, the idea and perhaps the reality of an adversary. Because both strategy and security can be properly assessed only as to their compatibility of fit within the context of international relations, it has to follow that there should be systemic discipline for the guidance of what otherwise would be all but autistic behaviour and feelings. In short, we cannot do strategy or feel secure in a political and strategic vacuum. Political process is capable of producing decisions about military capability that verge upon the absurd. But if we take a more reasonable view of competitive military preparation, we notice that polities tend to find that foreign menace is an expedient source of navigation on the contestable issue of 'how much is enough?'

Given that there are always competing demands for the use of ever constrained state budgets, political process inevitably seeks a level of resource commitment believed to be good enough to satisfy even the more alarming of insecurity anxieties. It has to be admitted, though, that political process does not ensure that adequate defence forces will be acquired, or that sensible strategy will be chosen and pursued. There can never be scientifically correct (i.e. known to be reliably correct in all circumstances, because of empirical testing) answers to the challenges about security that political process can meet only with guesswork. For example, will a large increase in the quantity of our long-range and nuclear armed missiles serve well to enhance deterrence, or instead might it provoke an enemy attack as he seeks to strike before we augment our forces? Wherever we look at strategic issues we find adversarial relationships that prospectively deny us certainty of political and strategic success. To note this fact is not usefully to identify a problem that might be solved; rather it is to recognize the nature of strategy and the ever indeterminate character of a value as uncertain as security.

Key points

1   Political process decides policy.
2   The political process is variably moved by the moral force of passion.

22   *Politics, power, and security*

3   Power is the ability to do and to act.
4   Security is a universal human necessity, but it is a subjective feeling rather than a calculable value.
5   Security, in common with strategy, only makes sense in relation to some perceived danger.
6   The value of a polity's security is revealed only in and by the course of its strategic history.

Further reading

Booth, K. (2007) *Theory of World Security*, Cambridge: Cambridge University Press.
Booth, K. and Wheeler, N. J. (2008) *The Security Dilemma: Fear, Cooperation and Trust in World Politics*, Basingstoke: Palgrave Macmillan.
Bull, H. (1997) *The Anarchical Society: A Study of Order in World Politics*, New York: Columbia University Press.
Clausewitz, C. von (1976) *On War*, ed. and trans. Howard, M. and Paret, P., Princeton, NJ: Princeton University Press.
Gray, C. S. (2010a) *The Strategy Bridge: Theory for Practice*, Oxford: Oxford University Press.
Gray, C. S. (2014c) *Strategy and Defence Planning: Meeting the Challenge of Uncertainty*, Oxford: Oxford University Press.
Mearsheimer, J. J. (2014) *The Tragedy of Great Power Politics*, upd. edn, New York: W. W. Norton.
Simms, B. (2013) *Europe: The Struggle for Supremacy, 1453 to the Present*, London: Allen Lane.
Smith, M. L. R. (2014) 'Politics and Passion: The Neglected Mainspring of War', *Infinity Journal*, 4/2: 32–36.
Thucydides (1996) *The Landmark Thucydides: A Comprehensive Guide to The Peloponnesian War*, ed. Strassler, R. B., trans. Crawley, R., rev. edn, New York: Free Press.

2 Peace and war: politics at home and abroad

> *Reader's guide:* Political context. The need for strategy in war and peace. Strategy must satisfy at home if it is to work abroad. Importance of political understanding, of adversaries and oneself. Politics rules through strategy even when it is poorly chosen and done.

Introduction: strategy is about politics

This chapter is all about political context, both that particular to war and its warfare, and that which precedes and follows the violence. All war, everywhere and at all times, has political context. Movies and some enthusiasts' literature on military topics are apt to be dismissive of, heavily sceptical about, or simply silent regarding this context. However, war is 'not a mere act of policy but a true political instrument, a continuation of political activity by other means' (Clausewitz, 1976: 87). Organized violence becomes warfare if and when its motives and its consequences are intelligible politically. The use of force in criminal behaviour cannot be understood as war because the motivation does not meet political criteria, even if the violence seems to approach a level and shows a quality of direction akin to military. War can be waged primarily for gold, glory, or for reputation (honour); indeed for a wide range of motives. But while motives will likely be disparate, what they will and must have in common is some political meaning. Politics is what war has to be about, whether or not the belligerents know it at the time. War and its warfare have political consequences, meaning they pertain directly and indirectly to the relations of influence among the combatants. This is not to claim that warfare is political activity; it is not. But it is activity that invariably has political meaning. The symbiotic connection between war and politics is a persisting source of misunderstanding as motives, intentions, and plans need to adapt in order to be tolerably compatible with the verdict delivered by action in the field. And unduly easy familiarity with such concepts as politics and strategy in daily use and misuse promotes an undisciplined and often faulty grip on the relations between these nominally, though not always practically, hierarchical activities.

The most essential function here is to explore and explain the relations between political process and strategy, with the latter concept approached and understood inclusively. From a general treatment of the fundamentals of political context, we proceed by considering the full spectrum of antagonism and hostility between political communities, and introduce examination also of the universal and seemingly eternal issue area of civil–military relations (a subject treated in detail at length in Chapter 8).

24 *Peace and war: politics at home and abroad*

Chapter 2 opens discussion about the politics of strategy making and conduct, and then offers comment on the longevity and essential continuity in the practice of the strategy function throughout the great stream of time (Neustadt and May, 1986).

Political context

Officer cadets around the world may not be much interested in political process. They are just beginning military careers that assuredly will be dominated all but exclusively for many years by their need to master tactical skills and doctrinal precepts almost unimaginably remote from high political purpose. The condition that I have just characterized admittedly is changing greatly in our current era, as warfare has descended in scale, though not quality of violence and danger. Indeed, changes in the character of conflict have come to pose challenges to military capability that are, as yet, far from comprehensively answered. The 'strategic corporal' may well be a sound idea, but it is a rather distant ambition, one typically frustrated by deep systemic limitations pertaining to young soldiers and their lack of life experience (Krulak, 1999; Simpson, 2012). There are difficulties in civil–military relations in all phases of the spectrum that encompasses contextual conditions from peace to war.

It is a significant challenge not to lose conceptual grip upon the necessary core of key ideas, all the while exercising sufficient flexibility and adaptability to capture the typical memories of historical experience. The clarity of definition that was so important to Clausewitz does have some ability to slide into a rigidity that can lead to error. What is needed is an approach to our subject that is accepting of some inter-categorical intrusions. Although we need to be clear about the distinctive meanings of politics, policy, and grand strategy, we should be unsurprised by occasional softness in the boundaries between these very high concepts. Similar flexibility is needed with respect to inter-categorical connections at every other level of behaviour (i.e. those interconnecting strategy, operations, and tactics). In Clausewitz's day it was common practice to fuse operational and strategic argument, a practice which tended to leave our contemporary understanding of strategic matters dangerously under-considered (Stoker, 2014: 33). However, Clausewitz leaves us in no doubt that his comprehension of strategy did include, when necessary and appropriate, subjects that today are labelled strategic.

The levels of conflict for understanding and analysis cannot help but provide context important for lower levels of effort. Politics provides meaning and policy decision for grand strategy, which in its term contextualizes and prioritizes for military strategy. Military strategy yields the contextual meaning for operations, which necessarily are performed tactically. The flow diagram of descending authority is obvious enough but each higher level in the descending order should be somewhat open to amendment, or even wholesale revision, if a lower implementing level is unable to perform as higher authority wishes and seeks to command. Strategic malpractice continues to be so frequent as to be judged unremarkable. Why is this so?

It is clear enough that the US and British experience with wars in Afghanistan and Iraq in the twenty-first century revealed an appalling strategic incompetence (Elliott, 2015). Whether we employ the austere conceptual architecture of strategy's general theory – ends, ways, means, and assumptions – or examine the experience(s) to consider what should be the dependencies among politics, policy, strategy, and tactics, the resulting analysis reveals an unflattering story (Strachan, 2013). It seems unarguable to claim that the challenges to strategic competence typically are not of a kind that should trouble too severely a professional military instrument supposedly world-leading in quality. As much to the point, civilian politicians and civil servants reasonably well schooled in experience of statecraft ought not to be as embarrassed as commonly they have proved to be.

Although this book finds high value in theory, it is more concerned with seeking to understand why strategic performance frequently is poor. On the evidential base of a lifetime spent in efforts to encourage strategic education, I must admit that the making and execution of both policy and strategy cannot usefully be regarded as a quest for perfection. Journey's end for the indissolubly linked subjects here can only be a good enough strategic performance that should enable a manageable level of insecurity for the longer term.

Rather than the unattainable goal of perfection in strategy, I am happy enough to settle upon the objective of improving official strategic performance. The relaxed standard of performance identified here should be understood as the 'good enough' rule (Gray, 2010b). So varied and many are the good reasons why strategic performance can fail to serve its purposes, that it is only sensible to grant that many things, including much that could not have been foreseen, are beyond the control, possibly even the influence, of particular strategic actions. One is likely to be surprised that the course of strategic history was not more painful than proved to be the case. For a major example, although Britain ultimately was a victor in 1945, it is hard to resist the suspicion that British statecraft and strategy owed altogether too much to German errors in policy and strategy. A strategic theoretical assessment of British policy, strategy, and tactical effort in 1914–18 shows an even more egregious display of incompetence. That level of poverty in statecraft is exceeded only by the arrangements made for post-war order in and as a partial consequence of the Treaty of Versailles (Macmillan, 2001). Extreme clarity of vision concerning world order is only ever granted in lengthy retrospect, and even then usually not without contentious argument.

To those who may believe strongly in strategic perfectibility, this book can offer little hope, I'm afraid. However, it might prove some consolation to recognize that the record of strategic folly does not show a marked depreciation over the centuries. I should underline, however, a particular reason for contemporary anxiety. Although the rough co-habitation, if not quite agreeable marriage, of politics with strategy always has been fraught with potential disaster – consider the appalling incompetence that resulted in the Athenian catastrophe before Syracuse in Sicily in the great Peloponnesian War, most specifically in 413 BC (Thucydides, 1996: 473–8). The defeat of the great Athenian expedition to take Syracuse is entirely explicable in the terms employed here. Indeed, ancient though the history most certainly is, contemporary students of statecraft and strategy can find just about everything of lasting relevance to debate about the consequences of folly in that appalling episode.

It is commonplace to pose the question, 'why don't we learn from history?' (Howard, 1991: Ch. 1). The answer is because there are too many undisciplined variables interacting unpredictably. Politics and its consequential policy is a creative art, not a science – notwithstanding extravagant claims to the contrary. The human race has not made notable improvement in its practice of strategy or in the political decisions that govern such use. The politics of and for war have varied widely among polities of distinctive type, and there have been social, possibly civilizational, trends in change. But, tempting though it is to cite the near global spread of increasingly liberal values in recent decades, there is a persisting reality of contingently possible tragedy today on a scale that would

26 *Peace and war: politics at home and abroad*

dwarf comparison with any period in recorded history. Whenever we incline to favour a relatively approving judgement on the contemporary world and its professed values, it would be well to remember that our world, critically and strategically regarded, is permanently hostage on the largest of scales to the skill, the prudential common sense, and even simply the luck, of politicians and their advisers. The political stability of the current (and future) world political system is fundamentally dependent upon policymakers and their strategists not believing themselves compelled to have to resort to nuclear weapons. Much ink has been spilled in extolling the virtue accruing deservedly to a 'rules-based international community'. Whatever the merit in that mantra-like claim, scarcely lesser importance derives from the sustainment of a balance in military power between polities.

It is prudent to take an inclusive view of context, even when one is focusing especially upon its political manifestation. In the same way political context should be understood as open to influence by factors not usually regarded as being primarily political (e.g. the creative arts, philosophy, science), so also the strategy in this book's title needs understanding as being 'grand' in scope and reach, rather than narrowly military. There is a good case to be made for privileging the idea of there being what amounts to a super context (Gray, 2010a: 262). When polities decide to take military action in support of policy and to forge and execute strategy as a vital enabling agent, most typically they find themselves both somewhat hostage to military fortune in the dynamism of warfare, and critically dependent upon the evocation and then the sustainment of domestic support. Just about every war in history has required of its strategists that they provide some narrative tolerably appealing to the values of the societies engaged in combat. Virtually no matter how dictatorial its political system and process, any and indeed all communities are required to acquiesce in, if not necessarily support enthusiastically, strategic projects abroad.

Peace, war, and episodic antagonism

Society and its strategists find themselves struggling to understand just how and why the global strategic context is changing, let alone whither it might be heading. Little about that context is entirely unprecedented historically, save for the admittedly nontrivial potential implications of nuclear weapons' use, and the all but instant prompt of global connectivity allowed by contemporary electronic communications. These technological features of the present day are both awesomely new yet significantly absorbable by a historical context that is nothing if not inured to substantial change.

We need to recognize the possibility that it was the twentieth century that was exceptional in strategic regard, rather than the current more 'fuzzy' context. The two world wars, and then the Cold War, made for an unusual clarity in strategic contextualization. Both in Britain and the United States, though especially the former, casual popular as well as serious professional mention of The War has not required further detail in citation in order to be understood as referring to 1939–45 (or 1941–5). In the 1920s and 1930s also it was understood that reference to The War could have only one clear meaning. Until quite recently, notwithstanding the passage of many years, strategic thought continued to be dominated by an understanding of war known to be rendered critically anachronistic because of the nuclear revolution, yet which seemed inescapable. The problem was not that nuclear facts and probabilities were ignored and neglected, because they were not. But, there was a dominant idea about historical periodization that proved paralyzing to strategic imagination.

Peace and war: politics at home and abroad   27

The novelty of the nuclear dimension to the Cold War, which persisted from 1946 until 1990, had the consequence of impairing recognition of those themes in that period which had lengthy strategic historical precedence. Superpower antagonism and therefore rivalry has a history traceable with variable clarity through two and a half thousand years. A principal balance of power struggle between hegemonic rivals and ambitious aspirants is entirely unremarkable historically. Indeed, it would be extraordinary were potentially regionally hegemonic powers not to have antagonistic political and therefore also strategic relations.

The novelty in the nuclear dimension to Soviet/Russian–American relations reduced the ability, perhaps the willingness, to log the Cold War into a grasp of the meaning of those decades in the great stream of time. Taking inspiration from Clausewitz's likening of war to a game of cards (1976: 86), we can see that acute awareness of nuclear danger is not dissimilar from the context wherein a frustrated card player chooses to upset the game table. It has been difficult for strategists to pursue their craft when they feared that the rules and norms of responsible behaviour were at risk to nuclear use as a wild card that most probably would render all strategy moot. On the one hand, it is all too reasonable to claim that in history the need for strategy has never been greater than since 1945. But, on the other hand, the reason why we have had such acute need of strategy is the very reason why its potential for harm is so great. There is unresolved irony in the high strategic value of nuclear danger, though that menace is so awesome as to render the nuclear instrument of strategy inherently problematic (Kahn, 1960; Schelling, 1960). The challenge that nuclear weapons pose for strategic practice, and the attempts that have been made to square the circle in identifying potential use for what perhaps ought to be regarded as unusable military power, comprise a subject contextual for this work.

It is necessary so to employ concepts that their meaning is unambiguous. However, such a sound precept is apt to fall foul of strategic practice that persistently declines to adhere tidily to distinctive categories of action. Fortunately for understanding, we have to appreciate that 'strategy never sleeps'. Strategy and its theory can be regarded as thoroughly indifferent to categorical context. In the first quarter of the twentieth century, arguably the two outstanding theorist-practitioners of strategy were engaged successfully in the direction and actual command of coercive action in contexts of notably irregular war. Specifically, Michael Collins was the outstanding strategist for the Irish Republican Army in 1919–21 (Gray, 2007), while T. E. Lawrence theorized about and practiced strategy on behalf of the Arab Revolt against the Turkish Empire in 1917–18 (Lawrence, 1991). Somewhat contestably, one might choose to add a third name to the strategic honour roll, in the person of Lt. Colonel von Lettow-Vorbeck in German East Africa. It is more challenging to attempt to locate outstanding competence in strategy in the more regular warfare waged in Europe for four and a quarter years from 1914 until 1918. There is always a need for strategy, though the record of strategic history shows unmistakeably that commonly it has been missing either or both in the planning and from the meaning of the violent action.

Military theorists are overly attracted to the idea of option purity. In other words, it is convenient to fix conceptual boundary markers around kinds and levels of military effort, indeed around contexts for polities with particular assignable strategic meaning. Such tidiness lends itself to relative simplicity and therefore ease of transmittal for military training, if not education. A trouble with the especially clear PowerPointable lecture is that it is likely to pay a price in loss of comprehensive exposition and

28 *Peace and war: politics at home and abroad*

understanding that should not be afforded. It is common for the strategic dimension to history to be all but airbrushed out of recorded sight over lengthy periods. There is a somewhat fanciful view of history that chooses only to register a strategic dimension with respect to a few notably occasional outbreaks of war. Such a perspective declines to understand strategy as comprising a constant element, albeit temporally variable, in history. This view has little difficulty understanding strategic matters, most especially wars, as effectively constituting mainly punctuation marks of occasional military unpleasantness. Wars thus perceived are treated as being only an episodic malady affecting history in the great stream of time. Strategy and behaviour that must have strategic consequences is a permanent element in history. From time to time, strangely it will seem to some people, wars do occur. They disturb the typically even flow of historical happenings. Rarely, war is understood as having led to momentous shifts in historical narrative. However, wars quite commonly are considered as strategic punctuation to the more usual ebb and flow of events, as observations. Whether a particular war was relatively large or small in scale – however one elects to measure the disruption – it is likely to be treated by historians as an irregular violent episode in the more normal character of political life, which is held to be typically peaceful.

Some scholars have noticed that the conduct of interstate war on a large scale would appear to have gone out of fashion in recent decades (Pinker, 2011). This issue intrudes as a difficult challenge for policymakers and strategists in the twenty-first century. They cannot help but notice the contemporary prevalence of different styles in largely irregular warfare, all the while that the possibility of major war remains within the bounds of plausibility. Some contemporary scholars of an optimistic liberal persuasion are convinced that war and its warfare are becoming obsolete, so irrelevant are they and dysfunctional for human needs.

Those persuaded that war in all its aspects is obsolescent, becoming obsolete, are making a fundamental error, notwithstanding the novel opportunities as well as alarms promoted by nuclear weaponization and global IT. Unfortunately, I do not believe that our species will frighten itself out of a context fraught with nuclear risk. Furthermore, it seems improbable that we will so connect ourselves globally with IT as to render competitive politics, strategy, and concern for security, strictly yesterday's subjects.

If we take the long view of history, it becomes plausible to appreciate that the ebb and flow of periods of little disturbance, interspersed with episodic alarm, should be considered normal for our narrative. This is not to be dismissive of the grounds for anxiety over nuclear possibilities, or of aspirations for improved trans-cultural, if not supra-civilizational communication, courtesy of globalized IT. But, it is to decline to be overimpressed by the potential influence for good and evil of contemporary science and technology. Some of the primary causes of today's exaggerated hopes and alarms also were present in the middle and later decades of the nineteenth century, when the steam engine and electricity seemed likely to revolutionize the course of human history. Efforts to impose order retrospectively on the many processes and irregularities of history always are liable to encourage interpretation that is seriously distorted and misleading.

An approach to understanding the roots, course, and consequences of war waged on the greatest of scales is much advanced if we contextualize such episodes in appreciation of the normal happening of history. This history has always been more, or less, strategic in cause and consequence. We make it unnecessarily hard for ourselves if we approach historical understanding on the firm assumption that wars and their strategies are only episodic interruptions to normal human life. What is much needed is appreciation of the enduring relevance of strategic consideration. Contemporary professional military instruments tend to be unwelcoming to the apparent evidence of radical change in national strategic context, in part significantly because their worldview largely has been ordered by a sense of primary duty to focus upon preparation for the possibility of major war. Given our history, this focus is readily understandable and even excusable. My argument is not to claim that a dominant concern to be ready enough for interstate warfare is significantly wrong. Rather is it important for our soldiers to appreciate that the polity has permanent need of their services because, to repeat, the need for strategy never sleeps!

Great wars of all but maximum strategic effort should now be consigned to the politically discarded file of history, for the obvious reason of nuclear hazard. This danger is permanent because both cause and consequence in its regard assuredly will continue to hold in the future. But, what will not hold in the future is a particular character of the strategic context for national and international politics. Given that all periods in the past have been characterized by their own unique political contexts in the eternal quest for necessary security, as a consequence strategic context too has been an inevitable and indeed necessary feature in our history. Attitudes and styles have altered, of course, quite recently with a relatively new global habit of conduct with strategic preparation in times other than, as well as, those of war. Such defence planning, pursued with variable political energy, cultural enthusiasm, and social effort, today occurs as official behaviour considered to be entirely normal and expected. States and even less formally organized bodies today 'do strategy' at all times. It is not an activity reserved exclusively for periods of acute political crisis or war itself. Language, including concepts with authority, tends to follow experience of practice. Strategy, in an operational sense as campaign planning for anticipated war, is by no means only a recent phenomenon. Political leaders and their principal military advisers have woven great and not-so-great designs for offence, and possibly defence, in periods of relative strategic calm, pending expected need in the near future (Kennedy, 1979). However, there is little doubt that leading states today are striving to adapt and adjust to a moving strategic context. The competitively and necessarily strategic search for security is conducted both in fear of nuclear danger and as a consequence in reaction to that recognition of risk.

War and peace have not lost their core meanings today, but as categories for clarity of understanding of context they are seriously inadequate. Recent peacetime, so-called, saw us at war for more than a decade. If we believe the 2000s-plus were a time of war, there is need to appreciate the major limitations in our policy ends, to our strategic ways, and with our military means. The long familiar concepts of war and peace, while retaining much of their traditional and popular meaning, are not satisfactory as elementary organizers for efforts to help understand the twenty-first century.

Home and abroad

For most Western democratic states, strategy typically is understood to relate overwhelmingly to the polity's plans and contingent intentions vis à vis the outside world. However, in practice it is so much a domestic product that it is necessary to risk besmirching the simple purity in some explanations of strategy that insist on according near exclusive primacy of importance to an alleged necessity of 'power politics' (Mearsheimer, 2014). This fearful and fearsome concept loses much of its ability to

30 *Peace and war: politics at home and abroad*

inspire awe when one realizes that the two words constitute a tautology that thoroughly compromises the authority hoped for in the use of the expression. All politics have to be based on relations of power. Moreover, power is the ability to act no matter the agencies that achieve it or the forms that it takes in action. It is necessary to understand both that all power necessarily is political, and strategy is not a subject that sensibly can be assigned solely to states' external relations. States do not have domestic arrangements thoroughly disregarding of their external wishes and behaviour. No matter the uncommon features of a polity at home, elements as a consequence of that distinctiveness are reflected in its preferences in strategy aimed abroad.

It is true to claim that the domestic context for policy, strategy, and in some cases (e.g. of civil war) even action, is notably different from the foreign context. The Charter of the United Nations is permissive with respect to the license it recognizes and sanctions with respect to political and strategic behaviour self-excused with reference to plausible claims for self-defence. The major difference between the domestic and the external politics of states does not lie in the respective weight and quality of relevant law. Instead, the critical difference, the one that affects state behaviour most critically, is the fact that domestic law, rules, and even simply norms, most typically around the whole world quite literally are both enforceable and in practice are enforced with variable severity. There is no police force ready and able to discipline behaviour that the international community, or some functionally similar euphemism, claims to deem unacceptable. Although it would be misleading to liken world politics to a realm subject only to the law of the jungle, nonetheless there would be truth in such characterization. It is worth recalling that the great Australian scholar, Hedley Bull, titled his classic study of world politics *The Anarchical Society: A Study of Order in World Politics* (Bull, 1997). The title lies on the edge of irony. It is an error to think of international order solely with reference to material agents. But, there is no doubt that the unenforceability of international law in the cases likely to be most menacing to international order needs to be comprehended clearly. The regulatory context is one with a night-as-contrasted-with-day difference between domestic and international situations. This can prove difficult if soldiers are required to obey the rule of law (which law?), and possibly act in ways acceptable to our idea of strategic ethics, when the enemy recognizes no such constraint: this is an asymmetry strongly characteristic of all variants of irregular warfare. ISIS-licensed jihadists in Syria, Iraq, and Afghanistan, for a recent example, attempt to be obedient to the law of war, but it is not a law recognized and respected by their opponents.

Scholars have some difficulty in their seeking to explain the relationship between home and abroad with respect to military strategy and the threat and use of armed force. It is generally understood and accepted that military action is a realm wherein hurt is inflicted deliberately by force, ultimately for political purposes (Clausewitz, 1976: 87). In addition it is well understood and required that soldiers should behave only in a manner of which we in civil society can approve. There is a necessity to grasp thoroughly some aspects of strategy in politically purposeful action that often in practice are neglected; three such are addressed in the paragraphs that follow.

The first great truth about the threat and use of military power is that it is unavoidably and egregiously illiberal. No matter how noble one believes the political cause to be, and regardless of the quality of legitimation acquired from a licensing body (e.g. pre-eminently the United Nations' Security Council), force is violence and generally is alien to the values of civilized society. Rewarded, warfare is always nasty in the doing of its

Peace and war: politics at home and abroad   31

consequences. Moral and political justification may be persuasive, but the violent deeds claimed to be required are never attractive.

Second, because war inherently is adversarial behaviour, the character of the force applied in warfare can never be controlled and constrained with complete confidence. Since war necessarily is a competitive activity waged in ways intended to produce satisfactory strategic, ultimately political, outcomes, its violent course inevitably is always to some degree dictated by the dynamic path of the struggle, one created in contest under fire. Given that motives in war are going to be serious, and are duly categorized as such by Thucydides (1996: 43), it is necessary to appreciate that a decision to fight is a vote for the unknown and unknowable. Most wars have a course, if not usually an outcome, not well anticipated in reliable detail in advance by their belligerents. Soldiers may find themselves obliged of necessity to act in a manner neither anticipated at home in advance, nor ethically acceptable when publicly revealed. The advent of global IT means that military organizations no longer can be confident that violence interpretable as excessive will not reach far beyond the strategic theatre, described both in colourful prose and shown graphically in digitized photography. In warfare conducted between state and insurgent it is commonplace for atrocity to be committed in order to tempt the state's soldiers to overreact with counter-atrocity. This is the conduct of war as political theatre, and in modern times was understood and employed effectively by Michael Collins, the leading strategist of the IRA in 1921. The assassination of Reinhardt Heydrich by Czech irregulars in 1943 similarly was intended to encourage the Nazi rulers of Czechoslovakia to respond with punitive repressive measures anticipated hopefully to spark popular resistance.

Third, the decision to fight is likely to oblige a society and its politicians to take a walk on the wild side. Because the course of war can never be anticipated with complete confidence, a decision to fight will in effect be a decision to go wherever the dynamic struggle that is war takes you. When a society chooses to roll dice and fight, it is undertaking a journey beyond the ability of friendly political or strategic navigators to plot, let alone control. Despite the aspirations of social scientists and the confidence felt by the friendly military instrument, war is always a gamble. My point is not to argue generically against war, because occasionally it will be politically necessary for the restoration of good enough order, but it is to insist that there will never be a war from which chance can be removed.

Understanding the enemy, and oneself

Although many learned treatises and supposedly expert theorists would disagree, prominent among the major errors that impair comprehension of war and strategy is the mistaken belief that these are sciences. This error is important because it cannot help but fuel the conviction that there are objectively determinable, even calculable, right answers to strategic challenges. Because strategy is an art and not a science, it cannot be decided on the wholly reliable basis of empirically tested, therefore verifiably replicable, knowledge (Grygiel, 2013; Gray, 2014a). The issue is the nature of both strategy and politics, and what their qualities should mean for sensible approach to their study. If one teaches strategy and politics, is one instructing about and for science? Should science be a realistic aspiration, its mysteries must be amenable to discovery by the application of suitable analytical method. For the acquisition of reliable knowledge there is no alternative to the conduct of controlled and replicable experimentation. Neither politics

32 *Peace and war: politics at home and abroad*

nor strategy lend themselves to trials in the medical sense for the testing of new drugs. In practice, strategy and its political master have to be realms ruled by understanding of what is possible, what is practicable, and hopefully, what is good enough to secure the prudent (?) goals then selected. Most probably these are best answers to key questions about politics and of strategy, but there is never a feasible way in which such clear superiority can be demonstrated ahead of time to be correct. Politics for policy is not a field of contention wherein the more weighty uncertainties can be delegated to those especially gifted or trained in numerate skills.

The immediate purpose here is to explain why certainty of knowledge is unobtainable with respect to both of the concepts, concerns, and activities in the title of this book. In politics as with strategy, the right answer always is one found by experience to be good enough. This is a realm wherein 'B+', or even just 'B', can win the prize. 'As' are desirable, but usually strictly not required. It is worth remembering that extra-rational elements afflict an enemy as well as oneself. There is no undisputed and accessible Omniscient Observer willing and able to reward or punish losers and victors, depending upon the rival qualities of their political and strategic performances. That said, however, it can matter profoundly just how well a victor performed in war, with reference to the post-war consequences, given that such should be what war is about.

A useful way in which to think about both the persistent nature as well as the changing character of war is to contextualize a particular armed conflict using Thucydides' familiar triad of policy motives – fear, honour, and interest. Following the Athenian, little effort is required to realize that state motivation is beyond calculable certainty. Guesswork educated by experience is the best that we can manage. Because the course of strategic history is played out only once, we are unable to implement true dry-runs of planned strategic episodes (Krepinevich, 2009). While it is necessary to understand what one can about an adversary, also it is essential to recognize that he will not function as might an automaton. Fearful persons deciding and acting under extreme stress in a context rife with accident, chance, and surprising moves by the enemy are not suitable candidates for cool and calculating analysis. In the apposite words of Lawrence Freedman: 'Plans may be hatched by the cool and the calculating but they are likely to be implemented by the passionate and the unpredictable' (Freedman, 2006: 36). Clausewitz sought to remind us of the salience of 'moral forces'. It is a general truth of strategic history that both political demands and strategic performance in their support are more than marginally hostage to the competency achieved in both material and moral assessment of the adversary. America's enemy in the 1960s in Vietnam needed assessment as to his material capabilities, but even more with regard to his moral strength and stamina. Whether it was the Vietcong in the 1960s, or militant Islamists in the 2010s, there can be little doubt that the Thucydidean trinity of motivations greatly helps encourage inclusive appreciation of the political fuel for strategy.

All strategy is made at home, and all politics are local somewhere. These are not reliably true all-case claims, given the globality possible in cyber warfare, but they are true enough to warrant respect. Argument about strategic culture, including whether or not this rather vaporous, if imperial, concept has sufficient reality to merit respect and command attention, I defer for consideration in Chapter 7. Generally it is a fact beyond serious dispute that there is always a political narrative, and often a moral one also, behind, and subsequent to, all war and warfare. Even in the historically unusual case of an acute international crisis propelled emotionally by the unbridled political will of a dictatorial leader such as Adolf Hitler over the Sudetenland of Czechoslovakia in 1938,

Peace and war: politics at home and abroad   33

there will be local political context it should be advantageous to understand. Hitler's willingness to fight over the Sudetenland might just have been sufficient to trigger the military coup against his regime that was discussed very seriously in the top-most ranks of the German Army by those who feared provoking a war they were convinced Germany would lose; their clandestine contingent scheme required Britain and France to be ready and willing to go to war. As it was, Anglo-French pusillanimity resulted in a Munich Agreement explained imprudently by Prime Minister Neville Chamberlain as meaning 'peace in our time'. Admittedly, this is an extreme case of political ignorance encouraging unwise policy and absence of strategy. But, the course of history is punctuated amply by episodes wherein poverty of political understanding had unfortunate consequences. For a more recent example of the peril in political ignorance, in early November 1983 the aged and seriously infirm Soviet leadership was convinced that the Reagan Administration had decided to launch a nuclear attack on the greatest of scales (Barrass, 2009: 28). Unfortunately, Soviet warning indicators were reinforced and even apparently confirmed by an unprecedented NATO command exercise on procedure for the general release of nuclear weapons. It is doubtful if Hollywood could have invented so lethal a script of inadvertent nuclear danger. When political understanding is as poor as we now know it to have been in Moscow in 1983, the consequences for military strategy may be catastrophic.

Strategy everywhere and at all times is in potentially sick, weak, or at least unlucky hands. Even if or when strategy is brilliantly conceived, well calculated, and ingeniously crafted, decisions for its implementation and subsequent execution will be tied to and by a political process the functioning of which may be less than smooth. Although the enemy's production process for strategy will differ greatly in local detail, it must share with our own a generically political contextuality, with a like possibility of proving seriously flawed in practice.

Strategy needs to be obedient to the interdependent logic required for tolerable compatibility among ends, ways, and means. But, it is not the product of de-humanized unilateral digital logic in command and control. Because war is the realm of chance, so also is strategy. Although war and its warfare are not politics, so pervasively are they inbred with political meaning that the confusion of inappropriate conflation of the two is readily understandable.

Politics both reigns and rules

There is all but systemic tension between the world of the soldier and that of the politician. So separate can those worlds be both in appearance and more deeply in reality that understanding of their true interdependence, as well as ordered hierarchy, may slip from public and professional view. The soldier knows that he serves at the pleasure of the state, or at least the political community that lives, feeds, equips, and directs him. Of practical necessity, most soldiers, at least in their military role and function, do not interact with the political process that should control them. The state delegates and licenses command and control to the hierarchy in a profession of arms. Particular military traditions vary, no matter what the character of military subordination to political authority; the nature of the relationship is not in doubt: the soldier serves the state in the form of its legitimate government, and follows such strategy as that military pursues as conceived, designed, and implemented as an agency of state policy. In high theory all is crystal clear, the military is an instrument of

34 *Peace and war: politics at home and abroad*

state. In practice, though, this has to mean that the military is and does what pleases the government of the day.

There is an integrity distinctive to political as compared and contrasted with military affairs, and this difference is not as well appreciated as it needs to be. The problem is that each of the two worlds requires the other to leave its comfort zone of professional expertise and venture inter-zonally into what really is alien territory. On the one hand, the military is expected and required so to perform in battle that friendly political interests are advanced as a consequence. On the other hand, our policymakers are required to ask of the military that it performs professional tasks in combat only of a kind and to an extent within its competence. Policy goals, or war aims, though possibly politically impeccable at the outset of hostilities, may fall victim to unexpectedly adverse military circumstances. Since military confidence can prove overconfidence fed by hubris, the course of military events is ever liable to spring unanticipated, unpleasant surprises. A competent military instrument necessarily is one that always performs well enough, a standard that usually requires it is able to innovate and adapt adequately to meet unexpected challenges.

Given the dominant role, properly armed if not always taken, by policy, and given also the universally necessary fact that political process generates policy, policymakers should deserve both praise and thanks, as well as be prepared to accept criticism and possibly blame. Policy needs a military instrument sharp enough to produce required strategic effect, while the military requires policy guidance confined to the practicably deliverable. These reciprocal demands are part of the core of difficulties that often beset the troubled relations between politics and strategy.

Conclusion: separate worlds?

There is no fully satisfactory solution to correct the more fundamental reasons why strategy and politics seem often to exist in worlds that scarcely meet to engage in constructive discussion. The best that can be done is to acknowledge and seek to come to reasonable terms with the undeniable facts of basic difference between the two realms. There are occasions when individual personalities, particular institutional fears (for example, regarding anticipated budgetary loss, leading to capability loss, leading to expected loss in public esteem), unexpected circumstances, accidents, and bad luck produce crisis in civil–military relations. Nonetheless, there is need to look beneath the surface of events and possible misdeeds. War in action as warfare is all about politics, that after all is what sets military machines in motion, but often it does not seem so to soldiers functioning tactically and operationally in harm's way. At those levels, warfare will be near wholly a personally dangerous business. At least in Western perspective, the political context of war usually is understood as requiring that action must only be legal and ethical, but it is not in the nature of war for it to be so regulated. Some commentators endorsed the proposition that warfare should only be waged in the interest of enforcement of legally sanctioned (by United Nations) rules, and in support of just cause, but such noble aspirations often are foredoomed to fail. In strategic historical practice war is akin to a ferocious beast that cannot be tamed and controlled, but which can, with much coercive effort, be somewhat constrained and disciplined.

War and its warfare are not simply one among many elements in grand strategy. Rather are they rendered different by their essential inhumanity, and also by the scale and range of challenge they pose to political process of any character.

Key points

1 All of strategic history has political context.
2 'Strategy never sleeps', even when it is hard to find.
3 Strategy is always made at home somewhere, even when it is wholly designed to meet challenges from abroad.
4 Global IT, and especially mobile phones that take photographs, mean that home and abroad are not as far apart as they were until recently.
5 Since strategy is the product of political process, political ignorance is apt to be strategically lethal.
6 There is political meaning to all strategic behaviour, whether intended or not.

Further reading

Bull, H. (1997) *The Anarchical Society: A Study of Order in World Politics*, New York: Columbia University Press.

Clausewitz, C. von (1976) *On War*, ed. and trans. Howard, M. and Paret, P., Princeton, NJ: Princeton University Press.

Gray, C. S. (2012) *War, Peace and International Relations: An Introduction to Strategic History*, 2nd edn, Abingdon: Routledge.

Gray, C. S. (2014a) *Strategy and Defence Planning: Meeting the Challenge of Uncertainty*, Oxford: Oxford University Press.

Howard, M. (1991) *The Lessons of History*, New Haven, CT: Yale University Press.

Lasswell, H. D. (1936) *Politics: Who Gets What, When, How?* New York: Whittlesey House.

Mearsheimer, J. J. (2014) *The Tragedy of Great Power Politics*, upd. edn, New York: W. W. Norton.

Murray, W., Knox, M. and Bernstein, A. (eds) (1994) *The Making of Strategy: Rulers, States, and War*, Cambridge: Cambridge University Press.

Ryan, A. (2012) *On Politics: A History of Political Thought from Herodotus to the Present*, London: Allen Lane.

Smith, M. L. R. (2014) 'Politics and Passion: The Neglected Mainspring of War', *Infinity Journal*, 4/2: 32–36.

Strachan, H. (2013) *The Direction of War: Contemporary Strategy in Historical Perspective*, Cambridge: Cambridge University Press.

3 War and warfare

Reader's guide: The vital hierarchy of concepts and activities. The inclusive central idea of battle. Varieties of war, but politics as usual. Continuity in nature of war, but change in its character.

Introduction: vital hierarchy

Strategic Studies is not a subject fixated wholly upon war, but such a focus would be understandable. In Britain, at least, some major university-based research and teaching efforts are organized under the flag of War Studies, rather than strategy or security. This chapter is designed both to explain the connections between war and strategy, and to explore the relative importance of war for our entire subject. It is particularly important to understand how a small number of especially key concepts relate to each other: the most vital of these are security, politics, policy, grand and military strategy, and warfare or tactics. It is useful to notice that these seven concepts commonly are employed incorrectly; such misuse can hardly fail to promote misunderstanding on the part of the speaker or writer as well as the audience.

In theory, even in law, there is a clear enough hierarchical relationship that explains the logic of their interconnections. The clearest and most convincing explanation of the core of ideas discussed here is offered by Hew Strachan when he writes that '[s]trategy is designed to make war useable by the state, so that it can, if need be, use force to fulfil its political objectives' (Strachan, 2013: 43). There may be better explanations of the basic function of strategy with respect to its duty of support to state policy, but they are unknown to this author. Strachan's explanation of strategy's function is arguably unduly restrictive, but nonetheless it targets by far the most troublesome of a state's duties conducted on behalf of its citizens.

Each of the seven concepts mentioned above plays a significant role in the whole narrative of strategic history. In the interest of maximum clarity, I offer short explanations of the meaning of these key ideas and also of their relationships one to another (Gray, 2010a: 18).

- *Security* is the highest purpose sought by politics and strategy, notwithstanding its subjectivity.
- *Politics* and political process decide which particular goals will be sought in the quest for security.
- *Policy* comprises the objectives decided by political process to be pursued.

- *Grand strategy* and *military strategy* are required in order to answer the 'how' question about policy. Grand strategy naturally is superior to its subordinate element, military strategy, but in practice the 'whole of government' approach and commitment in the idea of grand strategy can be notably subordinated to the military interest in time of war.
- *Tactics*, including *warfare*, refers to the means available to be used by strategy in pursuit of the politically determined goals of policy.

The hierarchy just specified is clear in its meaning, and also crucially important for the understanding of particular responsibilities in the hierarchy of authority in any system of governance. Rank ordering of these seven concepts is not offered in the naïve belief that the proper order of relative authority is a fair explanation of the way things are in the real world of official behaviour. However, this is one of those cases wherein misunderstanding as well as typical human and institutional mistakes are near certain to have severe adverse consequences. The British (and American) experiences in Iraq and Afghanistan in the 2000s provided an exceptionally clear example of poor performance for national security following as the result of unsound political process, poor policy choice, inappropriate strategy and unavailing tactics. In a recent book, retired Maj. General Christopher Elliott shows how and why the two wars came to be waged with cumulatively appalling ineptitude, despite the high tactical quality of many of the troops (Elliott, 2015). In the British case there were always too few of them, they tended to be poorly equipped to try to meet the severe challenges they had to seek to answer, and they had been tasked to achieve wildly unreachable policy goals. Unsurprisingly, as today is all too clearly revealed, they failed both in Iraq and in Afghanistan. Here we need to appreciate just how war and its defining activity, warfare, need to relate to strategy and politics.

Battle

Much, indeed almost certainly most, of what modern students of strategy write about is far removed from the grim and gory actuality of battle. While battle, meaning the violent clash of arms between politically sanctioned and legitimized soldiers, is not typically the most characteristic behaviour demanded in a soldier's professional life, even in time of war, still it has a defining authority in explanation of the soldier's existence and function (Clausewitz, 1976: Ch. 1). Strategic studies (and military history) are not all about battle, any more than soldiers' lives are characterizable very largely in terms of experience in battle. However, the idea of politically sanctioned and organized armed conflict is defining for war and strategy, while for good reasons the specific concept of a clash of arms on a major scale has been present in human anxiety throughout the course of history. In recent decades, the idea of battle has suffered a substantial decline in popularity for two reasons: the possibility of nuclear use, and the contemporary actuality of asymmetrical and irregular warfare. Battle has become too dangerous an idea to treat as other than a horrific possibility, while almost invariably irregular warfare offers no opportunities for the conduct of major battle. Such combat is unlikely today principally for the reasons just given. Nonetheless, war on a large scale remains possible, even if somewhat incredible, and smaller wars are a certainty. A book about the relationship between strategy and politics should not have to focus very heavily upon major war, because combat of that character ought to be so improbable a product of

38 *War and warfare*

contemporary political choice as to be all but unthinkable. That said, it is a fact that unthinkably great wars have occurred, though unanticipated, in the quite recent past, and there are worrisome reasons why it is necessary to retain some measure of preparedness for their appearance in the future. In modern strategic history, French and Spanish ambitions exploited the local desires of Italian city states at the close of the fifteenth century (1494–1559) and beyond; a war of shifting alliances but of fairly steady vaulting ambition was visited primarily upon what was known as Germany between 1618 and 1648; the final decade of the seventeenth century and the first fifteen years of the eighteenth saw the conduct of war on the grand scale as Louis XIV strove to assert and impose French hegemony upon Europe; nearly a century later the Wars of the French Revolution and Empire consumed the years 1792–1815; and more recently we have suffered from two world wars (1914–18, and 1939–45), and a great Cold War (1946–89) that might well have dwarfed in its awful consequences all else that I have cited so briefly (Simms, 2013).

The reasons to decline to be impressed unduly by the possibility of a very great war in this new century are impressive and generally persuasive. However, it ought to be difficult to forget the occurrence in the past of devastating wars that should not have been waged with the furious tenacity, or for the length of time that they were. One would like to be able to convince oneself that war of a major character is now passé, but, to date, this is not possible.

Although one might have expected the weaponization of nuclear physics to have led to radical change in world politics, the danger unarguably being so great, the problem of necessary respect for strategic history intervened decisively. Reluctantly, we cannot help but notice that the high calorific ingredients that persistently have resulted in major war at irregular intervals throughout recorded history are still extant. Moreover, the motives for armed conflict on all scales of possibility remains active. This is not to undervalue the worth of weapons of mass destruction as a massively discouraging, even dissuading, contemporary factor, but it is to register doubt as to the authority of claims for the demise of major war. It is worth remembering that a general (then necessarily) European war involving most or even all the great powers was believed widely in the later nineteenth century to be an impossibility. The concept of an effectively general war seemed to be banished on the pragmatic grounds both of the increasing globalization of trade and finance, and the experience and skill in statecraft demonstrated apparently convincingly in then recent decades. In short, in a nineteenth century proud, not to say arrogant, of the ability of leading politicians to chart a course for international order, major (meaning general) war anxiety looked to have been retired as a potentially live source of anxiety from strategic history (Howard, 2001). The inter-state wars of the nineteenth century post-1815 were few and far between, and were strongly characteristic only of the 1850s and 1860s and barely into the 1870s. There was war in the mid-to-late 1870s in the Balkans, as the Ottoman Empire collapsed, but the Congress System of European diplomacy, intended to preserve the balance of power and therefore a tolerable condition of international order, managed to perform well enough in order to preclude a slide into general European war. The principal conflicts of the century were all either sub-regional contests (e.g. Britain, France, and the Ottomans against Russia, 1854–6; Prussia with German allies against Denmark, 1864; Prussia again with German allies against Austria, 1866; Prussia and German allies against France, 1870–1), or were civil wars (the Taiping Rebellion in China 1850–64, and the American Civil War, 1861–5). There was no general, let alone 'world' war for a whole century (Gray, 2012: Chs 4–5).

The Congress 'system' of interstate diplomacy which had begun in Vienna in 1814, and limped on with a very modest half-life until the late 1870s (in Berlin, 1878), encouraged the belief that general European war had become an anachronism. The lack of merit in this conviction was demonstrated with the catastrophe of 1914–18, of course. Not unreasonably, there was no little faith in the unthinkability of a return match of general war through most of the 1920s and 1930s, which is scarcely surprising given the horrors of the experience suffered so recently. But the determination, 'never again', was not shared quite as widely as was necessary, with consequences revealed in abundance between 1939 and 1945. International strategic experience since 1945 might appear to have demonstrated empirically in protracted non-extant experience that the murderous record of warfare as battle finally had taken command of our history.

Unfortunately, the absence of evidence is proof of nothing (Taleb, 2007). Experience of battle and its consequences has been an episodic constant in history. Since battle does not serve as a concept adequate to convey the many practical meanings of war and warfare, it is not hard to understand why it should not be employed casually in a sense intended to be summative. The expansion of possibilities in warfare enabled by its politically fuelled democratization and industrialization had rendered the strategic quest for decision by battle hugely problematic. Although wars can be won by the strategic effect of what really is largely the tactical triumph of success in a single battle, commonly termed 'decisive', for the last three centuries such a descriptor has not often been appropriate as a valid characterization of a particular event (or episode). Even Waterloo on 18 June 1815, decisive though it proved to be, needs to be understood in its full political and strategic context. Many historians have commented on the futility of the search for political success through the achievement of decisive victory in battle, especially in a single such happening. What we know for sure is that because war is the product of political process, always and everywhere, the availability of the resources essential for its conduct will enable warfare to be protracted. Historians have observed that both world wars in the twentieth century were devoid of a truly decisive single victory/defeat that settled matters. But, just as Germany could function despite suffering cumulatively enormous damage in 1914–18 and 1939–45, great anti-hegemonic struggles have always been protracted. Decision has not been reached through the throw of the dice in combat in a single battle lasting only hours or a few days. In the greatest war of the eighteenth century, that of the Spanish Succession, Britain's Duke of Marlbo-rough won four major battles (Blenheim, 1704; Ramillies, 1706; Oudenarde, 1708; and Malplaquet, 1709), and still the struggle continued in a somewhat desultory way until peace was restored with the Treaty of Utrecht on 11 April 1713. The record of strategic history shows clearly that although the factors making for notable 'decision' by a single battle, particularly very limited exploitable military resources, were certainly more prevalent in pre-modern than modern times; the fuel of political will sufficed to deny the power of decision to a single clash of arms.

The combined constraints of limited available assets and modest political ambition, considered in a context wherein statesmen were attentive to arguments concerning the arguable prudence in contemporary strategic behaviour, typically sufficed to dampen the fires of war. Most often what is sought through war is advantage with political value, not the decisive defeat of the adversary. But, as a practical matter often it is difficult, if not impossible, to calibrate political ambition so as to match military effort, which means that battle is likely to acquire a value all its own. The political process that should be served may fall some way towards the rear for significant attention.

40   *War and warfare*

A central and always potentially dominant problem for strategy as the servant of policy and its politics lies in the often apparently autonomousless self-stimulating dynamics of warfare itself. Clausewitz alerted his readers to this phenomenon when he drew the possible distinction between the 'grammar of war' and its 'logic' (1976: 605). It is improbable that one belligerent would be able militarily so to conduct a war that his warfare calibrates closely with his initial, but not necessarily persisting, policy goals. War is an instrument of state that needs direction by strategy. But war also quintessentially is always a duel, which means both that in practice the enemy has a vote, and in addition that between them the combatant polities may well contrive to effect a substantially unanticipated dynamic episode of warfare. Such an episode may well not be designed predominantly by a single contestant, it will be a unique product, the result of their dynamic and even notably unexpected interaction.

We began this chapter by laying emphasis upon the concept and practice of battle because this rather inclusive idea is defining of our subject. As all roads sometimes are claimed as leading either to Rome or Jerusalem, so for a book on strategy in its military sense and politics it is necessary to recognize the presence of war, its strategy, and also its conduct in warfare as unavoidable context for discussion. In modern understanding, strategy designs direction for actions to be taken in support of the policy produced by political process; the focus usually is not upon strategy as military direction in battle. The concept of battle, however, even though it has been superseded by less emotive terms that characterize protracted conflict more accurately, retains high value. The concept, bearing the meaning of an event consisting of extreme violence conducted on a large scale, does lurk as a reminder of potential danger on the path that we are exploring. In all of the 'eras' into which historians have chosen to pour their packaging of strategic historical experience, war and its warfare have demonstrated the ability to escape close political control, particularly when assayed with respect to the efforts of a single belligerent. Loss of political control ever lurks as a danger. Wars always have the dynamically live potential to exercise their own militarily unique dynamics – to be all they can be. In states considering whether or not to resort to force of arms, it is essential for the historical experience of war's adventurous and probably unanticipatable character to be understood (Porter, 2009: 65, 170).

A critically important distinction needs to be observed with regard to war as contrasted with warfare. War is always about politics and it refers inclusively to context particular in the political life of a security community. The politically founded context of war has clear legal meaning, as well as economic, cultural, and military dimensions. The political and legal contexts of war are served by warfare as the instrument employed by strategy. 'Warfare', in Clausewitz's words, 'comprises everything related to the fighting forces – everything to do with their creation, maintenance, and use' (1976: 95). 'Fighting' thus is defining for the behaviour necessary for one to be sure it is war under consideration. In the messy reality of historical experience, we may choose to regard some war-like behaviour as not constituting warfare as strictly it deserves to be treated as the agency for the conduct of war. It is sometimes expedient, even prudent, to distinguish war-like behaviour from what we could choose to understand to be war. The concept of war has political and legal implications that security communities often have chosen not to recognize formally. Contemporary Russian misbehaviour in regard to Ukraine falls clearly into this category of happenings regarded (e.g. by NATO) as war-like, yet not claimed to be evidence enough of warfare for war. After all, warfare can only occur in war, and states understandably, if not always wisely, are loathe to declare being at war, with its deeply unwanted political implications.

Limited war: military command for political control

In characteristically logical and uncompromising a manner, Clausewitz insists upon the rightful dominance of political over military perspectives, given that the latter is, or should be, only an instrument of the former. In his words:

> Subordinating the political point of view to the military would be absurd, for it is policy that creates war. Policy is the guiding intelligence and war only the instrument, not vice versa. No other possibility exists then, thus to subordinate the military point of view to the political.

> (Clausewitz, 1976: 607)

With very few exceptions, wars are waged for limited policy objectives. Even when the political objective is of an absolute kind (e.g. defeat Nazi Germany), some constraints may be placed upon the character of warfare waged. For example, although the defeat of Nazi Germany was a goal on the high end of the spectrum of possible objectives in war, it was not a political licence granting *carte blanche* for killing all soldiers in German uniforms, let alone German civilians. International law has not proved especially robust in the face of the committed atrocity, but a combination of culturally imbibed norms of war, and also prudential self-interest, usually are adequate to achieve notable, if never absolute, constraint upon the possibility of warfare descending into an orgy of destructive violence. The possibility of military atrocity is an ever present reality because of the nature of the activity that is warfare. Young men, typically fearful, armed and generously enabled by specialized equipment for the purpose of doing violence, are not ideal subjects for constraint by discipline. Potentially lethal danger will be present reality, nerves will be on or over the edge, soldiers will be tired or worse, and strong drink and drugs may well have removed some usual inhibition. Also, the soldier's immediate combat context will be so remote from normal civilian life in peacetime, and the peril in his situation may be so alien to his more familiar situation, that inhibition and disciplinary constraint could pose a challenge they are not thoroughly fit to meet.

Although Clausewitz's justly famous, perhaps one should say infamous, 'climate of war' – danger, exertion, uncertainty, and chance – is authoritative in all geographical environments for combat, the land is probably the most challenging to aspirations for control and limitation (1976: 104). The Prussian's pervasive climate of danger that holds for all warfare is matched, and more, in human fear both physiological and psychological. It might have been sensible for Clausewitz to have added fear to his four climatological elements. Because the motivation for war tends to be as extreme in its way as the organized violence itself, the scale of menace to its careful calibration for fit with policy can hardly avoid posing serious challenge. It is no slight ambition, on the one hand, to seek sufficient strategic advantage through warfare as to incline an enemy to concede consequential political terms acceptable to us based on his weakened military situation. But, on the other hand, our warfare should be of so frightening a character that the promise, explicit or even only implicit, of 'worse to come, unless...' will be adequately credible. Civilian policymakers, innocently misreading Clausewitz and also probably over-impressed by staff college lectures and texts, probably can be forgiven for

42 War and warfare

believing too uncritically that war and its warfare are a readily controllable tool of state policy. In practice, war is always an extreme option in the playbook of policy action, and it has features endemic to its nature that are unfriendly to control for limitation by the political demands and needs of only one belligerent. When political authority decides that the dice of war will be rolled, in so doing it is leaving the familiar domestic comfort zone that is its only true zone of control. Because war is adversarial and is always the realm of chance, the familiar mantra of 'command and control' is apt to acquire unwelcome fully undesirable meaning. In principle, at least, command is not a problem for orderly and legitimate governance. However, the control part of the vital conceptual and pragmatic duo not infrequently proves to be a bridge too far.

War as a policy option for a state should not be approached as if it were a challenge in some important aspect of domestic administration. Leaving aside matters of law, it is necessary to appreciate that '[r]ules are inappropriate' in strategy, as the great Russian strategic theorist and soldier, Alexandr Svechin insisted (1927: 64). Neither strategy nor war occupy ungoverned space, but the fields of conflict that are theirs are not subject to entirely reliable constraint by regulation. This is not to demean the influence of law, principles, norms, and customary rules that can promote restraint. But, it is to argue that a security community typically will choose to do what it believes its strategic circumstances require, in effect largely regardless of legal or normative and customary points in potential constraint.

More often than not today, command and control are found fatally at odds with each other, as the political control over the use of state sanctioned armed force proves incompatible with the initially extravagant ambitions of high policy. In other words and with recent examples, both Britain and the United States, with NATO in Afghanistan, adopted policy in the 2000s that required strategic command of military behaviour that was politically infeasible. Neither in Britain nor in the United States were the nature or character of the challenges in Afghanistan or Iraq appreciated with sufficient accuracy (Elliott, 2015). The beginning necessary for wisdom in those recent historical cases is the subject of this chapter. The problem for policy and strategy revealed in and by Afghanistan and Iraq needed initial appreciation in the terms provided by enduring general strategic theory (see Chapter 4).

Mastery of local detail is always desirable and may even be essential for prudent statecraft and strategy. Nonetheless, it is yet more important to comprehend the persisting challenge in the nature of war to policy, strategy, and the politics needed to devise and sustain them. Although war is always likely to be limited by a host of factors that encourage restraint or which impose constraint, it is a grave error to believe that because war is about politics it is readily controllable by political process within a single belligerent state or coalition. In its function of direction over warfare, strategy is not to be thought of as a tap able to control at all closely the quantity and quality of interactive violence that is battle. Clausewitz alerted readers to this problem when he contrasted the proper 'logic' of policy with the 'grammar' that rules of practical necessity in war (1976: 605). The strategic conduct of war is far more akin to a creative art than it is to anything meriting description as a science. Every adversarial episode of reciprocal violence that we call warfare has a course that will be shaped and determined by many factors in every belligerent that has political meaning and influence.

For war to be useful to grand strategy as an instrument of state policy, it has to be limited yet tolerably satisfactory in terms of the Thucydidean motives identified in the three categories of 'fear, honor, and interest' (1996: 43). While there are always constraints imposing, at least arguing for, limitations on the conduct of war, those three motivational clusters from ancient Greece also, dangerously, are fuel for increase in combat effort. In most respects, it is imprudent to think of a war option for policy as being likely to be reliably controllable more or less strictly, as if it were an isolated and unilateral drive-by/fly-by event or episode. Furthermore, war and its warfare are not to be considered a 'spectator sport', notwithstanding the relatively minor involvement usual today for Western publics regarding the policy action commanded in their name and observed by the average citizen strictly on television (McInnes, 2002).

Arguably it is unfortunate that in wars commanded by limited goals for strategy, the military and consequentially the political results most typically are only very limited, and, one might say, deservedly. Because war and its warfare are a psychological as well as physical and material happening, a stronger will always are likely to succeed in conflict. The theory of limited war in respect of strategy was always at severe risk of falsification by a belligerent unmistakeably materially inferior, who was so high in motivation to fight that the obviously superior belligerent would be outlasted and outcompeted. In asymmetrical war, which is virtually a definitional quality in irregular conflicts, the theory and attempted practice of limited war frequently has resulted in the defeat of Western states. Every episode of war reveals strong similarities in experience. It is especially pertinent to recognize, for examples, commonalities among the United States in Vietnam in the 1960s, the Soviet Union in Afghanistan in the 1980s, and most recently America and Britain in Afghanistan and Iraq in the 2000s. Unilateral calibration of distinctly limited military effort, directed by constrained strategy in pursuit of limited policy objectives, is likely to fail if the enemy of the day scores highly on the index of motives to fight we can derive from Thucydides.

Varieties of war, but politics as usual

It is an empirically well founded belief behind this text that my subject can and ought to be understood as comprising two permanent themes in history, strategy and politics, and that there is no good enough reason to elevate either change or continuity as the dominant partner. Although strategies and political choices are ever changing, those changes must occur only within the fundamental and therefore persisting conceptual space appropriate to each. The politics most relevant here are those explained with reference to power, understood as influence over thought and behaviour (Lasswell, 1936; Mearsheimer, 2014: Ch. 2). In these terms, politics can be regarded as a function vital for all communities, particularly in respect of their need for security. The function of strategy has been required through all of history, even though this need has been expressed with different emphases in particular places and periods. The permanence of our political and strategic histories, considered functionally, is expressed most suitably in a common ironical French aphorism: *plus ça change, plus c'est la même chose* (the more things change, the more they stay the same).

Political and, controversially, strategic cultures can be manifested in a wide range, but politics and strategy, nonetheless, have been and remain essentially constant, even though in appearance it may appear that much is different. People in all places and periods, notwithstanding local variations, when understood functionally, perform politically and strategically. This argument can be upsetting to some professional historians who are not welcoming to a social scientist claiming that politics and strategy essentially have not changed throughout history. For example, Duke William of Normandy (later

44   War and warfare

known as The Conqueror) needed to think and perform strategically in order to secure the throne of England to which he believed he was entitled. Leaping forward no less than 878 years, General Dwight D. Eisenhower also and therefore similarly needed to function strategically, though in his case in a role subordinate to higher political and military authority, for the purpose of defeating Nazi Germany. Both examples lend themselves well enough to explanation in terms of a general theory of strategy, just as their military meaning is entirely explicable with reference to a theory of politics. The details of each historical case are vitally important, while their meaning in functional terms really is timeless and should be unarguable.

The special knowledge in the professional expertise of historians is necessary if we are to approach understanding of the course of history. However, insistence upon the significance of unique historical detail easily can be overemphasized. Although it is essential to secure some grasp of the historical context for Duke William's and King Harold's behaviour in 1066, also, at the least, it is highly desirable to achieve understanding of the political and strategic meaning of their respective behaviours. As Chapter 4 seeks to explain, it is feasible both to be faithful to the necessarily unique detail of historical data yet open to improved understanding of the whole category of events or episodes of which the happenings in 1066 and 1944 are only examples. General theory exists primarily for the purpose of providing navigation and to enable via education sound assessment of what can prove to be an indigestibly rich diet of historical detail. This is not to be disinterested in detail; rather is it only to be ready to seek understanding of what best may be understandable as evidence for classes of behaviour. General theories of strategy and politics aspire to achieve just that. As usual, Clausewitz captured the essence of the matter when he wrote as follows:

> A specialist who has spent half his life trying to master every aspect of some obscure subject is surely more likely to make headway than a man who is trying to master it in a short time. Theory exists so that one need not start fresh each time sorting out the material and plowing through it, but will find it ready to hand and in good order. It is meant to educate the mind of the future commander, or, more accurately, to guide him in his self-education, not to accompany him to the battlefield.

> (Clausewitz, 1976: 141)

The general theory of strategy serves the educational purpose that Clausewitz specified. While professional historians have been known to be unduly tribal over their claims to ownership of particular historical periods, so the scholarly strategist is not always as averse as he ought to be to overly bold generalization concerning specific events about which he may know little. The strategic scholar is always in need of empirical evidence as the base for his theory, while the historian should not be seriously unwilling to consider occasionally the persisting nature of his topics as well as their specific and therefore inevitably transient, if generically repeated, character.

Heated though debates can be among scholars moved to feel intolerant in their appreciation of the quality in statecraft or strategy of the historical figures they endeavour to hold in focus, the evidence from historical experience suggests the wisdom in a willingness to see virtue regardless of the variety in detail. Neither political skill in aid of superior statecraft, nor superior generalship in its strategic function, appear to be assignable to individuals or institutions associated with particular moral values.

Extraordinary political, strategic, and military competence seems, on the evidence provided by the record of strategic history, to be unconnected with specific political or ethical context. To hazard the unduly vernacular, ethically challenged people and flawed institutions are capable of producing competence and even genius.

Of course, political ideologies, institutions, and systems have varied widely throughout history, but what has not much altered has been the essential process by means of which politics functions. While political process entails registration of claims for commitment to public values, also it requires a disciplinary system able to reward or punish for individual and perhaps group performance. Political process can coerce or entice, according to the believed needs of contemporary governance. However, problems lurk for civil–military relations for two reasons in particular. First, the political process that always is the most potent source of war is not usually entirely domestic in character, with civil war of several kinds comprising a category of exceptions. This has to mean that the outbreak and then the character and course of war will be decided by political process that is never entirely ours to control. So, when war is defined, explained, and then described as being the product and indeed an instrument of politics, it is necessary to remember that it is an adversarial joint (plus) venture upon which we can embark. It might well be thought that the fact that war almost always is conducted in violent opposition to a foreign polity is so obvious as to be a needless banality. However, sensible respect for the great enduring truth that was so prominent in *On War* concerning the political engine for war frequently is mislaid temporarily or even apparently lost definitively. If, as here, one is considering the relationship between politics and strategy, it is important not to lose sight of the fact that war and its strategy can never be treated as though they are characteristic of a game of solitaire; they are not. When scholars and policymakers discuss war as a political instrument, they must always remember that it is a political instrument for all belligerents.

The second reason why even prudently would-be joint consideration of strategy and politics is apt to stray seriously is because the differences in nature between the two concepts are easily misunderstood. Clausewitz does not quite claim, and almost certainly did not mean to argue, that war really should be regarded simply as politics with violence, or even as political violence. Nonetheless, he did sail perilously close to the attraction of major error when he wrote as follows:

> We maintain that war is simply a continuation of political intercourse, with the addition of other means. We deliberately use the phrase 'with addition of other means' because we also want to make it clear that war in itself does not suspend political intercourse or change it into something entirely different.
>
> (Clausewitz, 1976: 605)

Unintentionally, I am convinced, Clausewitz at times risks overstating and therefore misstating the necessary connection between politics and war (with its strategy). Admittedly, this is a challenging connection, really a contextual dependency, to define and describe without misleading accidentally. Because war is political and certainly always about politics, it is easy to misdirect readers along the path that fuses together war and its warfare with the political process that launches, sustains, and gives them their meaning. Politicians as policymakers have understandable difficulty grasping accurately the true nature of war. Although war must be about politics and therefore justly can be understood to be political, nevertheless it is a category of coercive behaviour

46   *War and warfare*

substantially distinctive in and of itself. In this case, political parents do not produce a wholly political offspring. The violent connective clash and struggle between adversarial capabilities and qualities in historically unique context translates in practice into an event or episode that has character, possibly a changeable character, of its own. This character can be notably disregarding of major currents and themes in the political processes of the belligerent societies and states. My argument may well be a lot more than Clausewitz intended to present or imply with his insistence upon the distinction between war's 'logic' in policy and its 'grammar' in warfare. Hew Strachan is right in explaining that strategy should tame war so as to render it useable by policy and its politics, as quoted earlier (2013: 43). But, how useable is war, even if guided prudently by strategy (whose strategy? – ours, theirs, both?)?

It is commonplace for soldiers to believe themselves committed to action in a context that is either one of true chaos, or at the least one that appears imminently to be at risk of becoming so. We can hardly fail to notice that war as an adversarial operational and strategic exercise is always revealing of the fact that in its nature its higher conduct must prove to be the art of the practicably possible. And evidence for what is practicably possible can emerge only provably through demonstration in action. There is some value for improved understanding in considering war to be noticeably akin to a contest between two or more artists committed to produce a single painting, despite their distinctively different foci of main concerns and preferences on a host of matters great and small. Although one belligerent may come to dominate in shaping the course of the warfare, the unavoidable context and reality must be in the nature of a duel: the fact that that dominant influence nonetheless has to succeed against purposeful, if not necessarily well directed, opposition, or even just rather unintelligent harassment, means that the war for which the belligerents share responsibility is not likely to resemble the one originally intended by anyone. The political motivations that launch and sustain war and its warfare always are liable in practice to give birth to an offspring in a course of combat unanticipated at the outset.

This is not to argue that it is in the nature of war in effect to struggle to be free from direction and constraint, which is to say control, by political process. But, war is always so unpredictable an adventure that, notwithstanding its inalienable quality of political meaning, it is dangerous to believe that it is simply an instrument of policy. It is not entirely true to argue that it is in the nature of war to serve itself, but there is sufficient plausibility in that claim so as to warrant serious respect. Despite Strachan's apt characterization of strategy's function as a would-be tamer of war for the state, one needs to be alert to the probability of some failure of command in pursuit of impracticable control in that vital regard. Strategists convinced of their own cleverness, and policy-makers seeking reassurance that what they want to do will, in practice as a reliable consequence, prove feasible, constitute a potentially deadly marriage of errors.

In some contrast to the tone of the paragraph above, it has to be understood that we are only explaining the natures of political process and policy and of strategy. The difficulties of strategy are legion and indeed legendary (Gray, 2014a). It is inevitable and possibly desirable also that political process should challenge strategic imagination to conceive of ways in which the near impossible, certainly the exceptionally difficult, might be attempted with some prospect of success. In addition, strategic affairs often do not provide context in politics for policy to be amenable to the relatively easy answering of challenges. As Clausewitz warned, '[e]verything in strategy is very simple, but that does not mean that everything is very easy' (1976: 178). While individual genius will deliver prudent policy direction and wise strategic choices, by and large we are condemned to struggle on as best we are able, guided and misguided by people of good, though not exceptional, competence in contexts for decision often dominated by accident and chance. It may not be a source of much contemporary solace, but our reading and understanding of strategic history leads to the sad conviction that strategic matters were ever thus.

Conclusion: continuity in nature, change in character

If by use of the concept of revolution we seek to argue that the practice of warfare has been radically altered from time to time throughout recorded strategic history, there can be little room for serious dissent. Incontestably, warfare in its technical dimension has changed drastically in material ways over millennia. Indeed, the changes, cumulative and sometimes apparently sudden, can occur in only a bare handful of years, if that. Quite recently, in the 1990s, the American defence community, though largely strategically unchallenged in that decade, solemnly debated the meaning of the rapid emergence of new technical possibilities that the still very immature digital revolution was presenting for possible military exploitation. In the Western world, at least, revolution was the most exciting concept of the period. There was no very serious strategic contemporary necessity for a Revolution in Military Affairs (RMA), the principal acronym of the 1990s decade, but it appeared to be technologically on offer, so naturally it was accepted. Of major interest here is not so much the promise of militarily helpful change in the waging of warfare, but rather the much larger issue of the political meaning of such change when effected on a radical scale (e.g. gunpowder, nuclear weapons, digitization).

With the sole exception of nuclear weapons, there have been no changes in the character of warfare through the entire two and a half millennia of historical strategic experience to which we have some access for understanding that warrants description as revolutionary. We have come to use, most probably misuse, the idea of revolution in a way that diminishes its utility and is hugely encouraging of confused thought and understanding. This confusion has unfortunate consequences for public policy that are continuing. Specifically, casual reference to, or claims allegedly of, revolution understandably feed expectations of consequential change that are not realized.

Clausewitz's understanding of war and its conduct in warfare rested hugely upon his unquestionably deep and personal knowledge of its conduct from 1792 until the final fall of Napoleon in 1815. In his *magnum opus, On War,* he did not strive to range analytically over the whole of strategic history. What we know to be unmistakeably true enough is that, even if the Prussian had sought and been able to scour the entire historical record, he would not have been able to discover features in the nature of war notably dissimilar from those he could glean from his contemporary understanding. Greek phalanxes, Roman legions, and barbarian tribal war bands all fought for the same mix of motives as the three identified by Thucydides. Evolutionary and episodically even apparently revolutionary change in the means and methods employed in the conduct of war have occurred over millennia, but the general theory of strategy covers them all adequately. Contemporary would-be warriors need to know how to organize to fight effectively with the military technology available to them. But, to comment thus is to refer only to the often dynamic character of warfare, not to its enduring nature.

Even when organized violence is notably recreational and economically profitable (i.e. conducted with rape and pillage), still it will be substantially political in several

48 *War and warfare*

senses. Its conduct may be occasionally enjoyable for the warriors, but that conduct will have strategic consequences with political meaning. The fury of the Norsemen in the ninth and tenth centuries in particular may well seem a light year removed from the strategic diplomacy of Otto von Bismarck, but the fundamental ingredients for and of conflict were substantially the same in both cases: 'fear, honour, and interest' explains them well enough. If I am right, at least plausible, in arguing for the essential continuity of strategic history through the whole stream of time, the implications for our human future are reasonably clear, if not uncontroversial.

Because of the adversarial nature of strategy, fuelled as it must be by the political need for security, it is very likely to continue to be the case that wars and their ways in warfare will come and occasionally go, but little if anything of lasting note will disrupt the uneven but continuous flow of history. One cannot deny the possibility that the widespread and intensive use of nuclear weapons most probably would have consequences that would take the human race off the scale of political, let alone strategic, assessment, rendering most or all of such utterly irrelevant. But, that possibility aside, and because I am a working strategist, we can employ the evidence of strategic experience to help educate us for the future, though not as constituting judgement reliably of predictive quality.

Because we humans sensibly seek security, we are required to behave politically in ways that cannot fail to position us competitively in opposition to other necessarily politically organized polities. Polities need strategy in order to compete responsibly with other polities who are our adversaries. If we can resist becoming unduly excited by the advertised promise in changes in military technique and weaponry, we should be able to recognize the profound continuities that have underpinned all historical experience. At the high level of the meaning to events, if we are willing temporarily to suppress the 'what' and 'how' questions, the phenomena appropriately expressed by the French tag 'déja vu' is seen to be dominant. This is neither good news nor bad, it simply 'is'. Since the international politics of today with reference to Eastern Europe are all too easily comprehended with the educational assistance of a grasp of the course of the great Peloponnesian War of 431–404 BC, the argument for historical continuity is at least plausible. The character of battle changes with weaponry and to a more limited extent with the domestic context(s) for military organization. But, the all but organic and unique character of every war, the product of violent adversarial struggle, means that near constant change in character is thoroughly unremarkable. The factors making for an interactive constancy in the character of war and warfare need to be permitted to encourage us to be relaxed about changes in the character of violence, the uses made of force, which come, go, and always seem to come again, if in somewhat altered form.

Key points

1 The seven most vital concepts, from security (through politics, policy, grand and military strategy) down to tactics, are both logically and pragmatically necessarily hierarchical.
2 Battle may only be an episodic reality for soldiers, but its possibility is a permanent source of discipline for strategy.
3 Virtually all wars are waged for limited goals, though it can be difficult to restrain strategic command in the needed interest of political control.

4 The huge variety of wars and their warfare through the ages has not negated the subordination of military threat and action to policy that is always determined politically.
5 There is a permanent danger that warfare may escape from meaningful political control.
6 With the sole, albeit potentially critically significant, exception of nuclear warfare, war and warfare have proved to be as constant in their nature as they have been changeable in their character.

Further reading

Baylis, J., Wirtz, J. and Gray, C. S. (eds) (2015) *Strategy in the Contemporary World: An Introduction to Strategic Studies*, 5th edn, Oxford: Oxford University Press.

Black, J. (2009) *War: A Short History*, London: Continuum.

Bull, H. (1997) *The Anarchical Society: A Study of Order in World Politics*, New York: Columbia University Press.

Clausewitz, C. von (1976) *On War*, ed. and trans. Howard, M. and Paret, P., Princeton, NJ: Princeton University Press.

France, J. (2011) *Perilous Glory: The Rise of Western Military Power*, New Haven, CT: Yale University Press.

Gat, A. (2006) *War in Human Civilization*, Oxford: Oxford University Press.

Gray, C. S. (2012) *War, Peace and International Relations: An Introduction to Strategic History*, 2nd edn, Abingdon: Routledge.

Howard, M. (1983) *The Causes of Wars and Other Essays*, London: Counterpoint.

Mahnken, T. G. and Maiolo, J. A. (eds) (2014) *Strategic Studies: A Reader*, 2nd edn, Abingdon: Routledge.

Mearsheimer, J. J. (2014) *The Tragedy of Great Power Politics*, upd. edn, New York: W. W. Norton.

4 Theory for practice

> *Reader's guide:* The practice of strategic theory. The general theory of strategy. The function of strategic theory, explanation of the principal working parts. Education, doctrine, and training, complementary but distinctive. How strategic theory guides, even when it is not recognized.

Introduction: the practice of theory

Both of the two main subjects of this work, strategy and politics, are unrewarding to rules. People can be educated as to how they should reason strategically and politically, but neither field is promising ground for training. Those who believe they can teach what to think and how to behave, either in politics or strategy, are near certain to be disappointed by the subsequent performance of their pupils. These negative observations pertain only to general theory for strategy and politics, not to theory in the sense of doctrine for political activity, or that for military operations or military tactics. There are levels of military behaviour for which prescriptive manuals are necessary. Both operations and tactics have to be conducted with skills that can and should be taught and learnt. In regard to both operations and tactics there are usually right and wrong answers to standard categories and sub-categories of questions. Nevertheless, even at the tactical and operational levels of warfare, there is always some room for innovative and imaginative behaviour. Such non-standard action may well surprise an enemy who is faithful to a play-book that in substantial measure may be common among the belligerents. Even if the contending soldiers did not attend the same institutions of Higher Military Education, which can be the case in the event of civil war, it is likely that much, perhaps most, of the weaponry in a war will be accessible and usable, albeit variably, to both sides (Stoker, 2010). It is a military truth of enduring merit that how a weapon is used, especially in the moral matter of determination, is of greater significance than the technical issue of actual performance in destructive use. That said, it will always be true that even though strength of personal and group commitment to a fight may enable a greatly inferior unit to succeed against the material odds, the moral element should not be overvalued. King Leonidas of Sparta and his 300 elite warriors assuredly did not lack the will to fight on expertly, but they were simply overwhelmed by the numbers of the Persian enemy in 480 BC. Eventually, in all warfare, gross adverse asymmetry in numbers means defeat, if only for reason of the cumulative, even if disproportionally favourable, relative loss rate. Acute awareness of this remorseless fact of combat arithmetic was dominant in the mind of Britain's Air Chief Marshal Sir Hugh

Theory for practice 51

Dowding in the summer of 1940, when he employed the strategy of strictly minimal necessary engagement against the Luftwaffe (Gray, 2014b). In principle the RAF was fatally at risk to defeat by attrition if it was committed too carelessly in large number to combat. Dowding's strategy demanded that Fighter Command fight hard enough to keep hurting the German enemy and denying it a confident belief in victory, all the while staying in the fight sufficiently to discourage any practicable prospect of invasion.

Dowding could not reach for the general theory of strategy as a vital source to help him decide how, with what, and when he would conduct a Battle of Britain, should such a challenge need to be met. The general theory of strategy cannot be a source of advice on the crucial details concerning how to fight *now*. Such advice needs to be imported and absorbed as doctrine for tactics which is all about the best way understood now about how to fight. In wartime, certainly, doctrine needs constantly to be rewritten so as to reflect very recent experience in combat.

The better military historians have noticed that strategy inherently is more significant in its potential for net benefit or harm than are operations and tactics (Murray and Sinnreich, 2014: 3). The basic reason is that if a belligerent has a sound enough strategy, it is more probable than not that weakness in operational and tactical skills can be corrected, even if painfully, on a learning curve that can rise high enough that sees the wartime job overall through to eventual success. The American Civil War serves as a classic case in point. President Jefferson Davis is not known to have entertained any noteworthy thoughts that plausibly could be considered strategic (Stoker, 2010: 36). Unfortunately for the South, Davis' better generals were relatively superior only in the conduct both of operational art and battlefield tactics, but not in filling the vacuum that should have been Confederate strategy for the conduct of the war. The Emperor Napoleon, whose adventures were quite faithfully reflected in the writings of the most influential of military theorists in the first half of the nineteenth century, Baron Antoine Henri Jomini, had fallen terminally short of distinctively strategic acumen, as his exciting career revealed with appalling clarity. Napoleon, substantially via translations of Jomini's admiring prose, was the principal guide for generalship in America, North as well as South (Confederate) between 1861 and 1865. Serious deficiencies in strategic thought, education, and practice have more often been the rule than the exception in modern history. Often my use of the concept of strategic history is really ironic, because challengeable for the empirical reason that little, if any, conscious thought worthy of the strategic label is detectable from the record of events.

Here we proceed by explaining the meaning of theory for strategy; exploring the whole architecture of strategy; considering the relationships of dependency among education, doctrine and training; considering the argument and explaining that strategic theory is present as a guide for practice whether or not it is acknowledged to be an influence. Strategic theory in its several guises has practical authority in the guidance of soldiers that is more authoritative and pervasive than commonly is recognized. Hovering over all of this chapter is awareness of the inalienable presence of political decision and will. This presence may be hard to find at times, especially when the polity's strategic performance is less than exemplary; nonetheless it will be extant, even if only on life support.

General strategic theory

The library of first-rate studies over the course of millennia on general strategic theory is extremely small (Gray, 2010a: 244–6). Indeed, most probably it is no exaggeration to

52 *Theory for practice*

say that despite our species' permanent need to understand strategy, relatively little serious intellectual attention has been paid to the comprehension of military force both as threat and in action. Typically, no distinction is drawn between general theory and theory specific to a particular time, place, political and cultural parentage, and historical context. Here we draw a clear distinction between strategic theory as possibly eternal and universal truth, and strategic theory as a conceptual construction unquestionably specific to a time, place, and circumstance. In regard to the latter, it may be the case that some strategic theorists and their predominantly professional military audiences will believe they are reciting eternal and ubiquitous truths of strategy. However, in reality what they will be reciting and intellectually imbibing will be nostrums likely to be notably local to temporal, geographical, and possibly political and cultural circumstances. Both kinds of theory are necessary and essential, but it is important not to confuse them one with the other. As often as not, the distinction between general and more specific theory is not properly understood, which has to mean that the value of strategic theory is likely to be compromised fatally. As this distinction quite commonly is not understood, it is no surprise to realize that the worth of a general theory of strategy is not always well grasped by those most in need of its assistance.

The strategic theories particular to time and to often passing, though possibly temporarily dominant, conditions cannot prudently be designed or employed if the generals in authority are not confidently well enough educated by general theory (Elliott, 2015). The general theory of strategy is needed as conceptual preparation for specific theory design and choice. Only if and when the general theory is appreciated is the functional theory for contemporary strategy likely to be discovered and possibly applied with a superior chance of success. The functional theory of strategy for today is revealed admirably by Harold Winton, when he lays out with exemplary economy in functional terms what military theory should do (Winton, 2011). He advises that there are five principal functions of military theory: to define; categorize; explain; connect; and anticipate. These are not modest tasks in ambition for functional analysis, geared as they have to be to particular and therefore unavoidably transient circumstances in strategic history. Such functional theory has to be keyed to the dynamic narrative of tactical military capabilities and relationships. This is not criticism, because there is always a necessity to understand what should, or perhaps may be, possible tactically in warfare. Vital though this comprehension ought to be, it is not and cannot be a foundation upon which the understanding of strategy can be advanced. To define, categorize, explain, connect, and anticipate on the basis of what is known about the tactical military world in detail today certainly will not be safe as the footing for understanding why, how, and with what strategy performs throughout history. The challenge to the would-be general theorist of strategy is the necessity to navigate between, on the one hand, an all too dynamic material and contextual narrative and, on the other, claims for theory that are little more than platitudinous banalities. The general theorist has to avoid conceptual capture by details that have strictly only a particular contemporary claimed reality, and those so inclusive that their products are more akin to conceptual flatulence than to anything of educational value.

It is helpful to consider (military) strategy as having three distinctive meanings: (1) general understanding authoritative on all subjects of military importance, at all times and in all places; (2) understanding of the general meaning of distinctive military capabilities in particular places at particular times; and (3) the choices made historically in contexts that are always unique in detail, but will have much in common with

Theory for practice 53

other episodes of conflict during the same period. To summarize what we have just itemized amounts to an explanation of the roles of theory in educating for guidance in state practice. This can be expressed summarily as follows:

1 *General theory* provides the basic building blocks for understanding strategy.
2 *Particular general theory*, only superficially self-contradictory, provides understanding of distinctive categories of capability (e.g. landpower, airpower, and logistics).
3 *Strategies* comprise the choices made in particular contexts in order to achieve historically distinctive goals.

With respect to the connections, including interdependencies among these levels, each step on the ladder of increasing generality needs to be consistent with the truth expressed in the levels above. What this should mean is that the realm of practice in strategy selection is constructed with sound building blocks and just possibly also with binding material that will serve well enough to enable different military components to function to mutual advantage in joint endeavours. Steps (1) and (2) above are all about education, preparation for war perhaps, whereas step (3) moves from the world of theory very substantially into that of practice. The sole purpose of both general and particular general strategic theory is so to educate the practicing strategist that he is competent to undertake specific and unique tasks of the day. The logic here can be illustrated empirically by reference to any occasion of strategic need in support of policy in all of strategic history. Regardless of cultural and political variation across time and geography, people obliged to function strategically have had no choice other than to reason and behave in the terms just explained, notwithstanding the wide variations in language, belief systems, and material contexts. Whether it was an era with high-tech chariots, composite bows, gunpowder firearms, or nuclear weapons, strategists have needed to understand the basic logic of strategy, which is revealed most economically in the triadic formula of ends, ways, and means. This is general and all-purpose methodology for relating the capabilities of the military means available at their time and to their polity, and the ways in which those means could wage warfare in pursuit of military outcomes that should advance strategic and ultimately political ends (Yarger, 2008).

General theory is written and taught strictly for the immediate purpose of education. It can be likened to mathematics taught for the purpose of so educating scientists that they are enabled to analyze whatever specific problems will be their particular concerns. Particular general theory is an essential step in further education on the road towards readiness to tackle specific challenges for the state. For example, in all periods of strategic history it has been important, often vitally so, that generals and admirals should have sufficient understanding of each other's distinctive military world so that some mutually tolerable jointness of strategic endeavour should be feasible. Napoleon's lack of grasp of naval realities could prove deadly to French admirals who sometimes were ordered to behave imprudently, while in Britain the future Duke of Wellington could prove lacking in understanding of what was and what was not practicable by way of the seaborne logistics vital for his army in the Peninsula. Generically, this class of difficulty for strategy persists to the present day, when nominally joint operations, commanded from supposedly joint headquarters, are found in practice to require a specific form of military capability that is beyond its reliable achievement. The modern world of practice to which we refer is one wherein military forces specializing in operations on land, at sea, and in the air are obliged to cooperate to and beyond the point of critical mission

54 *Theory for practice*

interdependence. If soldiers understand land warfare, as they must, and, for example, the air force understands its distinctive aerial environment (with similar comments applying to the sea and to cyber), what does each geophysically specialized element comprehend about the others, and how much does that matter? The vital backcloth to the argument developed here commonly is one of near exclusive geographical specialization by service, typically until a level of career seniority is reached where joint perspectives are met seriously. Nonetheless, for nearly all of a military person's professional life, he or she has to be near totally absorbed by the 'grammar' of warfare in a single geographical environment (Clausewitz, 1976: 605). The unavoidable trouble is that although strategy, and sometimes operations, is intended to be joint today, neither geography nor, necessarily and as an unforgiving consequence, tactics can follow suit closely. This context for modern strategic history has implications leading to potential difficulty, most especially with respect to sailors and aviators obliged by geophysical necessity to be isolated from the land and all that it means in and to conflict. The professional demands for technical competence made of sailors and airmen persistently are so heavy that little time is available for some mastery of trends in combat capability or even argument in other geographies. Higher military education for competence in joint warfare is apt to be dangerously slight outside a particular individual's by then quite long experience on land, at sea, or in the air. Given this reality in experience, it follows that the general theory of strategy needs to provide as much education as it is able, in order to provide some compensation for the particulars of education in the geographical contexts missing from his professional resumé.

The function of theory: explaining the strategy puzzle

The core function of theory is explanation – whether it is simple or complex is of no consequence for its function, which is universal and eternal. Also, of course, it may be wrong, if and when new and different empirical evidence gives rise to demands for a change in theory. Strategy and politics have altered greatly in their more obvious aspects over the course of millennia, but scarcely at all when they are understood in functional terms as they most need to be. Strategy is about the consequences of efforts to achieve the goals that politics decides it wishes a community to pursue. In order to gain the necessary clear understanding of how strategy and politics complement each other, this section explains the nature and functions of the seven concepts that may be characterized as the strategy puzzle. There should be clear comprehension of the identities of the seven pieces on the board, their functions, and how they relate each to the others. These ideas are very familiar, but their meaning is not always grasped as firmly as it needs to be. The seven concepts considered here are: security; politics; policy; grand strategy; military strategy; operations; and tactics. Important ancillary concepts excluded from that list include assumptions and logistics. Security is about the reasons why politics, policy, and strategy strive to achieve what they do; policy concerns the goals selected by politics to be accomplished strategically; while strategy addresses the ways in which policy is pursued by force, and about the consequences of that pursuit (in the context of this book). Operations and tactics are about the execution of strategy.

1. *Security* is the conclusive purpose of strategy, even though it is a distinctly subjective idea or even feeling. Nearly all strategy, at all times and everywhere, is intended by policy to advance the security condition of a polity. This condition surfaces in public discourse usually with some physical reference. It can find translation territorially with

respect to people and their real or alleged ethnicity, or it may be manifested as demand for achievement of a particular competitive balance in armaments. As often as not there is no very credible metric for comparison of a state's alleged security vis à vis another state. Commonly it is adequate simply to invest more heavily than previously in the activities that tend to make particular communities feel more secure. Seriously troubled, even frightened, people are likely to attend church more often, and to pay more in taxes towards the cost of national security. Because of its subjectivity, feelings of insecurity can be hard to allay. Nonetheless, somewhat indeterminate though it is almost bound to be, security is what our subjects here are all about. The fact that a condition of security usually is desperately short on supporting evidence capable of verification with complete reliability does not suffice to dampen enthusiasm for this concept. The all but promiscuous use and misuse of the elevated concepts of international and national security have rendered this opaque and rather vaporous idea unfortunately popular. The United States led the way in the 1940s in official adoption of the concept of national security; Britain followed suit, as usual faint but pursuing, sixty years later (Great Britain H. M. Government, 2010).

Unfortunately, the inclusive vagueness of the concept of security is the quality that renders its charms so appealing to politicians. Since the grim world of strategy requires political translation before it can be presented in terms of security and insecurity, it has irresistible appeal to those who function professionally in search of public influence as politicians. It should be recognized that future dangers are likely to promote anticipatory anxieties and even fear. This means that the problem with security is not really with the empirical uncertainty of evidence about the future, but rather with the range of unpleasant happenings that we know for certain strategic history could send our way. The problem lies in ill chance, accident, and the violence consequent upon the dynamism of competitive and anarchic inter-state political relations, not truly with an innocent concept that expresses all too inclusively the sources of our anxiety (Booth, 2007). Those among us seriously dissatisfied with the vagueness and indeterminacy in the concept of security deserve to be challenged to suggest a more useful alternative.

2. *Politics* is the pragmatic shaper and driver of the policy that orders the world of strategy. Politicians are acutely aware that their authority in determining policy is issued under licence by political process. Of course, the process varies markedly from country to country, but my claim is largely indifferent to variety among domestic processes. All polities require legitimacy for policy to be secured by successful management of local political process. Strategists should not be misled by institutional appearances or unduly casual language into the false belief that their product, strategy, emerges in purified form from an orderly process of policymaking that rests really only nominally on the consequences of the rough and tumble understood to be in the nature of political process (Gray, 2014a). Admittedly, the relationship between careful administration and political process is not always clearly determinable. Indeed, so deeply enmeshed are strategic choices in political preferences, and so reliant can they be on political assumptions, that it is a challenge to try to determine the role played by evidence of need in the decisions taken and pursued. Once one considers critically competing claims for alleged strategic need, one realizes there can be a fundamental problem lurking in the function of politics with respect to the selection of strategy. If politics is the art of the possible, then so also must be the fate of policy and strategy. It should not be thought that politics and its process is simply one phase in the strategy narrative. On the contrary, political process can have influence all of the time and at all levels of behaviour. It is

56   *Theory for practice*

commonplace to believe that domestic political process has no authority over operational choice and tactical behaviour, both allegedly reposing comfortably in a combat zone free of politics. This popular view is incorrect. The permanent concern to secure political favour at home, especially in this new era of widespread social media IT accessibility, means that the keys to the kingdom with respect to the waging of its warfare are not handed over to the generals for the duration of a conflict. Because all military behaviour has some meaning for strategy, no matter that it is organized and identified in theory as being operational or tactical, it is always possible, even probable, that its strategic significance flags for political attention. The influence of political process may be felt on all military matters. Recognition of this contemporary reality simply is obscured by diagrammatic representation of the strategy process that inadvertently misleads by depicting a hierarchical flow chart that positions 'politics' as a phase that passes only down to policy. Intellectually and as a necessary matter of levels of authority and decision, there is indeed a hierarchy, but it is not one that demarcates and thereby limits plainly what is, and what is not, the zone for politics. Although this has been written with a simplified context of a single belligerent's domestic political process in mind, the influence of political process can be felt even more strongly through all the levels of warfare in the context of coalition and alliance warfare.

3. *Policy* is the product of political process, though other influences may be felt. It might be imagined that selections of policy objectives must be heavily disciplined by the influence of events beyond the reach, let alone control, of domestic political process. It should not be forgotten that although events more or less distantly abroad may themselves be entirely untouched by our domestic politics, that domestic political process will determine what, if anything, we strive to do about them. Therefore, our domestic political process can have a potent influence on the course and outcome of foreign war, since our politics will have to decide whether or not we should intervene, and how we might do so. The politics of policy means that the goals for achievement passed down to professional military strategists from policy process will almost always be a work still in progress. Politician policymakers, ordering a variant of limited warfare, always need to provide for some freedom of possible policy change in the future. This means that political instruction to the strategist will be restrictive in contrast to permissive.

Policy choice for the guidance of strategy usually can be influenced by foreign authored (mis)behaviour, but that is not the elementary and reliable conclusion to our possible policy dilemma. The political and strategic meaning of foreign behaviour often will not be clear. This means that our domestic and even Alliance-wide political process will not be tripped, as it were, automatically into reactive motion; instead it may be decided that there is less military menace in events than many people feared. This conclusion could well reflect simply a primarily political judgement. If there is no heavy role for strategic discipline to be enforced because of evidence of danger from abroad, political process can be shaped and steered very largely by the influence of domestic factors alone. We may be untroubled by external contextual hazard – until, that is, the foreign danger itself proves beyond argument that it means deadly serious business.

4. and 5. *Grand* and *Military strategy* is determined very substantially by political process for reasons that politically are easily intelligible. This analysis is not dismissive of the significance of influences on strategy beyond the normal scope of domestic political process; rather is it important to take an inclusive view of the relevant scope for concern of that process. This is not an elementary matter of binary choice, foreign as opposed to domestic priorities, or more as opposed to less resource allocation for

defence. It is a common error to confuse tactics with strategy by conflating the two. Almost invariably this results in the essentially conceptual and non-material phenomena that comprise strategy being neglected in favour of the more exciting and tangible action of tactics. Similarly, strategy is apt to suffer some demotion when it is conflated, though often actually confused with policy. Thus, understanding of our subject is apt to suffer because both the lower tactical step and the higher policy one attract attention and argument that ought to be more focused on strategy. It is perhaps ironic that policy choices often come to function as lightning rods for public notice, when the damage that they can cause more reasonably should be laid at the door of the political process that first produced and then subsequently sustained them.

Although strategy should serve as the bridge between policy purpose and warfare, it is necessary to resist its unwise, because imprudent, extension on to the distinctive activities and responsibilities on either or both banks. It is a persisting challenge to the strategist, on the one hand to select ways to employ force that should support policy, while on the other, choosing ways that friendly military forces can execute tactically and operationally. Since an instinct and inclination for strategy are rare qualities for soldiers, there is a frequent tendency for them to retreat from its possibly ill understood frustrations back into core comfort zones of apparently apolitical operations and tactics. Rarely, the gifted soldier is by instinct and perhaps preference more of a politician manqué than a true warrior. This translates as meaning that he will be eager to cross the strategy bridge almost definitively and function actively as a policymaker, with the political requirements that must accompany such a de facto professional transition. For powerful reasons both of circumstance and personal inclination, often it is difficult for a state to maintain integrity on its strategy bridge. Because it is critically important for a military strategist to remain current regarding the policy choices reflected in the military effort expended, there must be a perpetual need for the strategist to be able to function effectively with, if not quite in, politics (Clausewitz, 1976: 81, 605–10). Concerning the physical military action bank to the strategy bridge, no less pressing than the strategist's need to understand policy and its politics is the necessity of his understanding how well or poorly the soldiers are performing tactically, and why. There is a persisting difficulty in maintaining a sufficiently distinctive focus on strategy on and from the hypothetical bridge, because both banks of the river offer siren-call attractions and distractions. Though a professional and senior soldier, the strategist faces constant appeals and even demands for his cooperation in plainly political endeavour. Also, frequently, the strategist finds himself distracted by operational and even tactical concerns that more properly are the delegated responsibilities of subordinates with command responsibilities.

The soldier strategist tempted or morally obliged to function in a near overtly political role, or who is seduced by personal interest into addressing tactical concerns that were his perhaps a quarter-century previously in his career, will not find the time necessary to function adequately as a strategic thinker and planner. Strategy needs higher direction by the results of political process expressed as and in policy. Also, in its way as important, strategy needs to be informed expertly about the military capabilities on which it can rely tactically and operationally. That said, there must remain a core integrity to strategy that clearly is outside the conceptual and the corresponding physical categories of politics or of tactics. Strategy is neither politics and its policy, nor is it tactics with its warfare, but it is necessary for it to be able to connect the two, hence the suitability of the metaphor of a strategy bridge (Gray, 2010a). Dicta 1 and 2 are my definitions respectively of grand and military strategy (Gray, 2015b). Strategic

58 *Theory for practice*

history records much evidence of a breakdown, even a total non-appearance of strategy, because the person required to function as a strategist was unduly distracted by political concerns or by tactical challenges passed up to his high level by subordinates. The staff college simplicity of the formula that claims the essential structure of our subject consists of ends, ways, means, and assumptions has much to recommend it. Probably its greatest virtues are the clear distinctions it asserts. In practice, everything depends upon everything else, in the spirit of Alexander Dumas' *Three Musketeers*: One for all, and all for one! However, the undeniable necessity for each element among the three to rely heavily upon understanding of the pertinent contextual meaning of the others should never be permitted to excuse inattention to the capability to perform distinctive functions. As politics and policy decides what will be attempted, and tactics provides capability to fight well enough, so strategy must design ways in which to employ available fighting power for policy purpose. Political awareness and tactical understanding are necessary for a strategist, but those are not defining for his job description.

6. and 7. *Operations* and *Tactics* are the means in the standard triadic formula. All military units do tactics, while typically clusters of (necessarily tactical) units are organized and directed at the operational level of war. This level needs guidance by strategy and coordination for mutual support with other operational groupings. For example, in spring 1815, with the Emperor restored to power on 20 March following his all too brief temporary exile on Elba, the enemies of France had assembled in the field: 92,000 soldiers under Wellington; 121,000 Prussians under Blücher; 225,000 Austrians under Schwarzenberg (and another 85,000 in Italy and the south of France); there were 168,000 Russians slowly approaching, while Spanish and Portuguese troops also were invading France across the Pyrenees. With everybody counted, Napoleon faced a potential need to counter actions by close to 1,000,000 enemy soldiers (Stoker, 2014: 225). Obviously, the articulation of armies, let alone among the armies of more or less closely cooperating allies or coalition partners, required a kind of military skill that approached what often is understood by strategy. Operational art became a necessity during the Napoleonic Wars, when the scale of land conflict became so great that whole campaigns rather than individual battles were recognized as the new character of warfare. In the period 1809–13, belligerents were too powerful militarily to be terminally vulnerable to defeat in a single battle. From this time through to the end of the Second World War, the idea of a decisive battle remained popular, but in practice it proved elusive or, more often, impossible. If a state or coalition fought only for limited policy goals, it was not likely that military decision by combat would be sufficiently discouraging as to prompt urgent discovery of the virtue in peace. However, when the political motive in war was of an absolute kind needing the agency of victory to settle matters, wars typically were protracted by the strength of political will that enabled truly extraordinary commitment and sacrifice. In the major wars from the mid nineteenth century through the Second World War, the human and material contexts of major war required skill in operational art in order to translate large-scale tactical effectiveness in fighting into definitive strategic advantage (Olsen and van Creveld, 2011).

In theory, operational art organizes, directs, and employs tactical fighting power for the purpose of strategy, or at least with the benefit of strategic sense. In practice, however it is argued by some, operational art intrudes destructively into the realm of strategy, with the latter's goals being neglected or perhaps supplemented by strictly operational goals (Kelly and Brennan, 2009). In this critical view, operational art is pursued in a context agreeably free from politics for the professional soldier. Whereas tactical expertise can and must be taught, operational art usually needs to be exercised with some discretion particular to the whole military context of the period. This means that although there are, for example, logistical disciplines imposed by the physical constraints that beset issues of supply and movement, choices will need to be made over military objectives and the commitment of particular formations to chosen priorities. The priorities for operational effort should be commanded by strategic sense, though not necessarily directed explicitly by strategy as such. Operational art thus has to be used strategically in order to ensure that individual campaigns contribute usefully to progress in a war as a whole. The articulation of organization of armies into individual or sometimes entire corps (usually comprising two or three divisions per corps) was a necessity driven by the growth in size of forces and logistical realities, but also it proved a vital enabler of coordinated manoeuvre. Operational level manoeuvre can be a critically significant key to victory on the part of commanders skilled in its administrative direction and blessed with good luck. But, all too easily it can be a key element contributing to military disaster, or at best to stalemate. An army may be thought of as a mighty vehicle that purposefully is organized, deployed, and committed to manoeuvre for battle. The army has major working parts that need to act cooperatively in well enough coordinated ways. In other words, we will march divided, but we need to fight united. If command, even superior command, at corps level is not exercised under a strategic level of discipline bearing upon the whole direction of military effort in a theatre of operations, operational commanders may well be able and possibly inclined to play strategist themselves. Both command and control are essential if command in operational level warfare is to be prevented reliably from substituting for an absent strategy.

The potential challenge to the authority of strategy inherent in the exercise of operational art has to be preceded by competent provision of the discipline of strategy, both for a particular geographical theatre and for a whole war effort in a conflict comprising several theatres.

Education, doctrine, and training

Strategists cannot be trained, but they can be educated (Gray, 2009b). In order to train there is a necessity for doctrine, though not for strategy. Training manuals provide instruction, often mandatory, on how to perform standard military tasks, but exceptional needs calling for abnormal methods usually are admitted though certainly not encouraged. Although there are eternal verities that should hold for operational art and tactics, these critically important categories of military skills are both of them subject to near constant change. This has not always been so, but assuredly it has been true since the time of the Napoleonic Wars (France, 2011: Ch. 7). Agricultural revolution in the eighteenth century was enhanced and deepened by the Industrial Revolution early in the nineteenth century, which in its turn was partially enabled and accelerated by a revolution in communications. These changes were made manifest primarily by the power of steam generated from coal, and by the iron and then steel that steam allowed factories to produce. Since early in the nineteenth century, material change, usually judgementally termed progress, has been continuous and normal. Material, now principally immaterial electronic, advance with good reason is anticipated for the future. All too obviously, the substantial material dimension to warfare has periodically, if episodically, been a severe challenge to soldiers who have had no choice but to attempt

60 *Theory for practice*

to make tactical, operational, and strategic sense of near continuous technological evolution and occasional revolution.

Contrary to some widespread popular opinion, technological change, even revolution, does not much matter for strategy when it is regarded through the lens that seeks to detect general truth. But, fortunately or unfortunately, polities cannot usefully ask their strategists to turn the pages of their favourite, or at least most fashionable, general strategic theorist in order to extract or download eternal wisdom in answer to the ever vexed question, 'how do we fight this particular war?' The difficulty lies in the fact that the challenges to strategy in history, including our own, are always to a considerable degree unique in detail. Furthermore, the whole context of war, looking at a specific conflict at a particular time, is also both unique and ever changing. What this has to mean, as Carl von Clausewitz recognized unambiguously, is that better understanding of strategy's general theory should so educate the executive strategist that he can cope with the dangers and opportunities of his time. The selection of strategy for necessary command, and hopefully control in support of the ends of policy, is more likely to emerge from a mind trained in how best to think strategically, as contrasted with one easily satisfied by more common, perhaps formulaic, candidate solutions. For soldiers who have spent decades of their professional lives seeking to master tactical and then, on serious promotion, operational tasks, strategy can be a bridge too far to attempt to reach.

Strategy requiring imagination and a willingness to be prepared to reject long favoured formulae, including habitual responses to problems, is a creative art. Military minds cannot be well enough prepared to meet strategic challenge for reason of their having been instructed by 'how to…' practical manuals. In sharp contrast, such tactical questions as to how to deploy scarce troops for perimeter security, and operational issues such as how best to manoeuvre forces for mutual support, are permissive of calculation for demonstrably correct solutions. But, strategy has little in common with these fairly mundane tactical and operational tasks. There is no school (i.e. staff college) solution to the challenge of how to defeat Nazi Germany, Imperial Japan, North Korea and Red China, or the Vietcong as well as the North Vietnamese Army (NVA). Readers can bring this argument up until the present day should they so choose. Even if a polity is well peopled by military strategists who have read and understood the undoubted classics on strategy's general theory, there can be no guarantee that major advantage must follow as a deserved consequence.

The caution just expressed reflects the notably Clausewitzian, albeit simply common sensible, view that war and its warfare is a realm wherein some 'friction' is normal, and luck and accident may frustrate even the best laid plans (Clausewitz, 1976: 119–21). The realm of strategy is one characterized so heavily by irony that cleverness, brilliance even, is rarely a guarantee of strategic genius. Subtlety and nuance may serve diplomacy well, but for strategy there is sometimes much to be said in praise of readiness to act boldly and suddenly. This is not meant as criticism of intellect and imagination; rather is it offered as a caveat conceding the limited value of creative imagination and impulse not married to superior qualities of judgement and determination (Clausewitz, 1976: Ch. 3). The whole of strategic history can be raided in search of non-violent solutions to the challenges of the day that might well be deemed missed opportunities. However, we need to recognize that even though usually there are political solutions to conflicts, those answers often are inadequate to prevent war. Strategy can fail, even if it is chosen intelligently. Because tactics and operations have only limited domains, it can be difficult for those truly skilled in their practice to comprehend how it can be possible to fail in

Theory for practice 61

war that is well fought. Surely, one might enquire, if we fight well and typically success-fully, which is a tactical and possibly also an operational assessment, overall success in a war, in short strategic success, should follow all but automatically and inevitably by right of victory in combat? The tactician and also the operational artist need to understand that theirs is so heavily, even exclusively, a military context that they may not be able to gauge how the record in battle should translate into political consequences, indeed even if it can so do.

Operational artistry and certainly tactics can be taught and learnt, but – to repeat – strategy cannot. Operational challenges and tactical dilemmas commonly repeat in a particular historical context, but strategy usually does not. Strategy in practice so often disappoints its political sponsors and military author-executives because, although it tends to be fairly simple, it is populated abundantly by difficulties. In summary, to borrow again from Clausewitz, 'friction' frequently appears to reign and rule over the domain of the strategist (1976).

Conclusion: theory guides, even when unacknowledged

The proposition that strategic theory is a body of thought quite apart from the real world of practice is seriously incorrect. The idea that the world of the working strategist is one wherein theory does not hover over the course of events, potentially to harass the busy soldier or statesman, is seriously in need of revision. This author, who for many years occupied positions between the domains of strategic practice and strategic theory, has come to recognize that the common distinction usually drawn between them is misleading at best, and wrong at worst. Strategic practice is scarcely possible without assistance from theory. There is much to be said in praise of the argument which holds that strategic theory and strategic practice are but two sides of the same coin. When one explores the meaning of theory, as in this chapter, recognition of the umbilical nature of the mutual dependency of theory and practice becomes irresistible. Since the core meaning of theory is explanation, the role of strategic theory is usefully clarified, though not entirely without some trouble from irony and occasionally paradox. All strategic practice must rest upon accepted explanation of the anticipated causes of desired consequences. This cannot be scientific theory, because it is not empirically verifiable ahead of time. Even if there is empirical understanding of what should happen as a result of an exceedingly large seaborne invasion of Normandy, assisted by a paratroop and glider-borne descent on an unprecedented scale enabled by supremacy in the air, it will remain a sovereign fact that such a unique event is a practice of theory. Because there are so many dimensions to strategy, not least the adversarial, the antici-pation of future strategic history cannot be other than an exercise in theory (Gray, 1999: Ch. 1). Anticipated, even predicted causal connections leading to advantageous consequences, is an exercise of and in theory.

Once strategic theory is de-mystified from allegedly having a meaning usually that is rather abstract, and even esoteric, as contrasted with the more direct and robust appearance of actual strategic choices made real-time in definite strategic context, more sensible appreciation can proceed. The fundamental reason why strategy is a field governed by speculative theory is because the empiricism required for science is unavail-able. Strategic theory is an art and not a science because it cannot repeatedly be tested empirically in verification of its claims (Grygiel, 2013). Readers may recall that this text has argued that strategic theory cannot be taught for the purpose of training future

62 *Theory for practice*

strategists. Clarification of my meaning should be enhanced if we contrast the education needed for strategy with that provided for cooking. With respect to the latter, although individual flair (genius?), chance, and accident are all possible contributors to an event, nonetheless it is practicable to teach people in different countries and in different times how to cook the same dish satisfactorily (i.e. well enough). One can instruct concerning the necessary material ingredients, the heat required and its duration. Although there is usually scope for some individual variation by discretion, the basic process is open to expert explanation of the relations between cause and effect. The contrast between an attempt to educate about strategy and teach cooking, even at the highest and most demanding of levels, could hardly be sharper. In cooking, it should be possible to produce the right result, which is to say the dish intended, every time (albeit after considerable practice). For strategy, there can be no realistically approximate practice and no scientific theory, reassuringly empirically verifiable with safety. Nonetheless, strategic theory is needed in order to explain what ought to be attempted in order to secure desired results.

We function as strategic theorists because we have no other practicable and prospectively successful choices available to us. The theory used day by day and every day is not usually entirely bereft of empirical support from strategic historical experience, but such data needs to be appreciated as essentially unreliable. The problem is not simply resolvable by the accumulation and analysis of more data. The key indeterminacy pertains to the very nature of our subject. The politics that shape and drive strategic choice are not and cannot be controllable as is taught in cooking school. The Western strategist does not really know how much, and what kinds, in the way of economic and political sanctions, are required in order to deter Vladimir Putin from proceeding further with his campaign to undermine the viability and sovereignty of Ukraine. Furthermore, it is unlikely that Putin knows either. The process in question here in this contemporary example is organically dynamic, quintessentially adversarial, and is beyond the reliable reach of understanding by any variant of strategic theory that aspires to be able to anticipate. Although the situation in and with Ukraine is especially troublesome, it is deployed here simply because its very nature should make clear both the unavoidable necessity for strategic theory, yet also the limitations of such. The example of contemporary Ukraine with regard to the importance of theory invites speculation that the reason why NATO and the European Union have had little obvious success is because they have failed dismally to assess Putin's policy ends correctly. It is more than likely that his strategy is not so much intended to undermine Ukraine as an end in itself, but rather to advance the power and glory of a returning Great Power Russia. In the latter case, Ukraine simply is a convenient pawn; it is not really what is at stake in the international contest.

It is being argued here that strategic theory is as essential as it is unavoidable, while also that it can never be practised with complete confidence as to its reliability. If ever a country appeared to be ready enough to face up to, and see off, severe strategic challenge, it was the United States in the mid-to-late 1960s. The country was awash with theory that on the evidence appeared to be good enough concerning nuclear deterrence, the conduct of limited war, and arms control. The years from 1954 until, arguably, 1967 had some plausible claim to be regarded as a 'golden age' of (largely American) strategic thought for practice (Gray, 1982). Nevertheless, somehow the next decade, with the war in Vietnam, proved to be a strategic experience that was an extended nightmare. The theory of statecraft (politics) and strategy with which the war was conducted were shown unmistakably to have been unfit for their purpose. Moving on historically, though alas not upwards in quality, American-led statecraft and strategy failed again in the 2000s, in Afghanistan and Iraq. Empathically, this is neither to claim or even necessarily to imply that success should have been achievable, if only... The most important role of theory, its central function, is to explain the nature of strategic phenomena. In addition it is necessary for theory to reveal their working, their connection with extra-strategic elements, and their probable consequences (Winton, 2011). It is all too plausible to maintain that both in the 1960s and the 2000s the theory available as a vital guide for the practice of strategy and the politics of statecraft were inadequate. In both historical eras, however, it appears to have been the case that Western political difficulty was attributable more to the pragmatic choices made than to the body of theory on offer in explanations and as advice from scholars. As the saying goes, success is never short of claims to parenthood, whereas, in contrast, defeat is always an orphan.

Key points

1 There are no rules for strategy, which means that military students cannot be taught right answers.
2 General strategic theory is valid for all times, all places, and all circumstances.
3 The core function of theory is explanation; general theory provides education about how to think strategically.
4 There is in principle a clear hierarchy of authority in strategic affairs, reaching from security at the top, down successively through politics, policy, grand and military strategies, to operations and tactics at the bottom. Although this is a hierarchy of authority, in practice it needs to be a whole team effort, with each level of activity contributing uniquely and essentially.
5 While strategy can only be taught as education, operations and tactics require instruction and training for the imparting of correct methods.
6 Even though the fact typically is not noticed, most practice of strategy rests upon the theoretical beliefs of the strategist (or the strategy-making process).

References

Clausewitz, C. von (1976) *On War*, ed. and trans. Howard, M. and Paret, P., Princeton, NJ: Princeton University Press.
France, J. (2011) *Perilous Glory: The Rise of Western Military Power*, New Haven, CT: Yale University Press.
Gray, C. S. (2010a) *The Strategy Bridge: Theory for Practice*, Oxford: Oxford University Press.
Heuser, B. (2010) *The Evolution of Strategy: Thinking War from Antiquity to the Present*, Cambridge: Cambridge University Press.
Kane, T. M. (2013) *Strategy: Key Thinkers A Critical Engagement*, Cambridge: Polity Press.
Murray, W. and Sinnreich, R. H. (eds) (2014) *Successful Strategies: Triumphing in War and Peace from Antiquity to the Present*, Cambridge: Cambridge University Press.
Paret, P. (ed.) (1986) *Makers of Modern Strategy: From Machiavelli to the Nuclear Age*, Princeton, NJ: Princeton University Press.
Strachan, H. (2007) *Clausewitz's On War: A Biography*, New York: Atlantic Monthly Press.
Tzu, S. (1963) *The Art of War*, trans. Griffith, S. B., Oxford: Clarendon Press.
Winton, H. R. (2011) 'An Imperfect Jewel: Military Theory and the Military Profession', *The Journal of Strategic Studies*, 34: 853–897.

5 Making strategy

> *Reader's guide:* The whole process of making strategy. Strategy-making as process. The importance of context. Policymaking and strategy-making for Britain: key assumptions. The importance of surprise, accident, and non-linearity. Prudent adaptability vital for strategy.

Introduction: holistic understanding

Much of the writing on strategy errs in taking a still photograph of what is really a dynamic subject. The argument central to this chapter was expressed succinctly by historians Williamson Murray and Mark Grimsley in these words: '[s]trategy is a process, a constant adaptation to shifting conditions and circumstances in a world where chance, uncertainty, and ambiguity dominate' (1994: 1). The idea of motion, indeed even of change, claimed in the words quoted, is apt to make scholars uneasy and active policymakers and strategists potentially embarrassed. In common usage, policy and strategy often are regarded substantially as fixed items. While armed forces *do* tactics and operations, in some contrast usually, allegedly, they *have* policy and strategy. This contrast is not entirely mistaken, but nonetheless it is likely to mislead the unwary. Here it is argued that both policy and strategy almost always are required to be somewhat flexible and adaptable to the changing circumstances of context. Good enough policy and strategy should always be 'work in progress', at least to some modest degree. It can be difficult to argue thus, without as a direct consequence appearing to be dangerously willing to remove boundaries from what ought to be firm and clear intentions.

The argument here rests firmly on empirical evidence. It is no great challenge to historical scholarship to show that policy intentions and major designs in strategy often, indeed typically, are changed in the light of evidence from contemporary experience. More often than not, what scholars and others fail to understand fully is the continuous nature of the subjects analyzed here. The factor functioning most influentially on strategy undoubtedly is politics. It is a mistake to regard the two titular subjects of this book as products very largely settled in a particular historical context; often this is a serious misrepresentation of the course of strategic history. Of course, there are always practicable constraints that limit the scope for desirable strategic adjustment. For example, although Nazi Germany's Luftwaffe was both technically and tactically excellent, it demonstrated beyond room for doubt in the summer of 1940 that it was the wrong kind of air force for the circumstances of the times. Germany's bombers were not heavy enough for the anti-urban coercive task set them by Hitler, while the fighter force was far too short in range (Gray, 2014b). These were systemic limitations that could not be offset in the short or medium terms. For another example of a serious material constraint, the British Army in 1914 and 1915 was not equipped with the weight and number of heavy artillery pieces needed for the effective waging of warfare against an enemy well dug in. Virtually no matter how prominent is strategic genius, the practice of strategy invariably must require mutually enabling support among its ends, ways, and means. As strategy is made, the closest attention has to be paid to the material feasibility of chosen operations. Although general strategic theory is applicable to all of strategic history, chosen strategies need to accommodate every item in the standard formula comprising ends, ways, and means. Brilliance in concept is admirable, but feasibility of accomplishment by troops is a test that cannot be evaded.

The political process that generates strategy also must generate the military means to be employed. Time often determines the course of strategic history, its tempo at least. The time needed for the practice of strategy differs greatly among political ends, strategic ways, and military means. If, by strategy, one intends to refer principally to the political choices known as policy, the timescale for a shift in official emphasis may be as brief as a few hours or days. But, if one seeks to consider strategy more responsibly, there is no escaping the problem of lead-time. Even if the human and material resources to implement strategy are available and usable, neither of which necessarily should be assumed, the time frame necessary to transform basic assets into militarily useful capability can be *inconveniently* long. For another example from the First World War, until 1918 the British Army was not convincingly ready enough to wage the war that it found itself fighting. Politicians can decide in a single meeting that the country should or should not fight, while strategy for the war in question may be selected on the basis of inspiration and hope generated in a meeting or two. However, war always is waged by each of the three close relatives – ends, ways, and means – under the guidance provided by the assumptions fashionable at the time.

Chapter 5 considers the political process necessary for the production of strategy, and examines how that process functions. The context for the conception and development of strategy is discussed next, followed by the centrepiece for this chapter: consideration of the assumptions that shape the British task of strategy-making. Next is offered a review of some of the more important sources of problems for the strategist; I term these 'speed bumps', though they can be lethal in effect. Finally, on a somewhat positive note the chapter concludes with a terse re-emphasis on the merit of prudent adaptability for strategy.

Strategy-making as process

The interactive adversarial nature of war renders anticipation of its course a hazardous as well as potentially embarrassing venture into the unforeseeable and therefore unknowable future (Porter, 2009: 65, 170). When a state decides to fight it is moving from a context probably dimly lit, but still controllable in large measure, into a zone wherein no one really can be in control. It needs to be realized that a condition of war is one wherein there are almost always three major players, two (possibly plus) belligerents and the offspring of their violent antagonism, the war itself. This reification is a persistent reality in strategic history. When two politically sovereign states combine in

66 *Making strategy*

antagonism to fight a war, the violent offspring is near certain to have characteristics consequential from a particular unique clash of arms, resulting in a strategic historical episode true only to itself. The war may well merit objectification as an apparently organic happening and experience that bears little relation to the conflict that its belligerently adversarial parents originally believed they were undertaking. Not infrequently, states find themselves locked all but inextricably into a struggle over the course of which they have little control. The warfare and then consequently the war largely proceed as they must according to the dynamic net verdict of success and failure in battle. Because war is interactive and adversarial it can proceed whither it does, virtually regardless of all but hapless policy and strategic intentions.

What we are describing is a tendency to independence from political and strategic control common to all war. War is about politics, but itself is not politics, while strategy strives to render the threat and use of military force supportive of political goals. A major reason why strategy-making must be approached as process is because the violent behaviour in warfare it endeavours to shape, direct, and control is always obliged in the main to be responsive to the contemporary necessities of an interactive struggle. This statement would make no sense were war a violent episode that a polity could fashion and dictate unilaterally. In practice, always, there are antagonistic belligerents who, in effect, are making up the course, outcome, and consequences of a particular war creatively and emphatically contestably. As a general and universal rule, belligerents cannot know in advance just how a war will proceed and conclude. The logically interdependent structure of ends, ways and means, though essential to understand, also encourages dangerous fallacies. Although Clausewitz certainly is persuasive with his insistence that war should 'never be thought of as *something autonomous* but always as an *instrument of policy*', nonetheless there are severe difficulties with the condition that he defines thus (1976: 88). So important are these difficulties for the relations between strategy and politics that it is necessary to treat them with a respect that quite commonly they are not accorded.

1 The familiarity of usage and in basic logic with the bare formula of ends, ways, and means may all but anaesthetize an audience to the effect that the quality of discretion that applies to each element is not appreciated as it needs to be. What appears simple, even self-evident, in a lecture, serves to conceal an essentially undisciplined realm of choice.
2 The discretion possible with respect to any, or all among ends, ways, and means, typically will be uneven and therefore liable to be disruptive.
3 The uneven discretion in practice cited in (2) above may be manifested in large differences in feasibility of political, strategic, or military adjustment.
4 Only contemporary experience in, from, and about the field of action will demonstrate the relative worth of strategic ways and military means.
5 The formula of ends, ways, and means always is in need of competent contextualization with reference to particular circumstances and unique adversaries.

These points are intended to aid comprehension of the quality of challenge that faces the strategist. Above all else, these caveats should serve to discourage any naïve belief that the austere basic logic of strategy itself can be a useful source of guidance. A firm grasp of the E, W, M formula is necessary for strategic analysis, but it provides only awareness of the structure of practical needs and no more. In the real world of strategic

Making strategy 67

practice and malpractice, the sensible discretion that EWM must require is likely to be impossible to achieve. Since the decision for war inevitably is always a leap in the dark of the unknowable, urgent need for policy correction and probably for change in strategy is entirely normal. This may be difficult to effect, since it cannot be implemented by strategists but rather by the operational level commanders and indeed by soldiers necessarily behaving tactically. As so often in these pages, we must point to the problems that attend the need to behave at one level required by strategy in ways that have helpful consequences at another. Each level of military behaviour is given its functional meaning only by the next step up the ladder of authority in command. This means that tactics provide the military means for operations, which in their turn enable the military effort associated most directly with battle to serve the purposes chosen for the strategy, which is charged with enabling military power to register achievement significant for political reasons. The relationships on this hierarchy appear simple, but in practice the enabling potency of lower for higher levels needs a confidence to be placed by ever higher commanders in lower ones that frequently is neither felt nor expressed in a proper respect.

The challenge of necessary currency conversion by the strategist, which is to say for conversion of military advantage into the coin of political gain, is ill understood in theory and has proven a bridge too far for many would-be strategists in war after war (Gray, 2010a: 135–6). The core difficulty lies in the nature of the power conversion challenge, military to political. Nearly all soldiers called on by their political community to function as strategists are, ipso facto alas, over-promoted. Not only is there nothing in a professional military career that should educate a soldier to be able to function well enough as a strategist, in addition there is a great deal more likely than not to disable him from such. For more than twenty years the outstandingly successful soldier is required to be tactically competent if not better, and if he proves outstanding tactically, next to raise his game and shine at the operational level of war. Ideally, he will have or develop strategic and perhaps even some political sense, but those are desiderata only, not requirements for his lengthy professional advance. A large part of his problem is that performance as a strategist demands skills and knowledge that bridge what often is a wide gap between the military and the political domains. To function properly as a strategist requires a competence that cannot be taught or, just as importantly, learnt. Although all strategic historical contexts have much fundamentally in common, also, no less important, they are each significantly different in vital detail. The process of governance that invents, develops, and must adopt strategy commonly is peopled by individuals who are truly outstanding each in their professional field. Admittedly, there are a few, a very few, people able to function well enough from a professional base on either end of the strategy bridge, but that is so rare an occurrence as to be almost deserving of dismissal of importance.

Although the concept of process undoubtedly has a great deal to recommend it, it is necessary to acknowledge that it is not the only way in which strategy is made. Indeed, we should go further in recognition of alternative models in practical approaches adapted towards our subject. It is important to recognize that process is a concept that lends itself all too adaptably to conventions of convenience and prudence that may not contribute to the quality of strategy. Probably the leading alternative idea to that of process as the key desirable characteristic of a strategy-making system is the idea of instinctive inspiration (or, possibly, inspirational instinct). The sense of this model is conveyed well enough by the concept of individual genius, understood without its

68 *Making strategy*

typically often ironic connotations in English (Clausewitz, 1976: 100–12). In real strategic history, the past, as contrasted with a notional story wherein strategy-making was effected on one or another model of sound enough practice, option purity is discovered only very rarely. For both of the dominant contrasting alternatives, process and genius, each model should be considered a category, with historical examples varied in their closeness of approximation to the idealized type. What matters most is realization that there are two fairly distinctive models for the making of strategy, notwithstanding the historical reality of large local variation. Of greatest importance is the need to recognize that there always has been a clear enough contrast separating the making of strategy by process, usually *de facto* if not always *de jure* by committee, or by the instinct of one man possibly propelled by the inspiration of the moment. The former amounts to strategy by committee (pejoratively perhaps, by bureaucracy), while the latter is strategy by a charismatic individual – in their pure forms at least.

A wide range of alternatives have been tried and adopted in practice. There are obvious weaknesses inherent to both models, certainly in their purer forms. Nonetheless, the competence and personalities of major players stand out commonly as being the most significant factor in strategy-making. It is important not to be deceived and over impressed by appearances; often there is a noteworthy difference between process considered with respect to dignity as contrasted with efficiency. For political reasons, decisions on strategy may need to appear to be the outcome of discussion in a collective deliberative process (e.g. in a Council of War or a War Cabinet) whereas the reality of choice is decided on the basis more of dominance by personality, probably added to, or multiplied by, the respect, perhaps awe, believed owed to particular persons. Prominent among the reasons why the title of this book identifies strategy and politics as by implication being joined indissolubly, is that each literally is indispensable to the other. Moreover, the nature of the process that invents, considers, and decides strategy is always political. What varies is the detail of character about the political process employed. Near ideal types of the contrasting models of process presented here were to be found in the practice of strategy-making for the Second World War in Britain and Nazi Germany. Strategy-making in Britain was dominated by the larger-than-life Prime Minister, Winston Churchill. Yet even he allowed decisions to emerge, sometimes contrary to his personal and often impulsive preference, following exhausting lengthy night-time debate within the Chiefs of Staff committee. In sharpest contrast, the German leader alone made strategy, or, more often, operational art functioning hopelessly in place of strategy, because he enjoyed and exercised fully his authority as the leader (Führer) who was regarded as infallible, certainly by himself. Admittedly, this is a comparison of extremes, but nonetheless possibly there may be said to have been process in both cases of strategy-making. Even Hitler's charismatic leadership provided a kind of orderly process, albeit with an orderliness entirely obedient to the charismatic inspiration and will of a single man (all others, in effect, just took notes). His coterie of variably admiring generals and admirals were used to affirm his genius, not to review seriously what he decided. Churchill, and even Stalin, genuinely could be dissuaded from imprudent strategy, Hitler could not. However, the sufficiency test for strategy-making as a process strictly does not require a bevy of committees collectively overseeing the conduct of careful analyses for the purpose of comparing options for possible selection. The key requirement of the concept of process is orderliness in a series of focused activities directly relevant to strategy-making. Process requires a lack of confusion about relative weight of authority. Although there was much and prolonged committee work in the months preceding D-Day, 6 June 1944, the whole process needed a military Supreme Commander, General Dwight D. Eisenhower, to whom the Combined Chiefs of Staff and the governments of the Grand Alliances delegated the 'go/no go' decision (Smith, 2012: 290–317).

It is probably true to argue that the process of strategy creation and development always requires some assessment, be it ever so casual and inadequate, of the temporal dimension(s) to ends, ways, and means. This often unhappy appreciation is mandated logically by the unavoidable potential dominance of faulty assumptions. A strategist may reason sensibly, attending prudently to ends, ways, and means, yet commit egregious error because his assumptions prove as shaky as were those of the leaders of both Japan and Germany in 1941. In the Japanese case, the character of war unleashed upon the United States was mis-assessed in Japanese expectations of American understanding, because there was a critical deficiency in empathy for the enemy. Empathy does not require or imply sympathy, but rather simply comprehension of another's probable perspective and convictions.

The historical record of strategy-making is unflattering to many claims of genius. Even genius has an occasional day off. This is not to deny the challenge that undue caution is apt to apply in hindrance of timely and decisive strategy-making by committee. When the strategic vision needed for outstanding leadership is harassed and hindered repeatedly by the concerns (e.g. expressed annoyingly as 'what if...') of nervous and possibly overcautious subordinates, including Allies, the result usually is frustrating for the strategist. But, the clarity of political purpose and the strength of operational determination likely to be characteristic of a substantially personal process of leadership in strategy-making is vulnerable to the consequences of the mistakes that even genius can make.

Strategy context

Because all military activity in war has some strategic effect, it is an illusion to believe that strategy is avoidable. However, certainly it is possible to wage war without an explicit strategy. The United States and Britain so misconducted their efforts in Afghanistan and Iraq for a decade and beyond in the 2000s that they illustrated clearly the proof in this claim (Elliott, 2015; Bailey, Iron and Strachan, 2013; Strachan, 2013). Strategic effect is the concept that covers the consequences of behaviour, intended or otherwise (Gray, 2010a: Ch. 5). Improbable, perhaps ironic, though it can seem, it is possible to have strategic effect even though there may not be a strategy. Here when we refer to strategy, particularly when it is discussed qualified by a definite or indefinite article, we mean an intention in the particular sense of a plan, formal or informal. In historical practice, however, strategy in this objectified sense often has been seriously missing from the action. Although this does not, indeed cannot, mean that the course of warfare is bereft of meaning, rather is it the case only that the consequences of violent struggle are not guided by plans keyed to the belligerents' political intentions. One can simply manoeuvre and fight as opportunity appears to knock with the ebb and flow of events, and not bother to develop a formal or even an informal plan that would merit appreciation as a strategy.

Despite the generally high reputation that strategy enjoys, the practice of strategic history frequently, indeed commonly, has not been directed by explicit strategy. Strategy has to be executed by operations, which constitute the guidance and direction of

70   *Making strategy*

tactical behaviour. Neither neglect, nor even explicit rejection, of strategy can remove that sometimes elusive function from the course of history.

Since operations and tactics executed ultimately for political reasons must have strategic effect, even if unguided explicitly by strategy, success in war is possible in its absence. If an army is known to be highly effective in combat and if its commanders undoubtedly are skilful in the conception and execution of operational manoeuvre, the absence of a strategy worthy of the categorization may not even be much noticed and regretted, for a while at least. For example, the Nazi assault upon the Soviet Union in the years 1941–3 seemed so likely to result in the military overthrow of Stalin's regime that serious argument about military strategy in the East appeared close to irrelevant. It appeared all but self-evident to nearly all German commanders that there looked to be a variety of plausible and feasible operations that should promote a fatal Soviet collapse (Mawdsley, 2005). With Nazi Germany apparently spoilt for choice, it should not have much mattered exactly where and how the Wehrmacht struck home. Unfortunately for Germany, it was to be taught by the military course of 1944–5 what it should have learnt from the events of 1918. Specifically, war is not about tactical excellence or operational dexterity, rather is it about strategy, which has to be about the political consequences of battle and operational art. There is always a strategic dimension to history, be it relatively major or minor.

Not only is unarguable strategic genius hard to find in strategic history, in addition it has often been absent because it was simply not understood. To be fair, we need to appreciate the great difficulty there is in attempting to function as a strategist (Gray, 2010a: Chs 4, 6). It would be hard to exaggerate the practical problems that can impede the endeavour to threaten or fight to such strategic effect that political goals are at least approached and just possibly reached. In war after war in all periods of history the challenge of currency conversion from prowess in battle into political advantage has proved that its execution via the strategy bridge could not be achieved smoothly and inexorably.

To employ Clausewitzian argument yet again, the policy object in war can usefully be considered to be of just two kinds, total or limited (Book 8). The strategist's task in the rare former case is relatively simple to design, since it requires simply the complete military overthrow of the enemy: for obvious examples, 1815, 1918, and 1945. In principle, it is relatively easy to identify military ways and means needed in order to ruin a foe utterly. However, as Clausewitz understood completely, in practice all wars, probably without historical exception, are conducted in ways, with means, and for ends that are more or less limited. Genocidal annihilation is never the intention, prospectively not even in nuclear warfare waged on a large scale. This is not to deny that in modern times wars have been waged successfully that were intended by policy to conclude with the thorough and self-acknowledged defeat of the enemy. This was the meaning of the French defeat in 1815, the Confederate defeat in 1865 in the American Civil War, and the German defeats in 1918 and much more emphatically and consequentially in 1945. In contrast to the wars concluded militarily in those years, most conflicts are waged in pursuit of goals that fall far short of the unconditional surrender of the defeated belligerent. Typically, therefore, the struggle in a war consists of competing endeavours to raise the costs of continuing combat to an unacceptable level, in comparison to the anticipatable benefits of peace.

Strategy invariably is made for a context about which critically important assumptions must be made. Defence policy and the strategy chosen for its implementation can only

Making strategy 71

be guesswork, because states cannot obtain thoroughly reliable knowledge about the future. Even an excellent intelligence service cannot predict with certainty what policy will be decided in the future, and therefore what grand and subordinate military strategies will best suit for the years ahead. Although much about the near-term future, for example the next ten years, is known, there is so much that may prove critically important that cannot possibly be known today that the gross folly in the still popular concept of a 'foreseeable future' should be easily understood. So perilous can be the unknowable and therefore unpredictable features in detail of the future that it is only prudent for a national and alliance-wide strategy-making process to anchor its policy and strategy upon a few master assumptions. These assumptions should provide the basis in exceptionally sound reasons either that cannot change (e.g. Britain's geographical insularity), might need only a modest revision, or at worst would lose their validity only slowly. Because the future, even near-term, cannot be known with confidence, it must be prudent to adopt what we can identify as a contextual approach to the problems of national security. This approach has to rest upon twin principles: first, compatibility with contextual features reliably known to have enduring authority; second, a sustained ability to cope with change in circumstances by adaptation. This may appear to read as contradiction masquerading as irony, but the key to success in practice lies in the need for appreciation of continuity, while investing in a readiness to effect modest change. This dual tasking may appear to require an all but heroic prudence, but it should prove feasible. We need to lodge the caveat that electorates in popular democracies are prone to neglect the continuity theme in the dualistic theme of continuity and change.

Military strategy invariably is made in the context of a grand strategy that cannot be other than the notably particular cultural product of national political process. A major and possibly dominant response by the people in charge of the policy process for the permanent nature of strategic history is simply to assume a happy elision of wish with need. In other words, what is desired, and quite likely is possible, is assumed to characterize the future knowably. This is not quite an example of the triumph of hope over experience, but assuredly it is a case of hope under-disciplined by reliable empirical evidence.

Another caveat needing careful attention is that concerning the spurious authority of the inherently changeable. Electorates are all but trained to follow international happenings via mass media keyed professionally to the reporting of highlight 'news', rather than educated to understand the context for today's reported events. As a consequence it would be unsurprising were political pressure to rule policy choice virtually regardless of a lack of depth in supporting evidence. The challenge to a strategy-making process is the necessity to decide upon a course of action the value of which is proofed against temporary fluctuations in the political climate at home and abroad. For an example of the kind of contextually founded strategy-making believed here to be superior to leading alternatives, an illustrative detail is offered from the British case in the next section.

Strategy-making: assumptions for Britain

The guidance by policy that is the source of the ends for strategy shifts as a result of change in perceived circumstances. Nonetheless, most political communities make their strategy(ies) in a context understood as needing to conform broadly with some potentially important and fairly stable factors in their future. These factors vary hugely as to the confidence which can attend their anticipation, but they have in common the vital qualities of permanence, or near permanence, and of extremely high relative significance. If the

72   *Making strategy*

concept of a foreseeable future had net utility, it would embrace the major items discussed in this section. Britain is the subject only for the purpose of providing strategic illustration of argument.

1   The *physical geography* of Britain has profound and enduring geopolitical and geostrategic meaning. A position offshore but close to the continent of Europe has meant that England and then Britain has had no prudent alternative to being attentive to the balance of power in Europe (Gooch, 1994; Simms, 2013). From the War of Spanish Succession (1701–14) until the present day, Britain always has either led or at least been among the leaders of anti-hegemonic coalitions. France, or Germany, or Russia, the threat of the period has changed, but not the actual or potential context of unbalanced menace to British security. With vital reference to national security, Britain long has been, is today, and will continue tomorrow to be a power in Europe, though never quite a European power.

2   The Empire is now long gone, but the ultimate weight supporting and, if need be, enforcing security for Britain in NATO and the EU is the far offshore (from Europe) *United States*. Alliance with America is not discretionary for Britain, it is mandatory. Uncomfortable though it can be, there is and prospectively long will continue to be no practicable policy alternative to close political alliance with the United States. EU–Europe does not have and is not likely to develop a collective yet sufficiently unitary strategic identity for it to be able to substitute for American strategic leadership on behalf of European security, though in American interest, of course.

3   The geopolitical history of Eurasia has always been punctuated episodically by the menace of *unbalanced continental power*. The re-emerging peril to international order in Europe in the twenty-first century is taking the form of some Russian recovery from the nadir of its fortune as the collapsing and then defunct Soviet Union (Kissinger, 2014). Russia is not overly impressive as a returning superpower, save primarily for its very large nuclear arsenal, and its natural resources of oil and gas. The former should be deterrable, while the latter can be deprived of undue potency for reason of substitute sources of supply. Nonetheless, the solution to neither of these concerns is easy or free of serious risk. British policymakers must assume there is a permanence to Russian antagonism towards NATO. The Russian threat to the balance of power and therefore to international order in Europe was only resting from 1991 until Vladimir Putin's restored de facto tsarism matured by the mid-2000s. A Russian danger to British national security is likely to be a permanent feature of this century, as it was for much of the previous two, and its geostrategic implications have a shaping quality for London's attitude to defence. Russian antagonism is all about the balance of power and Moscow's deep anger at the humiliation it suffered, or believes it suffered, as a result of the competition with NATO led by the United States in the Cold War. It is far from certain that the contemporary Russian regime will have serious staying power for historical longevity, but the geopolitical and geostrategic bases of perceived potential menace from the East are certain to remain.

4   *China's appearance* in great-power, currently only candidate superpower, ranking is permanent, though, as with Russia, the political stability of the current regime is uncertain. However, it is an assumption of British national security policy that China's geopolitical and geostrategic ambitions are substantially confined to Asia,

which fortunately is far distant from Britain. Chinese financial and economic malpractice around the world, especially in South America and Africa, is noticed increasingly, but is expected to be largely self-harming in longer term effect. On balance, Britain regards China's relatively recent rise as being of net security benefit to international order. Cynically perhaps, though more likely realistically, fundamentally London considers contemporary China to be 'not our problem'. This is prudent, it is generally expedient, and it does rest persuasively on the facts of relative geographical location and geopolitics.

5   *Islamism* in extreme forms yet again is a menace, but notwithstanding its very modest domestic dimension internally for Britain, it is scarcely on the nursery slopes for security concern compared with the menace once posed by the German Luftwaffe newly re-based in the continental fringe of Europe, or the threat posed by Soviet Operational-Manoeuvre Groups on the North German plain (Bungay, 2000; Barrass, 2009). That said, militant Islamism will remain a challenge for Britain's security services for decades to come. In strategic terms there is no very plausible near-term solution to the problem of Islamic youth radicalization. Fanaticism comes and goes in strategic history (Burleigh, 2010). Education and worldly experience are the long-term answers, but neither is sufficiently available for youth today. For some people, education in favour of moderate belief will never compare to advantage with the excitement and fulfilling commitment on offer from the extremes. What the makers of British strategy have to understand is that the forcible reconstruction of seriously foreign cultures, as was attempted recently in Iraq and Afghanistan, is as likely to fail as one can be certain of any policy and strategy for the future (Elliott, 2015). Whether or not culturally far distant societies in theory might benefit from our efforts to reform them, such simply is not a prudently practicable strategy to pursue. To be blunt, neither Britain nor the United States will be able to effect the cultural changes we discern (possibly correctly) as necessary. It is a golden rule of strategy that impossible tasks are exactly that, and need to be recognized well ahead of time to be such (Gray, 2007: 86–9).

6   *Nuclear weapons* are here to stay, regardless of any change in their regard in British strategy. Moral and political attitudes towards these weapons are irrelevant to the basic facts of British security. The future strategic history of the human race will be influenced by the certainty of there being a permanent nuclear menace of unprecedented destruction. A few countries other than Britain assuredly will continue permanently to be nuclear-armed. We have to accept this as an unalterable fact, rather than as an assumption. Nuclear disarmament is not politically feasible, which means that it is not strategically advisable, while efforts to achieve nuclear arms control are certain to disappoint (Gray, 1992). The reasons why nuclear weapons are impossible to control meaningfully are exactly the reasons why they are so desirable to possess. As already noted, strategy is a subject riven pervasively by irony. In this particular case, nuclear weapons will not be subject to serious disarmament or constraining arms control agreement, precisely because they are found, or believed, to be uniquely valuable for countries' statecraft and strategy. Should that experience and belief fade and die, then nuclear arms control and even disarmament suddenly would become feasible, though ironically most probably it would scarcely be worth doing. For British strategy the issue is not over the persistence of a nuclear dimension to international security, rather is it the question, 'does our security require British ownership of these weapons?' To a strategist who

74 *Making strategy*

endorses prudence as the cardinal virtue in statecraft, the answer has to be in the affirmative. Respect for the experience of strategic history all but commands British retention of some nuclear capability. We can know nothing for certain about our national security in the future, but there is sufficient bad experience in the quite recent past to warn us against military imbalance and international disorder. Both of those dire interlocking nets of problems may be amenable to alleviation or preclusion by British nuclear ownership in the political and strategic context of extended deterrence effected by the United States in NATO. Nuclear weapons are so different from other kinds of military power that effective substitution for them is not credible or currently plausible for the future.

7 Strategy for *cyberpower* is coming slowly as the whole world learns how to employ the computer. At present it seems unarguable that electronic IT as a principal basis for communications is here to stay for the future. The British government accepts the proposition that cyber should be approached and treated as a generically distinctive domain of activity, though essentially a category of potential danger considerably below that of nuclear weapons. When we consider carefully what can and cannot be accomplished with the computer, it becomes obvious that the general theory of strategy applies as persuasively in cyberspace as it does to the land, the sea, and the air (Gray, 2013). The importance of cyber warfare is known to be high, but cyber defence and security is relatively easy to ensure, popular alarmist anxieties notwithstanding (Rid, 2013).

8 Adequate security for *global trade and its finance* is vitally necessary as a standing objective for British grand strategy. In practical terms, this trade will remain literally essential to the prosperity that such strategy requires. Britain might have been compelled to withdraw from war with Germany had its overseas trading connections ceased to be sufficiently secure. Overwhelmingly, international trade remains a maritime narrative, which has to mean that British strategy needs to help ensure good enough order at sea. Some officials and commentators have suggested that cyber weapons may prove as lethal in effect in their own (generally) non-physically destructive way as are nuclear weapons. Comparison between the cyber and the nuclear domains for strategy, though fairly popular today, is not credibly plausible. However, cyber now is recognized officially as a sub-category for all strategy, both military and commercial. It is understood that cyber power has become critically important and that as a consequence both defence and offence in this new geophysical domain are here to be mastered and, if necessary, exploited (Libicki, 2009). Nonetheless, recognition is slowly maturing with the understanding that the cyber domain is not seriously akin to the nuclear one. There is no question that breaches in cyber security could be extremely harmful, but also it is appreciated that the non-physically destructive nature of cyber warfare, directly at least, must cause us to refuse to surrender to cyber anxiety. Given that the international financing of trade today is wholly electronic, the issue area of cyber security is of major significance. However, it is important not to forget that while electronic financing enables international trade to flow, that flow is a story comprised very largely of maritime logistics.

The discussion above has identified and explained enduring factors of major importance to the process of strategy-making for Britain. Similar typologies could be assembled for other countries. A general argument underlying the analysis here is to the effect that the making and execution of strategy always is done with the light or in the shadow cast by all but mandatory principles that may technically only be assumptions. Although politics and strategy are both creative arts requiring imagination, they have to be at the least respectful towards implications that flow from the enduring factors explained here as assumptions.

Speed bumps on the strategy road

Studies that focus on the making of strategy need to beware the peril that lurks slightly off stage from the appreciation of order and method. The subject may appear more yielding to the prudent anticipation of future events than strategic history indicates to be appropriate. Although all consequences must have causes, and will themselves be the parents of future history, it does not follow necessarily that the great chain of causation is plausibly and reliably identifiably anticipatable far in advance. Political process and strategy-making happen in a real world that is not anticipatably linear in its narrative (Taleb, 2007). Three mutually supporting facts serve as caveats to much else that is written about the political process that produces strategy. Specifically, we must reinforce the previous expressions of doubt concerning the worth of future-assisted analyses; we need to endorse confidence in the occurrence of surprise; and finally, there is no avoiding recognition of the episodic and irregular occurrence of accidents with far-reaching consequences.

First, it is mandatory to be flexibly adaptable to the needs of changing circumstances, because the future is not foreseeable in much detail. Of course, a polity should not and cannot prudently simply be adaptable to whatever external events harass it in the future. An important reason why politician policymakers require education about enduring assumptions is because frequently there is need to help inexperienced people avoid imprudent choices. Tactical expediency in the interest of short-term electoral appeal, for example, or strongly personal conviction concerning what is believed to be right, can tempt vulnerable people into making unwise decisions. Senior generals sometimes stray from the strategy bridge by either privileging their own career or by mis-assessing what the government requires of them. The devising of military strategy is not necessarily a task natural to a person who is an expert tactician and then was an accomplished operational level planner and commander. Although the making of strategy should be a joint and seriously collaborative exercise by civilian politicians and civil servants and soldiers, it is inevitable that control both on and from the bridge will vary widely. In the face of a strongly determined civilian chief executive, frequently it has to be tempting to the soldier in effect to withdraw from much of his strategic role and play the part simply of a loyal operational level thinker and commander. After all, this would be where the soldier came from, only one 'star' previously.

Second, busy people locked into a political process that makes strategy insofar as it is able in an orderly manner obedient to a regular calendar are prone to neglect the possibility of surprise. It need not be that they are unable to conceive of events they have not anticipated seriously, but rather that they have not had reason to find the time for deep thought about the consequences that might follow on from contemporary events (Krepinevich, 2009). Scant effort is needed in order to understand that while anticipation of future first-order occurrences may be feasible, if nonetheless risky, further anticipation into second- and third-order consequences is so hazardous as to be scarcely worth the effort. It may appear ironic to argue that the military strategist and

76 *Making strategy*

civilian policymaker need to be prepared for surprise. The requirements just cited undoubtedly are extremely difficult to meet, indeed they are contradictory. Strategy often has to be made in alleviation of policy anxieties for which political process may well not have anticipated immediate need. Consequently there is permanent necessity for conceptual adaptability and practical adjustment in strategy. It remains a persisting fact of strategic history that surprise happens; moreover, it is unavoidable. What is not unavoidable, however, are many consequences of the damaging surprise. We cannot know what will surprise us, but we should know that there will be surprises in our future. Prudent strategy-makers should plan with sufficient flexibility against the surprising occurrence of happenings that will not be anticipated. Admittedly, this is a tough standard to adopt for strategic adequacy, but it is an important necessity. Contemporary strategic history, with the rapid rise of China, the geopolitical and geostrategic return of Russia, and the emergence of violent Islamism, have all been more or less surprising, even unanticipated. It is necessary to take note of the occurrence of true 'Black Swan' events; ones so unexpected they were not taken seriously. To many liberal optimists in the West, the aggressive revival of a geopolitically and geostrategically active Russia has been such an 'event'. We are particularly vulnerable to surprise by events or episodes that are believed to be impossible, until they happen (Taleb, 2007).

Third in this discussion of the irregularities in strategic history that disturb the self-confidence of strategists is the factor labelled inclusively as 'accident'. By definition, an accident is unplanned, and typically, though not necessarily, is laced with misfortune. Although accident is a category of surprise that can refer to an isolated happening, also it refers to unplanned or uncoordinated occurrences for which specific preparation was impossible or unlikely. Because accident needs context that yields dire consequences before it becomes tragedy, most items in this category I have labelled as speed bumps. These harassments should be appreciated as misfortunes and examples of bad luck. However, the strategist prudently well-educated as to the ever potentially critical significance of context is aware of the possibility of accident expanding exponentially in its possibility of lethal consequences into tragedy on a notable scale. For an exceptionally clear example of true tragedy, consider the grand scale of accident that was the outbreak of the First World War. While there was a cluster of unfortunate distinctive chains of events that resulted in a practicably unstoppable rush to catastrophe, a single accidental factor that stands out was the dysfunctional personality, character, and behavioural tendencies of the German Kaiser, Wilhelm II. By no means was he personally wholly responsible for the dread event of a general war, but it cannot seriously be doubted that his contribution to the events of the summer of 1914 made a malign difference in the course of strategic history, very much for the worse (Clark, 2012).

To advance the argument to the present day, it may be grimly appropriate to speculate that our contemporary strategic context, one that includes competitive nuclear armament, constitutes an accident on the greatest scale waiting to happen. The fact that this potential accident is not correctible definitively by likely political process, the only means that could be effective, does not yield comfort.

Conclusion: prudent adaptability

The silver standard for the making of strategy is awarded to those whose advice and decisions are shown by subsequent and significantly consequential events to have been both effective and prudent. In order to merit achievement of the gold standard for strategy, the strategy-maker needs to conceive, plan, and at least supervise the execution of military threat and action that secures worthwhile political goals. The most obvious problem attending the thought just expressed is that the strategist should not select his own political preferences as the policy goals for strategic guidance. If political ends are immoderate, and remain so regardless of the strategist's best efforts to secure their amendment, strategy is likely to be committed in pursuit of the impossible and therefore the unwise. The strategist should advise and warn against apparently imprudent policy adventures. However, the future cannot be anticipated reliably and some politicians hold value laden opinions blind to the critical difference between what is believed to be right and what is likely to prove feasible. The inevitable consequence is that forlorn hopes episodically occur in strategy and statecraft. Generals know that if they dissent from the deep conviction of policymakers they will be replaced by more compliant military servants of state.

Scientific certitude is agreeable, but the world of the strategist can offer nothing of that kind. The working standard for the strategist is good enough performance achieved by means of a strictly prudent conduct of warfare. For example, in the latter regard the strategist would have required Emperor Napoleon to agree to the terms of peace he was offered in 1813 (Stoker, 2014: 170, 191, 208), and that Adolf Hitler should settle for a compromise peace with Stalin in 1941–2. Of course, these events could not have happened for multiple reasons, preeminent among which were character flaws in the key individuals involved. In both cases the strategic context was mis-assessed to be one favourable to eventual victory. It is a sad feature in the nature of strategy and strategists that poor performance often encourages renewed effort, rather than discouraging and possibly terminating (if possible) adventures that are failing. Following Williamson Murray, in the main we have privileged the virtue of adaptation in the making of strategy (2011). However, the pervasively heavy influence of political process renders the making and execution of strategy a process inherently unwelcoming of adaptation that could be interpreted as a variant of political retreat. We must never forget that the second item in Thucydides' triad of key motives in statecraft is reputation or honour (1996: 43). When both civilian policymakers and military strategists have their reputations to protect, it is inevitable that the search will be on for identification of scapegoats for mistakes, should augmentation of past error fail to save the day politically and militarily, probably at the eleventh hour. To adapt strategically is prudent, but to lay blame on others is characteristically human.

Key points

1   Strategy is made in a largely political process of governance.
2   The lead-times for effective change vary greatly among the politics of policy, strategic ways, and tactical military means.
3   All strategy is made in and for a particular historical context.
4   It is necessary and feasible for a state to make a fairly short list of valid assumptions that should help guidance in choice of particular policy goals.
5   Surprise, including accident, is a permanent feature in strategic history.
6   The most advisable goal in the making of strategy is the ability to act prudently and adaptably.

78 *Making strategy*

Further reading

Clausewitz, C. von (1976) *On War*, ed. and trans. Howard, M. and Paret, P., Princeton, NJ: Princeton University Press.

France, J. (2011) *Perilous Glory: The Rise of Western Military Power*, New Haven, CT: Yale University Press.

Gray, C. S. (2010a) *The Strategy Bridge: Theory for Practice*, Oxford: Oxford University Press.

Heuser, B. (2010) *The Evolution of Strategy: Thinking War from Antiquity to the Present*, Cambridge: Cambridge University Press.

Kane, T. M. (2013) *Strategy: Key Thinkers A Critical Engagement*, Cambridge: Polity Press.

Murray, W. and Sinnreich, R. H. (eds) (2014) *Successful Strategies: Triumphing in War and Peace from Antiquity to the Present*, Cambridge: Cambridge University Press.

Paret, P. (ed.) (1986) *Makers of Modern Strategy: From Machiavelli to the Nuclear Age*, Princeton, NJ: Princeton University Press.

Strachan, H. (2007) *Clausewitz's On War: A Biography*, New York: Atlantic Monthly Press.

Tzu, S. (1963) *The Art of War*, trans. Griffith, S. B., Oxford: Clarendon Press.

Winton, H. R. (2011) 'An Imperfect Jewel: Military Theory and the Military Profession', *The Journal of Strategic Studies*, 34: 853–897.

6 History and geography

> *Reader's guide*: The power of context. A circular logic? The politics of history and geography: the United States; Russia/the Soviet Union; and Britain. A political narrative.

Introduction: the power of context

Strategy always is made in context; it does not spring entirely fresh from the imagination and reasoning of strategists. It can be a substantial feat to understand where the influence of context most probably weakens or even ceases, leaving room for individual and collective discretion. But, that discretion is exercised in the circumstances prevailing or anticipated, which must be regarded not unfairly as contextual for decision-making. We need to be very careful lest the concept of context be permitted so extensive a presence and role that it will devour itself, certainly its utility for analysis, by being unduly imperial. In the words of geopolitical theorist, Nicholas John Spykman, 'Geography does not argue. It simply is' (1938: 236). But, strategic historical experience leads to the appreciation, again one familiar to Spykman, that although geography is neutral in human affairs, its irremovable presence as context for politics and strategy cannot prudently be ignored. In Spykman's words:

> It should be emphasized, however, that geography has been described as a conditioning rather than as a determining factor. The word was used advisedly. It was not meant to imply that geographic characteristics play a deterministic, causal role in foreign policy. The geographical determinism which explains by geography all things from the fourth symphony to the fourth dimension paints as distorted a picture as does an explanation of policy with no reference to geography.
>
> (Spykman, 1938: 30)

Although there was, of course, physical geography before history could happen in it, it has been highly important through all human experience. Strategy must be made by political process, and that process is the product of historical experience, all of which must occur in the context of particular physical geography. With those empirical connections firmly made, it does not follow that geography necessarily is the primary, let alone the only, engine that produces history. Our difficulty is to explain the relative significance of both geography and history, without permitting either, or both in tandem, to function as the determinant of the course of that long narrative. Arguments concerning the consequences of geographical awareness and historical experience for

80   *History and geography*

culture as it bears upon, and may be reflected in, strategy, will be postponed until Chapter 7. Geography, history, and culture can be regarded as comprising a single grand category of influences upon strategic choice, but for ease of analysis without compromise of needed detail, it is appropriate to treat the contentious issue of culture independently.

The concept of context is as necessary as often it proves problematic. After all, everything has context; the idea potentially is so inclusive as to have no logically reliable frontiers. In other words, there is always context to context, without end. That fact granted, the practical problem remains concerning where to draw the line between sources of significant influence and everything else. Despite its problematic quality, it is recommended strongly that the concept of context be respected, and most especially that the problem of over abundant inclusivity be tolerated, because context is too essential to understanding for anxiety to be allowed to reduce its employment. Here we are examining the historical and geographical contexts in which political decisions about grand and military strategy are made. My argument is not that these are the only contexts relevant to the making of strategy. Rather, it is argued only that these factors have been and remain of primary importance. Many of the ideas pertaining to strategy and politics are to some degree problematic with respect to their proper boundaries. We may acknowledge this, but decline to be deterred by it.

By regarding and treating history and geography as contextual factors for strategy and politics, we have to keep constantly in sight what is meant by the concept of context. It refers to factors that can and probably should be considered to be outside the content of the main subject under consideration, yet having some noticeable influence upon it. Explained thus, it is fairly obvious why history, meaning the past as it is interpreted, and geography have to be treated as primary potential contextual sources of influence upon strategy and its politics.

A circular logic?

It is useful to recognize two apparently opposed ideas at the outset here. On the one hand, there is the belief that geography is of such fundamental importance that it is the very foundation, and more, of a state's choices in strategy. On the other hand, it may be argued that the course of a state's strategic history is always a golden key for anticipating its strategy in the future (Gray, 2013: Ch. 4). It is apparently paradoxical that geography and history require recognition as being simultaneously both fixed and also, in contradiction, often confusingly mobile. Physical geography is inert; in the words already quoted from Spykman, 'it simply is'. Nonetheless, the unarguable reality that physical geography is inert with respect to its playing a role relevant to human strategic history cannot mean that 'it' has an active role to play. The subject here is all about the politics of strategy-making and execution by humans who find meaning in physical geography. Does America's continental extent and location an ocean away from all political trouble in and about Eurasia mean that the New World can choose sensibly to distance itself from the squabbles of the Old? Or, is oceanic separation a source of net geostrategic benefit that can be exploited for US national advantage, possibly in the interest of international order as well as American national security? The meaning of American geography for the country's foreign policy and therefore its strategy has been debated episodically and heatedly from the days of the Founding Fathers. For another example, the physical geography of the Russian/Soviet borderlands in Eastern Europe has not altered greatly in modern times, but the meaning of those lands for Russian statecraft and strategy has changed radically as a consequence of politics of strategic ownership. Human thought and action give strategic meaning to a geography that does not play deadly human games. In Russian perspective, the strategic meaning of Polish geography altered dramatically as that country was resurrected. From 1919 to the present, successively Poland was independent but hostile (1919–39), in the main owned politically and strategically by Nazi Germany (1939–44), then owned politically and strategically by the Soviet Union (1944–89), and de facto became a ward of Western policy and strategy, eventually through NATO membership (1989–present). Admittedly, Polish political geography was shifted westwards at Soviet insistence in 1945–6. But, this particular example of the changes to the strategic meaning of a substantially unchanging physical geography makes the most vital point at issue here. The paying of close analytical attention to physical geography can tell us little about strategy in regard to Poland as contrasted with the shifts in meaning generated by politics. If there is a key to comprehension of Polish strategy, unquestionably it lies in politics, not physical geography, at least so it may seem.

If we think about Polish strategy and politics from a wider perspective than was taken in the paragraph above, physical geography all but rushes to engulf the analysis. Although politics would seem to dominate geography, as was just illustrated, unfortunately for a simple view of causation it is necessary to consider Polish politics and strategy in the context of the national and directly relevant international geography. Poland's fundamental security problem since 1919 has been its unfortunate geographical location between the two very great powers of Germany and Russia. When regarded with reference to that dominant reality, the case for being respectful towards the influence of geography is undeniable.

Moving to consideration of the other grand concept under examination here, it is popular to argue that history consists of what we choose to do and, in this view, geography largely has the meaning that we decide to make of it. The question of most interest here is the degree to which history influences contemporary practice in politics and over future strategy. The question pertains to the relationship between continuity and change. Sensible discussion of this matter is quite rare, the high ground usually being occupied by extreme rival views and assertions. On one side is the opinion that tomorrow can be almost as different from today as we choose to make it. This view need show no respect for the thoughts on behaviour of yesteryear, because allegedly we have the power to make our own preferred tomorrow. An essentially optimistic forward looking public and political culture such as that of the United States takes almost as a matter of faith the conviction that the future will, or even must inevitably, be better than today. But what does such a belief in the ability to shape a future we would prefer mean for strategy? Although arguably it should be true that appreciation of past mistakes in policy and strategy could lead to more prudent behaviour in the future, empirical evidence in support of this belief is hard to find. Michael Howard has written persuasively as follows about the alleged 'lessons of history':

[H]istorians may claim to teach lessons, and often they teach very wisely. But 'history' as such does not. The trouble is that there is no such thing as 'history'. History is what historians write, our historians are part of the process they are writing about.

(Howard, 1991: 11)

82 *History and geography*

With the words just quoted, Howard effectively dismisses the claims for history playing the role of a conscious animate agent of and for instruction. His pertinent thought here is not notably dissimilar in meaning from Spykman's dismissive view of physical geography as a purported agent for influence. The case of history is rather more likely to confuse, however, because unthinking reification is more prevalent with respect to history than it is to geography. We are unlikely to be persuaded that 'geography teaches... whereas the claim that 'history teaches...' is used widely with scant discipline. Both history and geography essentially are inert, they simply were and now are what they were and are. 'They' can teach us nothing at all, because quite literally they frame and pose no questions and therefore cannot provide any answers. But, ironically perhaps, both geography and 'history', meaning the past, are important sources of claims for influence on political process and its strategic products.

History and geography share an often critical vulnerability to lazy misunderstanding. Because of the common indiscipline with which the past is confused with history, it is rare for people to notice that usually what they refer to as history, really largely comprises stories about the past told by historians. Unfortunately, perhaps, historians' professional pride in their work often appears to inoculate them against full understanding that they are always able only to tell stories about the past as constructed narrative and somewhat speculative explanation. That past certainly was real in its day(s), but assuredly it is dead and gone as an active source of agency. Nonetheless, factual knowledge about human experience either has to come from or about the past (and present), because the future literally and inexorably is always 'out there' and can never arrive. However, even though the real past must be appreciated only through the stories told by historians, that does not mean the future can be made with scant borrowing from the past, whether or not it is recognized and acknowledged as such. In the pejorative wording of Karl Marx in his diatribe, *The Eighteenth Brumaire of Louis Napoleon:* 'The tradition of all the dead generations weights like a nightmare on the brain of the living' (Marx and Engels, 1962: 247).

The relationship between the historical experience of a polity and its geography is all but seamless. It is possible to tell a plausible story wherein geography was the primary cause of a political community's thought and behaviour, or whether the reverse was true. Imperial, nationalistic, and probably racist theories can be advanced explaining, convincingly to many, that the moral, political, economic and military virtues of their polity only exploited the physical geography that a blind nature donated to them. Although geography is blind as regards political opportunity or danger, being existentially inert and non-partisan in the human historical narrative, nonetheless it is disinterestedly playing a significant role in that strategic story. It is somewhat true also to maintain that a polity makes its own history. Furthermore it is true also, though to a lesser degree, to argue that a polity can make some or even much of its own geography. The geographical context for world politics typically is stable in the short term, but it is not necessarily that way in the medium or long terms. Even if the physical geography of a polity's homeland does not much alter, the political and strategic geography for which it assumes responsibility may change massively. For example, in the half-century from 1920 to 1970 Britain shifted and then shrank from strategic ownership of the largest empire the world had ever seen, to being simply a small number of rather small islands close offshore the super continent of Eurasia.

For a narrative of a very different character, consider the political and strategic geography of the United States. At the national outset in 1783, at the close of the victorious War of Independence, the new United States was a maritime oriented coast-hugging loose collection of former colonies occupying substantial beachheads on an almost totally geographically unexplored continent. Through some skill in statecraft, ruthless fraud, very considerable luck, relentless determination, and contextual opportunism, the country 'grew' from 13 seriously divided ex-colonies to 48 contiguous states, and beyond with the purchase of Alaska in 1867 from Russia and the annexation of Hawaii in 1898. However, America's strategic geography expanded almost as far as was practicable when, after 1947, the country knowingly and willingly accepted the role of political and therefore strategic guarantor of security over the Rimland of Eurasia. The containment of Stalin's Soviet Union was undertaken in the light of the strategic guidance provided pre-eminently in the books published by Nicholas John Spykman in 1942 and 1944 (posthumously). Physical geography had not altered greatly – change was imposed on nature by the opening of the Panama Canal in 1914 – but America's strategic geography was transformed for the Cold War by reluctant acceptance of strategic responsibility for the security of much of peripheral, indeed 'Rimland' Eurasia (Etzold and Gaddis, 1978; Gaddis, 1982).

The strategic geography of the Cold War and even beyond, thinking of today, was of course man-made by political process. But, that political construction and its strategic exploitation were very much the products of choices reflecting geographical definition. Menace from the East to Western values was perceived and discussed plausibly as reposing in unmatchable Soviet land power. This menace was readily recognizable in the policy and strategic terms continued in the writings of leading Anglo-American geopolitical theorists, especially Sir Halford Mackinder, since Nicholas John Spykman (who was Dutch–American) had died of cancer in 1943 (Mackinder, 1962; Spykman, [1942] 2007; [1944] 1969). Were the makers of the course of strategic history simply obliged to make use as best they could of their physical geographic circumstances, or did that context play a disinterested but still critically important role in the global strategic narrative as it unfolded? Although physical geography necessarily is politically and strategically neutral in history, it is never sound to argue that it is only a context devoid of influence over our strategic affairs. The inert neutrality of physical geography always finds more than ample compensation in value added, or multiplied, by highly committed human strategists.

The politics of history and strategic geography

The United States

Discussion of geography, history, and strategy often is conducted in terms and with choice of language that has the effect of suppressing the human element. This element should never be neglected, even at an individual level. Authors inclined to theorize about political process and strategy often stray too far from the individually particular in favour of the immoderately general. This book might appear to view the course of strategic history as being the rather abstract consequence of both high and sometimes morally low machinations of seemingly de-humanized political process and strategic design and calculation. Political process and subsequently its manifestation in strategy are not and have never been the result of pre-programmed thought and behaviour by human automatons. While national military strategy may occasionally be a 'grand design' worthy of that choice of words, to quote the main title of Donald Stoker's excellent analytical history of strategy in the American Civil War (1861–5) (Stoker,

84   *History and geography*

2010), frequently it is nothing remotely of the sort. It is important to remember the challenge of currency conversion between distinctive categories of action, to which this text has referred already. In theory, strategy should enable the political ambition of policy to be realized, while strategy itself is actually enabled in the military workshop of tactics. Quite often in what generally merits being understood as the course of strategic history, tactical behaviour by troops, with or even without much direction from those high up the operational military command chain, will over reach or under reach the original intentions of strategy. Given that by inexorable definition strategy has to be done tactically, when the latter misbehaves roguishly, de facto it will itself be in the command chair, for good or more commonly for ill. The strategy–tactics relationship, in the context of political process, has been critically important to the course of history generally, not only in the strategic regard.

The distinction between strategy and policy often is claimed by theorists to be clearer than the record of events reveals to have been the case. The United States, in sharp contrast to the legal and political contexts in Britain and modern Russia/the Soviet Union, assigns to the President the role and duty of acting as Commander in Chief of the armed forces. Given that the majority of American Presidents had not been professional military men, obviously they found themselves severely challenged by the need of leadership in war with respect to strategy. Policy choice and its political enablement has been relatively easy to devise and even sustain, but strategy typically has proved to be a bridge too far for the White House to master. In the Civil War, Abraham Lincoln sometimes provided exceptionally effective political leadership and guidance, but the great struggle undoubtedly was unnecessarily protracted by the inability of the Union to appreciate fully and therefore realistically just what was 'the kind of war on which they are embarking' (Clausewitz, 1976: 88). The course of the war over its first two, even arguably three, years eventually compelled President Lincoln to recognize that he was commanding in a war against an effectively united (very largely white) Confederate nation. To win such a war, the only strategic aim that could produce the political outcome desired had to be the decisive defeat in the field of the principal army of the Confederate enemy (Cohen, 2002: Ch. 2; Stoker, 2010). Cunning plans for the strategic discouragement of political support for the war effort in the South might well have been secured through tactical and operational level victory in 1861 and 1862, but by late 1863, following defeat at Gettysburg in early July, the South needed to understand it had been beaten and could not survive, endure, and possibly rise again. Unfortunately, the Union Army, and Congress, was not overly blessed with strategically talented people. This is a quite normal wartime context in most lands, not only the United States. In the Civil War, at least, the country was led politically by a President who proved willing to learn and occasionally was able to think and act strategically. Whatever the limitations of Lincoln's grasp of strategy may have been, his record of performance as political leader on the contemporary American 'strategy bridge' was exemplary when compared with that of his opponent. President Jefferson Davis was knowledgeable on military matters, more so indeed at the outset of the conflict than was Lincoln, but in the judgement of historian Donald Stoker:

> He was predominantly a tactician, which is not surprising considering his tendency to focus on detail. He never sat down with anyone and tried to figure out how to win the war, nor, in the vein of Lincoln, did he ever articulate a clear vision for how the South could achieve its political objective of independence.
>
> (Stoker, 2010: 409)

In the twentieth century, Presidential leadership tended to be admirably clear – towards Europe (and Asia, in 1941–5), defeat Germany militarily and thereby win the war. American policy with respect to the First World War was somewhat propelled by nationally characteristic grand appeals to liberal values and virtues, but the strategic guidance provided by President Woodrow Wilson to General John J. 'Blackjack' Pershing in 1917 was zero. The Treaty of Versailles cannot credibly be held responsible for all that happened that was negative for international security in the 1920s and particularly the 1930s. But, the US' unwillingness to commit to participation in the preservation of international order under the aegis of the League of Nations was plain evidence of political and strategic neglect. Throughout the interwar period the United States in effect ignored and denied the worth of the substantial sacrifice its citizens had made in 1917–18. The country essentially did not function strategically in those decades, at least with respect to Germany.

American Presidential political guidance for Alliance strategy in the Second World War was admirably focused and terse. The country's military commanders were ordered to take the war(s) to the enemy and win: unconditional surrender consistently was the requirement. It has to be said, however, that the political purpose for which the war was waged did not quite receive the attention needed for prudent statecraft. In the context of 1945 and 1946 it is not self-evident that much could have been done strategically by the United States to shape a post-war order in Europe very different from that imposed east of the River Elbe by Stalin's Soviet Army. Nonetheless, war should only be waged for political reasons; it is all about politics. In its nature strategy is about the consequences of battle for the political results that will or ought to ensue. There is a great deal to praise about the political structure of NATO in particular that was enabled by the American commitment to European security. But the awkward fact does remain that nearly all of Eastern and Central Europe was consigned by the verdict of battle to a Soviet tyranny that endured until 1989. It is undeniable that the complete strategic and political victory achieved over Germany by May 1945 was succeeded by nearly forty years of acquiescence in surrender to Soviet imperialism.

The negative view taken above is, we can recognize, an Olympian one that takes hugely insufficient account of the political and military realities of the post-war context of the mid-to-late 1940s. Notwithstanding the belligerent militarism of General George Patton, the principal undeniable American strategic fact of 1946–8 was that the American public – in common with other publics – did not reason strategically. The really 'worst guys' in Europe and Asia had been made to suffer for the egregious moral error of their evil ways, and now peace was the order of the day, with 'the boys' returning after a job apparently well enough done, to enjoy the rewards of life, liberty, and the pursuit of happiness. Post-1945, even to the British public, (almost) in Europe geographically, contemporary warfare came to be seen as a temporary irritation attributable largely to the great difficulty of devolution from empire, not as symptomatic of a lasting context that must always be strategic. The idea of a Soviet menace, military as well as political, to international order in Europe and Asia was not easy to sell to an American electorate justly proud of their country's success in the very recent war against German and Japanese imperialism. In regard to the latter, in 1945–6, many, probably most, Americans wanted the Japanese punished for their evil deeds, not least because of the 'day of infamy' that was 7 December 1941 at Pearl Harbour in Hawaii. While the theory of strategy is not encouraging of emotional motivations for military actions taken in war, a demand for revenge is an exceedingly potent motivator. In

86 *History and geography*

1944–5, Russian soldiers wanted to hurt Germans for reason of the suffering caused in Russia by Hitler's invasion. For their part, Americans waged warfare across the Pacific with scant regard for humane principles, even for the just war standard that commanded proportionality in response. Thucydides records and claims many instances of brutality during the great Peloponnesian War, but his wonderful triadic summary of motivation for statecraft – fear, honour, and interest – might mislead us into discounting the terror that belligerents commonly have found strategically useful to impose in times of crisis and war (Thucydides, 1996: 43). Despite the fact that the central enduring themes of this book are the reciprocal relations between politics and strategy, truly powerful but astrategic factors stemming from human emotion cannot be ignored. A leading emotion is anger. In the Second World War, Americans were angry with Japan because the hurt they had suffered had been without just cause, in American estimation. Anger was not necessarily incompatible with strategy, but effectively it was independent of it.

Relations of dependency in the hierarchy of military effort are not hard to illustrate. A major example of tactical failure frustrating operational ambitions and political hope was illustrated by Robert E. Lee's untypical less-than-stellar conduct of the three-day Battle of Gettysburg (1–3 July, 1863). Although luck, determination, and sound tactical decisions contributed significantly to the Union victory, a larger lesson of the battle was that when an army fights well, but is not commanded well enough tactically, the tactical failure must confound pre-battle operational intentions. Such weakness cannot help but thwart the military strategic aims of the venture. Strategic failure certainly will nullify political hopes that rested upon the military effort, most necessarily at the tactical level of the fighting. The negative view just expressed concerning Lee's battlefield command at Gettysburg needs to be contextualized with reference to his invasion of the North in the absence of any very compelling theory of strategic success in the war (Stoker, 2010: 303–4). Lee was a greatly gifted soldier, but those gifts were not noticeably strategic in kind.

In Vietnam in the 1960s, and Afghanistan and Iraq in the 2000s, the failure of American strategy – or, most precisely expressed, the failure of America to have a robust strategy – resulted unsurprisingly in consistent failure (Hennessy, 1997; Gray, 2012: Ch. 17). Tactical competence, even occasional excellence, could not reap high operational reward, let alone strategic success, as the basis for a post-war political settlement compatible with US understanding of its interests. Vietnam, Afghanistan and Iraq were all episodes of clear strategic failure that can be hard to understand if one lacks a grasp of the meaning of strategy. Possession of such a grasp cannot guarantee strategic success, but it enables its possibility. In all three historical cases the principal, decidedly deadly American failure lay in an inability to conceive, design, and implement strategy appropriate to the immediate case of need. The repeated American failures were not principally political, nor were they tactical or logistical. Instead, the politics of these three wars were never matched by strategies for their satisfaction likely to promote success. This can be difficult to understand if one believes that American policy was not inherently flawed, in other words the cause(s) for which Americans committed to action were good enough, and if one finds that, Americans certainly fought well. The failures were strategic, and they had the effect of delivering political frustration and tactical stalemate at best.

When strategy works as it should, but only rarely does, it directs the choice of operational level military objectives by advancing the whole consequential strategy narrative of a war, with the merited result that a tolerably favourable political order is enabled, and the soldiers who did the fighting are able to believe their mortally dangerous efforts were worthwhile.

The problem for America in the cases from the 1960s and 2000s was that the hierarchy of logic in the theory for the practice of strategy was not applied. Along with some others, I have argued that strategy is simple to explain, yet exceptionally difficult in practice (Gray, 2010a: Ch. 4). The invention of new policy options and actual fighting are relatively elementary tasks; inspiration can be a vital resource for the former, while training followed by experience in the field are critically useful as practical enablers for the latter. However, neither inspiration nor training are at all reliable as education for making, let alone trying to conduct, strategy. In regular conventional war the enemy has generically a similar structure of armed forces in the field, and he will have a territorial homeland with a capital city, industry, physical and knowable lines of supply, and other major assets that can be targeted. It is rarely easy to know reliably in advance how to fight even a symmetrical war, but time and experience usually provide the education needed for choice of good enough strategy. Unfortunately for materially superior regular forces committed to the conduct of asymmetrical war, the enemy of the day will be partially in and among the (local) people, he may have no capital to be taken, nor any similar physical or even emotional assets to threaten (Smith, 2005: Chs 7–9). Also, the enemy is likely to benefit from some cross-border support from interested 'Others', who will not be readily targetable by our forces. In a conflict of the kind just outlined, there is usually an absence of operational level military goals identifiable as targets for tactical efforts. In its turn this means that there are no achievable operational goals up the logical hierarchy of strategy from which strategic and then political victory can be constructed. There cannot be strategy in such a case and the whole venture, as in Vietnam, Afghanistan, and Iraq, must fail, which duly it has done and will continue to do so.

The wisest judgement bearing directly upon the American case has been offered by historian, Elliott A. Cohen in his study of the problems of supreme command in time of war, with particular reference to Union leadership in the Civil War:

> Lincoln had to educate his generals about the purpose of the war and to remind them of its fundamental political characteristics. He had not merely to create a strategic approach to the war, but to insist that the generals adhere to it.
>
> (Cohen, 2002: 50)

Russia

Russia is a great continental power, arguably still a superpower, with a long tradition of leadership by men who were not confused, or seriously tempted for long, by the attractions of sea power (Till, 2009). Leonid Brezhnev made an extravagantly expensive effort to improve Soviet military competitiveness at sea, but that decade-plus endeavour was brought to an abrupt halt in the early 1980s, when Mikhail Gorbachev surprisingly assumed command of the failing ship of state in 1985. The Soviet navy was a 'luxury fleet', to borrow an appropriately analogical concept from Holger H. Herwig, in his study of the Imperial fleet constructed overambitiously to satisfy the vanity of Kaiser Wilhelm II (Herwig, 1980). The security of Russia, whether Imperial, Communist, or quasi democratic, as it appears to be today, always has been understood by the leaders of the country as being dependent primarily upon foreign and domestic perceptions of its land power. The nuclear revolution endorsed and pursued over-excitedly by Nikita

88 *History and geography*

Khrushchev in the mid-to-late 1950s and then until his fall from power by political coup in 1964 introduced some challenge to traditional Soviet/Russian military thinking. In practice, if not entirely convincingly in Marxist compatible theory, the nuclear technological revolution was accommodated and tamed well enough. The supreme relative importance of mass in Soviet military planning did not appear to be confounded or confused by the coming of nuclear weapons. The first Soviet atomic test was conducted on 29 August 1949, but the balance first of atomic, then of nuclear (with the arrival of deployable thermonuclear weapons in 1954–5) weapons, and of their delivery vehicles, was quite a slow process. Only by late 1968 did the Soviet Union achieve some approximation to strategic nuclear parity with the United States. American acknowledgement of this new condition was flagged by the readiness of the Nixon Administration to open focused dialogue with the Soviets in the Strategic Arms Limitation Talks (SALT), which began in 1969.

The political leadership and military establishment in Russia have understood clearly that their security has been underwritten by the potent combined effects of space and mass. In modern times, sheer distance has saved the state repeatedly, in 1812, arguably in 1918, and unarguably in 1941–2. The extent of Russian territory and its populace has meant that, given time, an army of unmatchable strength (in numbers, certainly) could be mobilized in order to survive and recover from foreign invasion. All too obviously for political comfort, the army saved the nation. This undoubtedly was the case in 'The Great Patriotic War' of the Soviet Union against Nazi Germany from 1941 to 1945, and it had been true for the shaky Bolshevik Republic that appeared surprisingly from the general wreckage of tsarist Russia in 1917.

Russian geography in the continental Heartland position at the centre of Eurasia, inaccessible from the sea, required command of an army that could hardly fail to be regarded with suspicion and anxiety by its neighbours. Nonetheless, Russia has never bred a tradition of rule by the professional military. One can only speculate as to the reason for this long continued experience of civilian political ascendancy in a country that has had desperate need of its army repeatedly in modern times. A plausible reason why the strategy bridge in both Russia and the Soviet Union has never been demolished or ignored in favour of a strictly military dictatorship is that until late in 1991 supreme power always has been legitimized and exercised by variants of divine right (Fuller, 1992). The Romanov dynasty (1613–1917) that emerged as the rulers of Russia after a time of troubles in the sixteenth century was believed by a credulous and substantially illiterate populace to be divinely sanctioned to rule. In a vital sense, the political power of the tsar over Mother Russia was regarded, generally sincerely as far as one can tell, as a holy duty.

It is hardly surprising that the divine mystery that sanctified and protected tsarist political and strategic leadership was replaced, bloodily, by the all but mystical nonsense of Marxism–Leninism. Effectively, the new mandate from heaven for rule over Russia was to be found in the sacred texts of Marxist pseudo-science. Since skilful and ruthless politicians could interpret the Marxist theory to suit themselves and for adaptability to current circumstances, the greatest gangster won the struggle for political power following the all-but-divine Lenin's convenient demise in 1924. When Soviet military leaders acquired high reputations and prestige that might be translated into political strength, they were, literally, shot. The year 1937 was the highest (or lowest) point in The Great Purge, when Stalin either cleared the strategy bridge violently on its military side, or at the least paralyzed it by the creation of fear. In Stalin's purges, innocence was no protection because guilt was usually simply the product of Stalin's anxiety. That insecurity found ample focus on individual soldiers, but it is clear enough that Stalin's principal purpose was to cow by means of terror. A strategy of terror does not strictly require that its victims should be guilty as suspected and alleged. There is political value in punishing those objectively innocent, especially if they are generally believed to be so, because in that way the political leadership tells its public that no one can assume certainty of safety.

There is no doubt that the enormous casualties of 1941–5, approximately 9 million dead soldiers, lent moral strength to the counsels of the professional military that could be a danger to the civilian holder of the purportedly Marxist golden key for understanding historical change. Stalin managed to side-line, rather than purge fatally, the most prominent of the successful generals of The Great Patriotic War, most especially Marshal Georgy Zhukov. Following Stalin's death in arguably suspicious circumstances in 1953, the political leaders of the Soviet Union typically bent over backwards to meet and appease the ambitions and anxieties of the military establishment. Partial exceptions to this rule were practised, first by Nikita Khrushchev, who permitted his nuclear missile enthusiasm to get the better of his respect for senior military opinion. In critical addition he presided over humiliation in the Cuban Missile Crisis for which incontestably, he was most to blame. His successor, Alexei Kosygin, and Leonid Brezhnev, who had organized the Kremlin coup that replaced him, were far more tolerant of professional military preferences than was their predecessor. The Soviet military, including – unusually – the navy, enjoyed a relatively brief golden era in the 1970s and briefly beyond. The Soviet Union had no fewer than four political leaders between November 1982: Brezhnev died on 10 November 1982; Yuri Andropov died on 9 February 1984; and Konstantin Chernenko died on 10 March 1985. The new leader, Gorbachov, succeeded to rule in March 1985 as best he could over a severely ailing Soviet economy, and over-expanded military establishment. Also, inevitably he had to provide leadership over soldiers and secret policemen who would not be very amenable to statecraft that produced literally, if inadvertently, the demise of the Soviet state itself.

Relatively weak political leadership in the post-Communist Russia faced an appallingly difficult challenge. Territorially greatly diminished as well as deprived of its traditional quasi-divine crutch of Marxist ideological authority, political rule was 'up for grabs' by the most cunning and ruthless contender. Opportunity duly knocked, and Vladimir Putin succeeded to the political 'throne', in Russia in 2000, courtesy both of much criminal financial support and sincere backing by a military structure eager to be well funded again in pursuit of some return to glory for Mother Russia. Putin was able to bribe the military for their support with the profits that flowed from a 'boom' in the price of oil and natural gas in the 2000s. The 'boom' is now over, but its military consequences are still emerging in Russia, notwithstanding the recent oil price collapse. Putin's political authority may appear quasi-tsarist, but his rule is not backed by any mystical authority or holy texts. It is instead dependent upon a military acquiescence that rests upon convenience and is conditional. Also, in contrast to Soviet times, Putin must keep the Russian public on side for his rule with a 'guided' version of carefully administered democracy. However qualified by arguable adjectival modifiers, democracy is still an adventure in political narrative for Russia.

Geography and history were both the product of political process in Russia. Russian geography was not in any vital sense 'given', rather it was taken by ruthless political determination. Mother Russia has always been in danger of geographically physical

90   *History and geography*

subtraction by predatory neighbours and near-neighbours. Russian territorial and population loss for reason of the collapse of the USSR as a centralized state was always going to be a major source of anger fuelled in part by irredentist pressure demanding the return of (recently) lost lands. Given the absence of compelling natural frontiers facing Europe, the physical geography of Russia is and will be wherever the political process that fuels strategic history places it.

Britain

The physical geographical context for the politics of British strategic history necessarily has always been both European yet also significantly maritime. British history does lend itself to some plausible misinterpretation when it is dominated by 'Our Island Story' as the dominant theme. However, a more convincing narrative determinedly emphasizes the episodically critical intervention of forces from the near abroad in continental Europe. The politics behind and of British security have nearly always been populated by continental concerns. From the time of an initially remote menace of Roman aggression, through all the centuries until today, the politics of strategic security for those living in Britain have been more or less impregnated with anxieties about possible or actual threats from continental Europe.

Contemporary evidence in support of the argument advanced above plainly is evident from the whole strategic history of the islands that were only truly united politically in 1707 with the Act of Union that combined England and Scotland (until Irish independence was secured formally in 1937). In the Roman centuries (55/54 BC to ca. 410) Britannia prudently was considered to be a vile and exceptionally dangerous place. Britons usually were not found in the higher ranks of imperial governance. The Roman abandonment of Britain was succeeded by nearly 500 years of largely tribal polities and periodic warfare among both petty and more substantial kingdoms. Principally Angles, Saxons, Jutes, and Danes struggled for ascendancy over the two provinces left to their own insecure devices by the rather sudden Roman evacuation under threat (on the continent). The dominant Saxon kingdoms that had emerged by the eighth century were themselves of course the product of muscular and sometimes military intrusion from the continent. Scandinavian menaces, including invasions, not merely raids, persisted episodically for the next two and a half centuries. As late as 1066, King Harold Godwinsson of England, the legally somewhat controversial half-Danish successor to Edward the Confessor, fought and thoroughly defeated a powerful Danish Army in the Battle of Stamford Bridge. This notable strategic achievement was succeeded much too hastily by his acceptance of battle with William of Normandy near Hastings in Sussex. The Norman and then the Angevin and Plantagenet (1154–1485) Kings of England either held, or aspired seriously to hold, continental land in France. Indeed, from the time of the Norman Conquest in 1066 until 1453, English strategic history was an integral part of continental European strategic history. England lost its last remaining continental possession only in 1558, when Calais was taken by France.

Although English, Irish, and Scottish mercenaries fought in continental Europe in the sixteenth and seventeenth centuries, England had no territorial holding on the mainland of Europe in that lengthy period. The first new continental acquisition by Britain was Gibraltar, secured in 1704 by force of arms, and legally in the Treaty of Utrecht (1713–14). The strategic history of England has been marked, even arguably marred, notably by an episodic but persisting fear and very occasional reality of invasion from the continent. From the time of the War of Spanish Succession (1701–14) until the present day, Britain has striven never to be left alone to fight a great continental European power. From Marlborough in the 1700s, through Wellington in the 1800s and 1810s, leading on to the two world wars, Britain feared invasions. The Cold War, and now a context of some renewed menace from the Russian political and strategic renewal, has revealed a strategic historical narrative of anxiety that essentially is unchanged. Britain behaves, albeit often belatedly and sometimes minimally, as a part-time European strategic actor. The British military commitment to security in Europe is as modest a deployment as alliance politics allows.

Britain and the politics of its policy are not at all confused about the contemporary necessities of the country's security. Close alliance with, meaning critical dependence upon, the United States is politically accepted in Britain as a regrettable necessity. This dependency was demonstrated to be an unavoidable if not unmixed blessing by the all too extensive and intensive British strategic experience of nearly the whole of the twentieth century. Strategic independence from America died in 1918, and was reaffirmed by the insecurity of the late 1930s and then by the early years of the Second World War. Political process in Britain sought continental European, then transoceanic American, alliance in vital support of a national security that could not be founded reliably solely in a proud insularity. This has been always very substantially a strategic solution mandated by geography.

Conclusion: a political narrative

Politics should be understood as preeminent in the eternal and universal multi-contextual trio comprising politics, geography and history. Politics, in the case here meaning a struggle for relative influence, is inseparable from the human condition. The wide variety of forms that political process can assume may confuse people as to the nature of the phenomenon. It does not matter for my argument whether the historical subject is a variant of democracy, popular or much less so in a 'guided' version, or of authoritarian rule. Emperors, kings, claimers and presidents have all occupied the topmost seats of power through the centuries, and as an unavoidable consequence they have all needed to play the often dangerous game known and practiced generically as politics. This has never been discretionary. For better or worse 'The Game of Thrones' is an eternally necessary human pursuit.

Both geography, in all senses, and history are huge permissive factors for political and strategic behaviour. However, neither determines the course of strategic history. Both physical geography and a polity's historical narrative are subject above all else to ever dynamic political process. A polity's physical geography is not mandated by Heaven or Nature, but typically will fluctuate somewhat as a result of political choices, including decisions for war. Most countries in the world, both old and relatively new, enjoy sovereign rights over territory that has expanded or contracted, or indeed both. Political geography is not usually an entirely obvious reflection of noteworthy physical geography, because the course of strategic history has much to answer for. Although there has been a unique past course, the history that most typically is the stuff of supposedly historical argument is not likely to be identical to the actual past. The reason is because the 'past' to which we commonly refer freely is an interpretation constructed to provide particular meaning. We cannot help but see and try to comprehend Rome or High Medieval England in terms that make sense today. More, and

92 *History and geography*

many less, vigorous efforts are made to achieve helpful empathy with people 'then', but some guesswork is unavoidable. The trouble is that few of the undoubted facts about the past are completely self-evident as to meaning and implications in their own terms then, for us to be able to certify the consequences to posterity. While both geography and history are of immense importance to the course of strategic events, they need treating with caution lest they be permitted to explain too much. Theory at its core is only about explanation, while history, in contrast to the real past, really can only be at least partially theory.

Strategic geography is a concept with universal validity, but only since the eighteenth century has it been unified global reality. The maritime empires of European powers reached from the Atlantic around Cape Horn and the Cape of Good Hope into the Pacific, the Indian Ocean and the Arabian Sea. Maritime commerce had stretched between the Mediterranean basin and Asia even in ancient times, necessarily either around Africa or by transhipment on land to and from the Red Sea. Although there was some very modest level of maritime traffic between Europe and Asia prior to Portuguese ventures early in the sixteenth century, that effort was dwarfed by the regular flow of landward traffic from the Middle East to Persia, eventually to India, and even to China. These commercial contacts noted, still it was a fact that prior to what we term the late-Middle Ages, the closest approximation to global strategic history was the landward invasion product of the dazzling power of the horse armies of the Mongols. Hellenic influence generated by Alexander of Macedon and his successors had reached into Central Asia and modestly into Northern India from Afghanistan by the fourth century BC, but it cannot be claimed plausibly that the strategic history of the times in question were worthy of characterization as global. Strictly understood, although some claim can be made for war in the eighteenth century having being modestly global, truly the case for the globalization of strategic history is beyond much dispute only in the 1940s with the Second World War. It is important to note, however, that even that great conflict was two separate and distinctive conflicts, waged half a world apart. Of the combatants in that war, only the United States was heavily continuously engaged both in Europe and North Africa, and Asia–Pacific simultaneously. American strategic geography compelled transoceanic logistics and combat, eastwards and westwards (Spykman, [1942] 2007). Until the 1940s, the United States had behaved, generally contentedly enough, almost exclusively as a solely North American continental land power. In its earliest decades of growth in the twentieth century, the eventually mighty US Navy was conceived as a potential or deterrent power for good with particular, though not exclusive, reference to the Empire of Japan. The new navy was not anticipated to be instrumental in support of an American view of tolerable world order. That American view, though ideologically extant, was not fuel for a policy, let alone a global policy, of possible enforcement of global order. The United States was by no means as politically or culturally isolationist as careless commentary may claim, but certainly it was a light year from global strategic engagement – until Pearl Harbor was attacked on 7 December 1941. According to some political scientists globalization is substantially mythical, even today (Porter, 2015).

Whereas Americans like to think of their country as a polity best defined and understood by the concepts of law and liberty, in sharp contrast Russians favour the idea and physical reality of geography. If Americans respect and aspire to practice the intangible and rather ambiguous grand idea of liberty, Russians relate tenaciously to the idea of space (land, territory) and its terrain. The strategic history of Russian national security is one dominated by the repeated experience of territorial gain and loss. The politics of Russian strategic history is nearly all about physical space: the strategic experience of invasion from East and West, enabled with relative ease by the absence of geographical barriers. This physical reality shaped an enduring national reverence for the holding and control of territory. Political systems come and eventually go, but physical geography persists.

The geography of Britain periodically is challenged by the ideational preferences of Britons who wish to reject what the national strategic experience teaches. Occasionally it has been exceedingly strategically valuable (e.g. in 1805 and 1940) for Britain to be insular, but strategic isolation from the European continent generally has been strictly a regrettable necessity caused by continental failure, including strategic coerced expulsion; it has not proved a viable condition for sustainable security. By the time of the Second World War, Britain's splendid seeming and unquestionably global empire was a source of net insecurity for the home islands. Opportunistically, Britons seized an empire that was there for the taking in the nineteenth and early twentieth centuries, but it had never been acquired most substantially for strategic reasons. Certainly it added weight to Britain's voice in European politics, but the primary, though not sole, motivation was commercial. Recognition of the scale of the potential strategic vulnerability of Britain with its greatly dispersed global empire was the primary reason fuelling the inspired theorization in Mackinder's geopolitical nightmare of menace emanating from a Eurasian continental Heartland (Mackinder, 1962). The contemporary British security dependence on America is the inevitable and inexorable consequence of a national physical geography that unsafely is located closely offshore the super continent of Eurasia.

For the final words on the two subjects of this chapter, we turn to an experienced British soldier, General Sir Rupert Smith:

> History is the context of the battle, whilst geography is the context of the battlefield. Geography dictates the physical contours of the battlefield. Even with all the technological advances of our age, the location of a battle, and the limitations and advantages of that location – from contours through climate to the nature of the soil – will affect the battle, and very possibly its outcome. Technology has not made the globe an even surface: a missile will always be launched from one location and land in another – and both are hugely relevant to the successful application of the force. The discipline of geography therefore, as the study of the globe and its interaction with the people on it, provides us with the means to understand the battlefield and predict its nature so as to use the elements to advantage. This has always been the case.
>
> (Smith, 2005: 153–4)

Key points

1 All strategy is made in the contexts of geography and history.
2 Neither history nor geography determines a country's strategy, but their mutually reinforcing influences can be important in strategy-making.
3 Historical circumstances and physical geographical realities drove American strategy after 1941.
4 Russian and Soviet strategy has always been most concerned to acquire and control physical geography.

94 *History and geography*

5   British strategy always has been shaped in order to try and prevent the domination of continental Europe by a single power or alliance. It has been assumed that such a development must be incompatible with security for Britain.
6   The 'Game of Thrones' that is world politics is always strategic.

Further reading

French, D. (1990) *The British Way in Warfare, 1688–2000*, London: Unwin Hyman.

Fuller, W. C., Jr (1992) *Strategy and Power in Russia, 1600–1914*, New York: Free Press.

Gray, C. S. (2012) *War, Peace and International Relations: An Introduction to Strategic History*, 2nd edn, Abingdon: Routledge.

Mackinder, H. J. (1962) *Democratic Ideals and Reality*, New York: W. W. Norton.

Murray, W., Knox, M. and Bernstein, A. (eds) (1994) *The Making of Strategy: Rulers, States, and War*, Cambridge: Cambridge University Press.

Porter, P. (2015) *The Global Village Myth: Distance, War and the Limits of Power*, London: C. Hurst.

Simms, B. (2013) *Europe: The Struggle for Supremacy, 1453 to the Present*, London: Allen Lane.

Smith, R. (2005) *The Utility of Force: The Art of War in the Modern World*, London: Allen Lane.

Spykman, N. J. (1942, 2007) *America's Strategy in World Politics: The United States and the Balance of Power*, New Brunswick, NJ: Transaction.

Winters, W. (1998) *Battling the Elements: Weather and Terrain in the Conduct of War*, Baltimore, MD: Johns Hopkins University Press.

7 Culture and circumstance

> *Reader's guide:* Cultural context as an imperial concept that can be all embracing. Unsettled argument, a case for culture. Unsettled argument, the discipline of circumstance. Saving the encultured patient.

Introduction: cultural context reigns, but rarely rules

All politics and strategy are the product of those who cannot be other than people who are cultured, but not by culture alone (Geertz, 1973). In addition, often they are the product of circumstance that was neither intended nor expected. Over the past forty years scholars have debated the relative weight that should be assigned to these two partially rival categories of explanation of thought and behaviour (Sondhaus, 2006). The present author has participated in this debate throughout these years and reached a tolerable conclusion, to my understanding, that is advanced in this chapter (Gray, 2013: Ch. 3). The idea of culture in its arguable relation to strategy has attracted some extreme views over the decades. While truth does not necessarily always reside in the middle of a full spectrum of opinion, it is usually prudent to consider seriously the possibility that it does so in a particular case at issue.

The starting point has to be recognition of the human quality to all strategy and politics, a quality always both individual and collective (Rosen, 2005). It is convenient, indeed generally necessary, to lose identifiable people in the interest of explaining the structure and process of the grand narrative that strategy and politics comprise. This is an inclination that can be costly, albeit inevitable. As social scientists we can be guilty of ignoring trees in favour of the better understanding of forests, just as military historians are ever apt to lose sight of the forest because our attention is focused unduly upon the next battleaxe among the trees.

Close to the surface of this discussion is the persisting reality of notable disharmony among the several levels of strategic activity that can be categorized so as to accommodate their multiple interdependencies. We distinguish among the political, the policy, the (grand and military) strategic, the operational, and the tactical fields of endeavour. Also, we claim that each level and kind of effort depends upon the quality of performance in the others. Edward Luttwak, in particular, has argued convincingly that a condition of disharmony among the levels is a normal state of affairs (Luttwak, 2001: xii). The matters of most acute concern at each level are distinctive to itself; this persisting situation constitutes a fundamental disharmony that can undermine strategic endeavour.

96 *Culture and circumstance*

It is necessary to proceed beyond simple recognition of the distinctive layers in the hierarchy of strategy-making, into consideration of the human agents involved at each step on the ladder of authority comprising the chain of command. However, it is difficult to advance far without taking serious notice of the possible influence upon the thought and behaviour of people who try to adapt to fit their situation. Here it is necessary to provide some useful contrast for the sake of comparison between two rival claims. On the one hand, it can be argued that people think and behave as they do largely for reason of their human and arguably somewhat distinctive cultural inheritance. On the other hand, it is claimed that strategic thought and behaviour pre-eminently are the result of the circumstances in which people and their institutions find themselves. Although the topic may appear at first sight to be rather arcane and most suitable for scholarly debate untroubled by real-world concerns of policy and strategy, we can attest to its live relevance to strategic matters of the highest potential significance today. For example, in NATO's efforts to unwrap the meaning and purpose of Vladimir Putin's political and strategic intentions, there is much scope for rival theorization over Russian motives. Is there a grand design shaping and driving aggressive, even thuggish, behaviour towards Russia's post 1991 'near abroad', or rather is the Kremlin exploiting opportunities that we in the West would appear foolishly, if naively, to have donated?

Both culture and circumstance, or context, are super would-be explanatory concepts that beg to be overused and with indiscipline abused. These are imperial ideas that threaten balanced understanding. The important challenge is the need to decide what potency to expect from the possibly rival influence of culture as compared with circumstance. Our subjects of prime concern here are strategy and politics, both of which can be influenced and possibly even dominated by either of the concepts central to explanation in this chapter.

Unsettled argument: a case for culture

A case in favour of recognition of the contribution of culture to strategy and politics has to open with acknowledgement of its unavoidability. The point is not necessarily that culture always has to be influential, only that it is an inalienable presence in and about all people everywhere. It is possible to concede the presence, even possibly the influence, of culture, without necessarily granting it a substantial role in policy or strategy-making. One may consider the fact that a particular policymaker is in some respect physically disabled without arguing or implying that that physiological hindrance has to have consequence for his selection of policy or strategy. The concept of culture far transcends in its theoretical potential the restrictive implications on thought and behaviour of most kinds of physical disablement. The point is to suggest that policy and strategy-makers may be unaffected by beliefs, urges, and habits of mind and possibly behaviour that commonly could be regarded as cultural. The clearest way to express this is by deploying the strategist's principal canonical question, 'so what?' If we understand this question not so much in a literal serious sense, but rather to be expressive of disdain in exclamation, understanding should be signalled well enough. When comprehended as a genuinely open question, rather than as an exclamation and barely concealed negative comment, 'so what (?)' enables us to probe for the presence of evidence of cultural content in the people and by the institutions of interest.

We are unlikely to register satisfactory progress without first nailing down just what is meant here by this big imperial idea of culture. Demystification is important.

A critically significant issue of difference between schools of debaters is, on the one hand, between those who insist that culture must pertain only to the ideational realm, as contrasted with those who profess to see evidence of culture in choice and practice of behaviour. My preference is for the latter category of understanding, but I am respectful of those who disagree. What follows is the definition of culture that governs my employment of the concept: 'the persisting socially transmitted ideas, attitudes, traditions, habits of mind, and preferred methods that are more or less specific to a particular security community that has had a unique historical experience' (Gray, 2013: 110). Here, I was defining with respect to the idea of strategic culture, but the core content of my definition is considerably robust and inclusive, if not entirely uncontentious. If we pose the 'so what?' question with respect to any security community, the otherwise plain implication that culture should be expected to figure importantly in the analysis can be suitably deflated. If anything, the prompt demotion of culture as an agent for influence over both thought and behaviour can be effected too speedily. In scholarly debate today, exaggerated claims on behalf of culture as the key to the understanding of national preferences in strategy have been exposed for the probable nonsense that they appear to be on the ever arguable evidence. But, the possibility or probability that cultural explanation does have value for our understanding has, by and large, gone down along with the more poorly evidenced assertions (France, 2011). It is easier and more satisfying to make a strong argument pro or con a controversial proposition than it is to argue carefully on behalf of their being substantially, if troubling, by elusive merit, even in a case that has obvious leakage.

There is no correct definition of culture. Many years of argument and direct debate thus far have failed to deliver a clearly majority opinion with respect to strategic culture. Definitions divide clearly into those that seek to capture behavioural preferences, and those that limit their inclusivity to the realm of belief, thought, and feeling. I have never been able to persuade myself that it makes sufficient sense to eschew the evidence of deeds, confining attention to the non-behavioural. This is a matter of scholarly choice. The intellectual leader for the less inclusive view that differs from my own can be found in the insightful scholarship of Alastair Iain Johnston (1995). Although there is no watertight case favouring a welcoming attitude towards a cultural theme in analysis, there are important considerations of which one should be aware. These points are raised as follows:

1 *Existentiality and unavoidability.* Whatever use we choose to make of cultural argument, there can be no plausible denial of the presence of the phenomenon. Whether or not we believe that cultural identity and its dependent feelings are allowed to influence thought and behaviour on matters of national and international security, it must always be a fact that the human players in strategic historical drama will be encultured persons. Claims that culture is an irrelevance may well look convincing, but I have yet to be satisfied that that is a safe position to adopt. This is not to claim that culture necessarily occupies the highest ground dominant in an individual's decision process, only that it can hardly be other than a detectable presence likely to carry some power of influence.

2 *Evidence.* There is available no litmus test for the influence of a cultural urge or restraint. As a general rule, judgement on the pertinence of culture, contrasted with circumstance, can only be subjective. Scientific study worthy of the title is not feasible. Empirical evidence may be evidence of alarm over national security that is the

98 *Culture and circumstance*

product of an expert's analysis, regardless of his cultural affiliation. There is no obvious way in which we can separate cultural influence from professional analysis naked of cultural preference or even bias. This thought lays emphasis upon the sheer pervasiveness of culture, whether or not evidence for it is readily recognizable. With reference to the contrast we draw between an approach friendly to arguments that consider culture, and a view that is systemically sceptical, we admit that evidence, empirical or other, cannot settle the argument. The reason is because plainly alternative explanations are likely to be equally plausible. To illustrate hypothetically, if we seek to understand why Untersturmführer 'Heinz' behaved heroically on the long road back from deep in Russia sometime in 1943–4, we might, with equal plausibility on the evidence of bloody deeds, conclude that he undoubtedly behaved as he did because he was a warrior in the racial and political elite of the Waffen SS and he loved the Führer. As a good German he could have done nothing other. Or, was 'Heinz' simply trapped in desperate circumstances wherein his only hope of survival he understood to rest upon bold personal action? When there may appear to be an unmistakeably dominant motive for thought and behaviour, it is usual for a clear alternative explanation to be worthy of careful consideration also, even if it is of lesser apparent merit.

3 *Culture and past circumstance.* For an argument more than a little subversive of the value in the distinction that we are using here between culture and circumstance, I need to advance the thought that today's culture has not been purchased or otherwise acquired all but pristine from the internet. Memories about, legends concerning past circumstances are the stuff with and from which culture is constructed and adapted for today and tomorrow. Once the past experience of a security community is processed for understanding in the 'great stream of time', it is likely to contain a mix of outright myth and fairly plausible legend, as well as much that is well enough attested empirically to be carefully believable (Neustadt and May, 1986). Far from being merely the vaporous musings of the empirically challenged, argument for and with some cultural content can hardly avoid critical dependence on the popular national narrative of historical experience with security and strategy. It may appear in the apparent contemporary form of culturally coloured preference, but that would be to misunderstand the provenance of the phenomenon. A cultural guise is likely to be entirely understandable as an accurate reflection of what a security community has chosen to believe about itself in its past historical performance. After all, that will be the official national narrative taught to most of the nation's children. While the strategic history in question may not be uniquely entirely distinctive, given the likely frequency of an alliance context in defence preparation and war making, every country's strategic historical experience is bound to be to some degree different from that of all others. Countries acquire habits of mind by accretion and through some occasional soul searching over the course of decades and centuries. That will be the cumulative creation of noticeably national preferences in ways of war, notwithstanding the inevitable fact of occasionally aberrant thought and behaviour.

4 *The domestic political pull of culture.* We need to register the fact that strategy and statecraft are activities of governance always made at home, wherever that may be. Domestic political process both reigns legally and typically rules effectively over strategic issues. The fact that usually foreigners are targeted in threats and actions is not usually much of a critical constraint upon the power of domestic political

Culture and circumstance 99

process; typically perhaps it should be, but that is a different matter. Occasionally, a threat or actual war will be recognized, at least be expected to pose an existential menace to a polity. In this unhappy but rare event, the external context is likely to provide so powerful an incentive in favour of potential military effectiveness that long-standing partially cultural preferences have little if any traction with the relevant political process of governance. The unprecedented introduction of conscription in Britain in 1916, and the command and comprehensive control of the labour force in the Second World War, spring to mind as thoroughly un-British behaviours deemed essential because of strategic need believed credibly at the time to be desperate. However, nearly all wars for nearly all countries are to a greater or lesser degree ones of discretion (Porter, 2015). Situations for which a polity can choose how much or how little it will do are likely to be serious candidates for influence by a host of beliefs and feelings – i.e. brief over-enthusiasm and excitement, leading on inevitably to disappointment and attribution of blame – that may well warrant an ownership sticker assignment attracting mention of culture (Elliott, 2015). In a period not beset plausibly, as yet, by existential threats, it is normal for domestic political process in many countries to be unmoved by genuinely strategic argument bearing upon allegedly urgent issues in statecraft. Indeed, there may well not be any strategic issues for political process that credibly can be portrayed as urgent. For a major example, the British election campaign of 2015, though conducted in the context of at least a medium scale of crisis in the relations between Russia and NATO, was scarcely permitted by its domestic functionaries and would-be electees to stray from the matters that the electorate were known at the time to regard as vital to their well-being. Those issues were almost entirely domestic, parochial even. The only grander issue with contextual relevance for this book was the ever poisonous subject of continuing national membership of the European Union (EU). The possibility that British departure, including possibly defection from, the EU might well have a significant effect on the critical politics for credible deterrence of Putin's bullying in Eastern Europe, was not detectable in the heated domestic debate. Unconstrained by notable alien political influence, the typical domestic political process that cranks out strategy is apt to decline to allow itself to be much troubled by concerns about 'abroad'. After all, abroad does not vote in our elections. This is an enduring political reality, and is founded on the condition of popular political sovereignty fundamental to our political system. Today it is truly cultural, not merely one chosen pending the discovery of a better way of legitimizing the system of governance.

5 *Strategy must follow policy, which has to be political, which necessarily is somewhat cultural.* The presence of culture does not necessarily mean it has heavy influence. For example, to notice that an American soldier looks and appears to behave, at least sounds, in a style and manner commonly believed abroad to be typically warrior-type American is likely to mislead those not already tribally processed, let alone unwary foreigners. The quality of a person's thought, his sophistication and understanding of nuance and even irony cannot reliably be assessed on the apparent empirical evidence of how he talks to his combat troops in the field, or how short he wears his hair. I speak from a professional lifetime's length of personal experience in this regard. There is much tribalism in the military in many, probably most, countries, and successful professional soldiers need to be able to switch cultural appearance and style of behaviour in order to fit their particular audience. The

100 *Culture and circumstance*

challenge to understanding is to know how accurately to interpret the general that one meets or reads, given the cultural elements including clothing he is wearing, perhaps principally necessarily and expediently for the situation immediately at hand. We are not suggesting that an American general officer requires the often confused malady of multiple personalities, only that a successful person's cultural persona is certain to contain several different suites. However, the fact that he is American, undoubtedly since his late teenager years encultured in encouragement to think and behave as a warrior, in whatever organization and branch he serves, cannot just be dismissed as an irrelevance when times requiring professional decision are pressing and dangerous. Although the soldier as warrior occasionally will need the ability to talk intelligibly to civilian politicians and officials, his habits of mind and world-view are bound to be culturally tribal to some degree, even if suppressed for the occasion of meetings with non-military masters. Since policy guidance for strategy must be political – that is where it comes from after all – the potential of cultural phenomena to play some roles at every level of concern is considerable, if rarely measureable with certainty.

6   *Education.* Many critics of what has been called the cultural turn in strategic analysis fail to appreciate just how deep and pervasive what amounts to cultural conditioning is bound to be (Black, 2012). Simply growing up so as to be able to live tolerably well in a national community requires that home, school, and the local context beyond find a person's behaviour and beliefs acceptable for normal social intercourse. There are good looking reasons for being sceptical of the apparent promise of cultural analysis as an aid to understand strategic choice, but because a challenge is difficult to meet, in this case probably impossibly so, does not mean it is absent. Think of particle physics and the immense scale and weight of 'dark matter', if only we could find and measure it. We know it is there, but we do not know, really know empirically, much more than that. Culture is similar to 'dark matter'. It is pervasive and ubiquitous, but currently not permissive of reliable direct study. Too much recent scholarly study of culture in respect of strategy simply has failed to understand that culture is a conditioning factor for strategy making, and not necessarily, or even necessarily often, a significant determinant of final choice.

7   *Stereotyping and other sins against good analytic order.* Much of the better critical care that has been triggered of recent decades in objection to the cultural turn really misses the obvious point that we are striving to register. It is essential to take an inclusive, indeed an holistic, view of the subject. The case for culture as an influence and beyond on domestic politics, its policy and therefore also its strategy, has occasionally been overstated by cultural enthusiasts. Such people predictably have found cultural explanation too convenient an explanation of complex challenges (e.g. 'what else did you expect, after all he is Russian', and so forth). It is the task of careful scholarship to show up shoddy, simplistic analysis for the sometimes dangerous nonsense that it is. Culturalism is unavoidable, ironically almost regardless of a person's attitude toward the practice, because we humans are socially encultured (and possibly biologically programmed) from the earliest age to be able to know who, what, and where our group/tribe lives, and to what norms of decent behaviour our society requires us to show respect. Because of the great complexity of our social and professional lives, we are obliged to resort to short-hand comprehension of the apparently more prominent features about people, not excluding our country's/tribe's enemies. Young soldier warriors sent under orders to

fight on our behalf amidst the people in societies hugely alien to ours are certain to indulge in stereotyping, including negative characterization, of lands that do not much resemble West Virginia or California (Johnson, 2013). Expedient and often insulting stereotyping of 'Johnny foreigner' is an eternal and global strategic historical reality, not simply an American malady. Our soldiers are sent by us often to distant lands principally for the purpose of combat, not on-the-job preparation for a scholarly career in cultural anthropology. If we insist on foreign military deployment, the inevitable reality of the stereotyping of foreigners outside our home-grown tribes is an unavoidable potential evil with which we have to live. To notice its undoubtedly frequent ugly consequence may sometimes be helpful for an institutional push towards greater human contextual sensitivity on the part of immature young warriors, but really it is inevitable and essentially irremediable. We cannot expect 18- and 19-year-olds to be cultural ambassadors to thoroughly different societies.

8 *Common sense.* The final point here on the case for some cultural awareness across societies is simply the compelling attraction of common sense. This is not necessarily helpful to the makers of strategy, but it is nonetheless important for them to recognize what they cannot help but know about who, what, and where they are, somewhat contrasted with what is readily knowable about Others beyond the national tribe. Writing as a person who has some scholarly training in social anthropology, I confess to feeling a frequent frustration in reading criticisms of the alleged 'cultural turn' in strategic scholarship that does not rest on empirically founded comprehension of the pervasive ubiquity of diverse cultural phenomena. The still unsatisfactorily answered challenge to the peremptory strategist's question/exclamation of disdain, 'so what?', proves a demand too far for many strategic analysts, and for good, but alas admittedly often unfortunate, reasons. Culture is in 'here' and 'out there'; it is everywhere and to some degree it is in and about most things. But, it is multiple in personality, often shared fairly commonly among supposedly independent sovereign tribes (i.e. Scandinavian, Arab, and suchlike gross oversimplications). Because we cannot isolate the role(s) played by culture with great reliability in strategic history, it does not follow that we should pretend it does not exist as one or more causative factor among others.

Unsettled argument II: the discipline of circumstance

Although we contrast a tilt towards cultural awareness and perhaps sympathy, though only rarely empathy, this distinction relates all too inclusively to very broad categories of explanation that are irrevocably and permanently porous. Although the better among professional historians are tolerant, if often not comfortable with the notion of a crowded and usually chaotic strategic historical narrative, social scientists usually are mandatorily encultured by strict disciplinary requirements, for order, method, and, wherever possible, theory for measurement. The goal usually is to seek out order in a search for knowable empirically testable certainty in understanding. This is a foolish quest for certainty of knowledge, one that has little promise of success for scholars of strategic history. The past, the actual course of strategic history, is and has always been a more or less confused and even a chaotic mess; this enduring reality of 'events, dear boy, events', in the immortal words of then British Prime Minister Harold MacMillan.

102 *Culture and circumstance*

The conceit of believing that a scientific quality of therefore certain understanding is attainable would be laughable for the analytical fad and fashion that it is, were not so many of my social-scientific colleagues so persuaded of its feasibility and utility.

Although I have made no secret here of my belief that culture nearly always has a part to play in strategic history everywhere, decades of scholarly and popular debate on the subject have left me almost painfully, certainly regretfully, aware of the many genuine and largely irremediable weaknesses in the cultural argument. Indeed, it is now fairly clear there cannot sensibly be a distinctively cultural argument about strategy and its politics, because the subject really is holistic with open frontiers. There is culture in politics and therefore in policy and its enabling strategy. The preferred definition of culture presented above knowingly and perhaps unmanageably is naked of firm border controls. But, this analytically unsatisfactory fact is mandated by the nature of the subject. A desire or even demand for rigorous categorization and sub-categorization is all too understandable in the eternal quest after a scientific quality (i.e. empirically reliably repeatedly testable for certainty of correctness) of understanding, and often it is highly praiseworthy. The trouble is that the intimate relationships among strategy, politics, and culture cannot usefully be studied in that manner, no matter how careful and disciplined the scholarship. Both strategy and its fountain source in the politics for policy are creative arts, not sciences, social or physical (Grygiel, 2013). For the sake of fairness in debate, now we must explain why so many competent strategic analysts have examined culturalist argument and found it too seriously flawed to be helpful. Indeed, a few years ago I began a book chapter on 'Culture, beliefs, and strategic behaviour' with the following unpromising words: 'If the ambitious concept of strategic culture was an aircraft, one would not issue it with a certificate of air worthiness' (Gray, 2013: 80).

It is ironic that the case strongly critical of a noticeably cultural flavour to strategic analysis is relatively so easy to make, and yet also is so wrong. The key contrast here is that between the exaggerated hopes and expectations of die-hard culturalists, and the more moderate and measured aspirations of those of us content to see value in appreciation of the potential influence on politics and over strategy of the cultural factor. The scope for useful research and debate is not as wide as once it was believed to be. Enthusiasm for a cultural turn in analysis descended rapidly and expediently into the adoption of cultural explanation as a convenient default position, when more specific explanations of thought and behaviour were found wanting (Black, 2012). But, sensible debate conducted to explore and decide on a vital issue area cannot be conjured up out of a heated debate that showcased two extreme positions, neither of which betrayed much promise of evolution towards a useful middle ground. Sharp critics of the cultural turn had the more persuasive arguments at their command. However, given that they were criticizing an unsound and often extreme variant of cultural argument, it is scarcely surprising that it has been an unbalanced contest. The debate required was that between sceptical critics, not frankly hostile detractors, and moderate advocates. Each side found little difficulty in believing that it won the debate, because the opposing point of view typically was only a caricature of the sensible cases pro and con that could be made. The strategically useful truth in the debate described here does not lie somewhere close to the middle of the spectrum of possible attitudes towards culturally flavoured analysis, but rather resides plainly, if somewhat uneasily and perhaps surprisingly, on the cultural side. In order to attempt seriously to be fair to the position that in the main is not my own, what follows in the remainder of this section is identification and explanation of the anti-cultural case.

Culture and circumstance   103

1 *Necessity.* Political communities invariably are compelled by the anarchic structure of international politics, and the unavoidably adversarial nature of strategy, to accept discipline over their policy choices. On the one hand, such discipline is imposed by an unhappy domestic public, which naturally favours success, but only when secured cheaply. On the other hand, discipline certainly will be applied by foreign polities who insist upon a balancing of power as the basis of tolerable political order. What this complex structure of domestic and foreign constraints upon polities' more primordial wishes and ambitions means is that cultural attractiveness in political and strategic matters can only ever be but one factor, not a unilateral determinant of state behaviour – at least, not safely for very long. Anxious neighbouring polities have an enduring history of forming defensive coalitions or emergency alliances for the purpose of frustrating assertive powers deemed to be menacing. History does not teach lessons, but its course does show beyond doubt that states (city, democratic popular, people's, guided, or whatever) worth counting as having been successful over a lengthy period have had to find some mean between assertiveness and tolerance of the claimed interests of Others (Howard, 1991: Ch. 1). All polities fail occasionally and a brand of over-optimistic 'victory disease' or, in contrast, perilous passivity, sees them succumb to more successful aggressive statecraft and strategy from abroad (or even at home, in the event of some domestic secession and dissolution). The very structure and working of world politics, regardless of cultural variation among individual polities, requires that the politics of high policy and its strategy accepts limitation upon freedom of action. In the now conventional phrase, we recognize and usually seek to obey the norms and laws of a 'rules based international community'. Polities that resist acceptance of this potentially constraining regulatory context are widely condemned and sometimes punished as 'rogue states'. Of course, strategic history is a light year removed from being a morality tale. Nonetheless, political communities usually have been brought by grim and probably inexorable circumstance to realize there is a realm of necessity that often is willing, and all but invariably eventually will be able to discipline those apparently cultural urges that lead to excess in policy and strategy. There is much that can be said in frank recognition of the common sense in Imperial Germany's Chancellor Theobald von Bethmann-Hollweg's words in 1914, when he sought to excuse his country's invasion of Belgium on the basis of the principle that 'necessity knows no law' (Walzer, 1977: 240). A substantially, even just partially, cultural urge is not an uncommon feature of world strategic history, but it is unlikely to prosper for long as the front for the policy guidance driving strategy. Attempts to thwart it almost regularly succeed, because in a world of necessarily competing states, outward pressure on Others must have the consequence of fuelling growing anxieties abroad concerning the security of their homelands. From Athenian aggrandisement in the fifth century BC to the Russian revival that currently is underway following the hubris of NATO's arguably imprudent expansion in the 1990s, the political and strategic story essentially has been the same. Polities accept constraint and other pain when they must, often ironically because they fuel anxieties abroad that can be appeased satisfactorily only by counteraction. Cultural impulse, even strong preference, does not usually determine state policy and strategy, because it tends overwhelmingly to lead to tragic errors in statecraft. Vietnam in the 1960s and most probably Iraq and Afghanistan in the 2000s attest to the true modesty that is the proper role for the cultural element in policy and strategy.

2 *Undefinable boundaries: uncertain evidence.* It is a paradox that although everyone appears confident in their understanding of the meaning of the expression 'culture', the

104 *Culture and circumstance*

term is missing authoritative definition. What are we talking about (Geertz, 1973)? My own inclusive preferred definition was offered above, but that cannot readily serve purpose for scholarly enquiry. If culture is evidenced in the thoughts and deeds of a political community, and indeed commonly even across different communities, to what does it not apply? Culture, not unlike geography, politics, and strategy, has become a portmanteau concept so useful in everyday discourse that it becomes all but impervious to what should be careful analysis. But, if culture, rather strangely in common with physical and even psychological geography, potentially is everywhere and possibly influences all thought and behaviour, how can it be understood? If all is in some measure unavoidably cultural, political, or strategic, what should, and should not, be studied? This reason for acute scepticism does not amount to a denial of the existentiality of the phenomenon of culture, rather is it acknowledgement that it is not permissive of close disciplined study for understanding. If we are unable so to define culture that we can isolate evidence of its probable presence or absence, we cannot construct a useful theory to explain its functioning. It is probably ironic that it is the ubiquity of cultural influence that defeats our efforts to be responsible analysts. To practical effect, cultural influence that is probably everywhere, including within us ourselves, might as well be nowhere for the scholar, because it transcends any practicable feasibility for disciplined study. Unfortunately for the self-satisfaction of many scholarly would-be social scientists, the fact that we are not able to find wholly convincing evidence of cultural influence does not mean that the basic argument in favour of recognition of culture's influence has to be false. It is notoriously difficult to prove a null hypothesis, and this is a classic example of such. Even if we could show unarguably that something has not happened, that cannot stand as evidence proving that it could not occur. The longstanding scholarly and public debate about nuclear deterrence is a clear example of the 'Black Swan' challenge (Taleb, 2007). Because there has never been a bilateral nuclear war, is this evidence for its impossibility, or should we add the frightening word 'yet' to the sentence?

3 *Pervasive yet indeterminate.* If all people everywhere and at all times have to be the product of their genetic and circumstantial inheritances, what can we mean by claiming that they are culturally programmed to respond to particular stimuli in a particular way? Even if we choose not to halt further enquiry on the grounds that the subject of culture cannot be sufficiently distinguished and therefore isolated as to permit disciplined study, it is not obvious that we will be making progress towards answering the vital strategist's question, 'so what'? It could be a giant leap to attempt to proceed from cultural finding and mapping to a theory of behavioural causation. Indeed, a little reflection reveals that although culture spotting and possibly respectful observation is occasionally helpful for the conduct of political relations and strategic affairs, it is unlikely to be critically helpful, let alone reliable as a predictive guide for action. Most of us, much of the time, are aware of what we would like to do, if only we were able. The live question for statesmen and strategists is not, hypothetically, 'are they Chinese', or 'how Chinese are they?' Rather must it be, 'what if anything is likely to be the practical consequence of this adversary's Chinese identity and attitudes (culture)?'

Notwithstanding the occasional utility I find in refreshing my cultural awareness of other people in other places and at other times, this study takes a more casually holistic view of the subject of strategic history (Gray, 2012). While acknowledging the real or at least apparent differences between political communities, it is certainly no less necessary to recognize often deep and extensive commonalities among human beings. Whatever

Culture and circumstance 105

the culture and circumstance of disparate peoples, they are all members of the species *homo sapiens*. There is a physiological and psychological inheritance we all inherit, though admittedly with particular consequences that may well be stimulated by extraordinary historical and other contexts. A great debate is needed in order to attempt to secure a meaningful grip on genuinely separable motivations for thought and behaviour. Major difficulty lies in the obvious existence of multiple cultural personalities. That troubling caveat has to be set alongside the argument just made concerning the elements of humanity that precede culture, deriving from physiology and psychology. All people may or may not be equal, but assuredly they are all human, which has to mean they all have a great deal in common, regardless of particular cultural acquisition. Nature as well as nurture must be allowed a role in this analysis (Rosen, 2005). Through all of the accessible history of the human race, the two interdependent concepts of politics and strategy, treated as functions, have never been dispensable. This means that there has always been necessary political and strategic context driving a human search for security.

4 *Circumstance as context*. The contextual argument sceptical of culturalist theory is especially damning, not least because it takes the terms of debate beyond the bounds of possible settlement by deployment of any explanation of behaviour bearing some resemblance to evidence. By analogy, argument about culture versus circumstance is near certain to pertain to a context akin to a terminally corrupted crime scene. The grand narrative of strategic history usually is not hampered by lack of possible evidence, but rather by its contradictory overabundance. People and governments commonly do not have what is known as a narrow focus in option purity, a clear hierarchy of valued interests pursued rigorously in an orderly and often sequential manner. In the 1960s, spokespersons for American policy in Vietnam seemed always to manage to cite approximately half a dozen semi-plausible reasons for US actions, while forty years later exactly the same happened with respect to policy motives in Afghanistan and Iraq. Some explanations were to a degree dishonest, but in the main it is reasonable to conclude that the many, often contradictory, claims concerning national political and strategic motives and intentions were just confused as well as confusing to their audiences. Everywhere there are always multiple and somewhat alternative explanations for policy and strategy. If professional politicians, civil servants, and soldiers were unable to discover a variety of reasons to justify the decisions taken, probably they would be better employed in some other walks of life.

Our purpose here is not to be critical of those who attempt to explain what is being done in their and my names, and why it is being done. A vital key to understanding the course of strategic history must be willingness to tolerate attempted explanation of the genuine reality of happenstance – one damn thing occurring after another, uncontrolled by us! Strategic history is close to being a joke at the expense of the human race, if it is considered seriously to reveal the admirable consequences of well-considered and executed plans. Most polities conduct defence planning, but unwelcome surprise is a grimly episodic but repeated reminder of the limitations to foresight (Gray, 2014a).

The meaning in strategic history of the potential power of circumstance, an unexpectedly changing context, can be deadly for the authority we might like to assign to cultural preference. Stated directly, polities typically do what they cannot help but realize they need to do in order to survive while vulnerable in an essentially disordered world political system. In practical terms, even when national security is not commonly assessed as being under unusual threat, culture plays, at best, only a modest role in strategic decision-making and possibly in attitudes as well. The questions of highest

106 *Culture and circumstance*

moment for government are not 'what would we like to do, and how would we like to do it?' – questions that all but invite substantially cultural answer. Instead, the questions of the hour include affordability, appeasement, and bribery of some domestic critics. This is not to claim foolishly that cultural icons usually are ignored, but rather that there are always several or more reasons for spending ever scarcer tax revenue in alternative ways. Moreover, even when a national strategic decision is advertised and explained not implausibly as being 'the right thing to do' (e.g. as over the British Coalition Government's decision to replace the four Vanguard class SSBNs, like-for-like, with new submarines bearing Trident SLBMs), the political and strategic motivation is near certain to have been more circumstantial than cultural in any meaningful sense. A government will want to make the moral (in a Clausewitzian sense, not necessarily ethical) point that it is proof of determination and worthy of international respect. Cultural claims to leadership in ownership over policy and strategy nearly always are fatally vulnerable to assault by plausible alternative explanations that belong in the relevant, if confusing, category of redundant causation.

To help ensure a fair hearing for the view sceptical of cultural claims in strategic analysis, we close this presentation of contrasting opinions by quoting an inclusive negative judgement offered by the idea's most rigorous recent critic, Antulio J. Echevarria II. He is a serious scholar who has considered the issue area of culture in respect of strategy in considerable depth, and his opinions command and deserve attention.

> By Geertz's criterion [Clifford, cultural anthropologist who requires of the fictions of culture that they should achieve their purposes: Geertz, 1973], the fictions surrounding American strategic culture have failed. They have informed discussions of different national, political, or military perspectives in misleading ways having misrepresented or invented traits that are supposed to be either enduringly or uniquely American. This is true despite the fact that some of the interpreters of American strategic culture are part of the culture they purport to interpret. These efforts have succumbed to cultural determinism brought on by the concept's basic definitional vagaries and remain unresolved. In still other cases, the concept's popularity has induced individuals to assign the label of strategic culture to their works unnecessarily. Strategic culture, in short, went from being something fashioned, in Geertz's words, to something fashionable. While the concept may remain intriguing to academics, its flaws make it too risky for policymakers and strategists.
>
> (Echevarria, 2014: 44)

Echevarria is, in my view, considerably mistaken in the words just quoted, but he does raise valid and plausible objections to the undisciplined deployment of the concept of strategic culture. In particular, his negative view of the potential utility of the concept for policymakers and strategists is well taken by this theorist. Much of Echevarria's hostile critique concerns weakness in definition of the subject, and as a consequence the impracticability of employing it with precision. That said, his eschewal of respect for the idea of strategic culture, albeit with its 'warts'n all', is imprudent. The idea of strategic culture, with its fragilities freely conceded, is one we cannot afford to discard in the garbage heap of failed and failing concepts. In the Conclusion to this chapter, we identify the reasons why there is need for culture to be admitted for our education, even if it must come with an analytical health warning attached. What Echevarria has accomplished with his customary ruthless insight is to score goals across the undefended and really indefensible all too vague frontiers of the category of strategic cultural context. This context, alas, he appears not to understand properly or even recognize. If true, this fact must disable the power of his otherwise potentially deadly critique. Strategy and the politics from and with which it is made is always assembled unavoidably in a cultural context. Is this vague? – yes. Is this difficult or even impossible for scholars to employ very usefully? – possibly also yes. But is the organizing idea of cultural context therefore false as a logical consequence? – no. As the great geopolitical theorist Nicholas John Spykman wrote of physical geography in 1938, 'geography does not argue. It simply is' – cultural context should be accepted for much the same unyielding reason (1938: 238).

Conclusion: saving the patient

Unsurprisingly, culture in strategic mode fares badly when it is considered inappropriately. Echevarria among others has shown beyond serious question why the concept fails under close empirical and philosophical assessment. This author was troubled for some years by the conviction that the idea of strategic culture somehow was both unsafe at any speed, yet all but miraculously seemed too valuable to discard. Eventually, I came to realize that the subject here is an irony, not a contradiction with competing evidence. Ironically, the better apparent answers to cultural questions were owned by the concept's scholarly detractors, but common sense told me that they were fundamentally wrong. The concept of culture, strategic culture more specifically, has been mis-assigned by analysts as potentially determinant material that may be key to political and strategic choice and actions. I do not exclude all possibility of largely cultural explanation of behaviour, but am convinced that that is not the way in which culture should be considered. Culture does not make an isolated contribution to political and strategic thought and behaviour. Instead, it needs to be understood as a steady ingredient flavouring the mixture of motives and interests that we perform and sometimes have to confront as policy and strategy. By analogy and for example, American strategic culture can be considered a permanent component of American policy and strategic debate. It requires understanding as a standard, indeed inalienable, spice that always is there or thereabouts in the political and strategic dish that America serves itself and the world. When considered in this way, as an enduring contributor to public thought and behaviour, we recognize that it is always likely to help shape the political and strategic products, though it will only be one among many contributing factors.

When approached as immediately above, the concept of culture in its potential strategic relevance is shorn of the necessity even to masquerade as social science. Echevarria is right, of course, about its definitional uncertainty, but we need not care much about that weakness. Indeed, the sheer porosity of the cultural category of influences upon policy and strategy is probably as much a strength as a fragility. What is required for the necessary purpose of saving strategic culture from murderous would-be scientists is a greater tolerance of indeterminacy regarding attainable empirical evidence. Much of the criticism of culture in the strategic regard on balance is quite well founded. However, the relevant challenge is the necessity of realizing that the sins of this adventurous sounding concept really do not much matter when they are compared with its potent merits.

The principal reason why culture tends not to be treated satisfactorily by defence analysts is because typically they do not know how to attempt to understand it. Culture requires understanding as an inalienable quality required by an individual as he or she grow up. It is a vigorously holistic idea that refers to a person's social learning over the course of a lifetime. While cultural learning may influence opinion and attitude on particular matters, the more seriously enduring influence of culture is felt on approaches to challenges. Culture will not usually pick the winner from a short-list of pre-digested political options, but it is always likely to have served usefully in the marked reduction of possible confusion on the part of responsible policymakers. To pursue my short-list of thought a little further, culture is likely to affront decision making towards a particular part of the possible policy spectrum of response – towards a shorter short-list, in fact. Culture tends to confuse, even baffle, analysts because it is a potent seeming concept that is frustratingly bereft of meaningful boundaries. When policymakers and military strategists assess culture's role as a source of influence, they have difficulty grasping the fact that it is really everywhere in a society and cannot be considered as a disciplined source of attitude and opinion. An appropriate view to take of culture is one that considers the cost of its potential loss if it were to be expunged from all consideration. Also, debate over the domestic politics of defence preparation typically is heavily flavoured with attitudes and opinions that are plainly intended to have domestic impact, not strategic influence abroad.

Strangely, perhaps, the definitional weakness, uncertainty even of the highly inclusive concept of culture is a signal strength for our study. Echevarria and others are right in pointing critically to the uncertainties of definition that can render cultural, as opposed to other, identity uncertain. Strange to say, perhaps, but this definitional vagueness happens to be a strength in the concept's nature and character, not a weakness as one might expect. Both politics and strategy typically summon a wealth of innovative imagination that may lend itself to advantageous adversarial exploitation. The makers of policy and strategy frequently must attempt to cope with challenges that are unprecedented both in basic purpose and in precise detail. Because of its frequently broadly permissive nature, subject to expediently friendly interpretation, the nature and the local character of the relevant culture may well provide a vital source of inspiration for influence and action. With culture intelligently approached and used, we are dealing with a pervasively human dimension to this subject. The matter here comprises attitudes based somewhat upon local authority concerning what is rightful and justified behaviour, and those possible misdeeds that are not. Scholars and soldiers need to understand that culture is a broad inclusive concept that effectively does not have frontiers that social scientists can patrol. To employ an idea that I first employed many years ago, culture provides context for all policy and strategy-making (Gray, 1999b: Ch. 5). More often than not, its influence will be felt via a modest political intervention to nudge a distinctly modest alteration in the intended course of policy endorsed officially.

It is ironic that a pervasive and only occasionally decisive cultural influence upon the politics of policy can be distinguished amidst the chaos of competing urges and other emotions that fuel the policy train. However, the undoubted uncertainties about definition – concerning what is, as contrasted with what most probably is not, cultural – ought not to serve as fatal discouragement of cultural alertness in and to scholarship. Notwithstanding the still healthy flow of analyses that do treat culture with due seriousness, it is the judgement of this author that scholars continue to fail in understanding the true pervasive, indeed contextual, operation and influence of beliefs, attitudes and habits of behaviour that demand to be considered as cultural. I do understand all too well how frustrating, even discouraging, it can be to realize that this concept is so inclusive that effectively we are almost obliged to disregard the issue of specific frontiers to analysis. I do not wish to go quite this far, but am prepared to defend the big ideas that a great deal of our personal, certainly political, thought and activity is somewhat in debt emotionally, if not necessarily intellectually, to influence that it is plausible to understand with the label cultural. In practical effect, it is being suggested here that scholars need to shape their awareness of cultural influence, particularly when there is a shortage of popular icons that may serve as flags signalling a cultural contribution.

Those who reject this argument are challenged to look closely in the analytical mirror. If one rejects cultural influence as a potentially noteworthy contributor to national (or tribal) political and strategic behaviour, the result effectively is a black hole devoid of the motivations conditioned by historical and geographical circumstances that contribute to a polity's definition of its persisting interests and desires. Of course, politics, its policy, and strategy, are decided in the hope they will answer the more urgent national needs of the day. But, that understandable aspiration does not mean that policy and strategy are invented and pursued as if from a national context of understanding utterly unsullied by historical memories, geopolitical concerns, or enduring interests. Culture is not the entire national team, but it cannot be other than on the team permanently as one important source of influence among others.

Key points

1 All politics and strategy are the product of encultured people.
2 There is no authoritative concept of culture.
3 Unarguable evidence for the influence of culture is missing.
4 Culture today is the consequence of historical experience, memory, and legend.
5 Politics and strategy cannot be other than partially cultural in origin and motivation.
6 Polities think and act as they must in a world where necessity restricts choice.
7 The argument sceptical of culture as influence on policy and strategy is a strong one, but ironically it is wrong because typically it fails to understand the contextual nature of the subject.

Further reading

Barnett, R. W. (2009) *Navy Culture: Why the Navy Thinks Differently*, Annapolis, MD: Naval Institute Press.
Black, J. (2012) *War and the Cultural Turn*, Cambridge: Polity Press.
Booth, K. (1979) *Strategy and Ethnocentrism*, London: Croom Helm.
Creveld, M. van (2008) *The Culture of War*, New York: Ballantine Books.
Echevarria, A. J., II (2014) *Reconsidering the American Way of War: U.S. Military Practice from the Revolution to Afghanistan*, Washington, DC: Georgetown University Press.
France, J. (2011) *Perilous Glory: The Rise of Western Military Power*, New Haven, CT: Yale University Press.
Geertz, C. (1973) *The Interpretation of Culture*, New York: Basic Books.
Gray, C. S. (2013) *Perspectives on Strategy*, Oxford: Oxford University Press, Ch. 3.
Hanson, V. D. (2001) *Why the West Has Won: Carnage and Culture from Salamis to Vietnam*, London: Faber and Faber.
Johnson, R. (2011) *The Afghan Way of War: Culture and Pragmatism: A Critical History*, London: C. Hurst.

110 *Culture and circumstance*

Johnston, A. I. (1995) *Cultural Realism: Strategic Culture and Grand Strategy in Chinese History*, Ithaca, NY: Cornell University Press.

Katzenstein, P. J. (ed.) (1996) *The Culture of National Security: Norms and Identity in World Politics*, New York: Columbia University Press.

Porter, P. (2009) *Military Orientalism: Eastern War Through Western Eyes*, London: C. Hurst.

Sondhaus, L. (2006) *Strategic Culture and Ways of War*, Abingdon: Routledge.

8 Civil–military relations

> *Reader's guide:* This chapter explains the fundamental issues that trouble civil–military relations worldwide. In particular the relations are considered in terms of political power and the assignment of blame for failures. Civil–military relations are a key to effective jointness in strategy. Cooperation is as necessary as some competition is always inevitable.

Introduction: chain of command

Undoubtedly, policy is wholly owned by the professionals who devise, manage, and adjust political process, usually with periodic reference to the public ballot boxes that legitimize their licensed authority. In a truly tidy and orderly world this could stand as a proper, terse statement of what ought to be obvious. But, in the real, messy and ever somewhat chaotic context of policymaking, apparent roles may well not indicate the subtleties or perhaps the contradictions that lurk between what should be the case and what usually actually is so. At the core of the argument here is an elemental truth that Eliot A. Cohen expressed as follows:

> In fact, the study of the relationship between soldiers and *statesmen* (rather different from the relationship between the soldier and *the state*, as a famous book has it [Samuel P. Huntington, *The Soldier and the State*, 1957]) lies at the heart of what strategy is all about.
>
> (Cohen, 2002: xii)

In this chapter, as throughout this text, we argue and insist that formal roles and seemingly well-established practices of bureaucratic management tell much less than appears to be their promise. Individual human and collective cultural influences typically have roles to play in the making and execution of both policy and strategy. This point is not a dazzling insight, but it does have implications notably subversive of straightforward standard explanations of how matters allegedly are and ought to be. In military, even strategic, theory, the dividing line between policy and military strategy, with its enabling operations and tactics, appears sufficiently plain as to preclude unhelpful confusion. Historically, in practice though, much is and remains seemingly perpetually more chaotic than orderly. The aridly austere realm of social science theory is apt to be disinclined to recognize that the human factor in policy and strategy-making is not just an episodic, perhaps rather eccentric, actuality, but instead is a vital persisting reality that

112 *Civil–military relations*

always may yield substantive variants to what one might otherwise have anticipated to be the most probable consequence of events.

Here we are suitably respectful of what all culturally enlightened opinion in nearly all polities has chosen to consider the proper relationship between civilians in governance and their, meaning our, uniformed military servants. But, that respectful attention needs recognition bearing only upon a somewhat formal, even abstract, theoretical representation of political reality.

This introduction will close by quoting the pertinent judgement offered by Donald Stoker in his exemplary unique analysis of strategy in the American Civil War. Stoker offers the plausible opinions that are sharply contrasting:

> Lincoln's genius lay where it all started – in the political realm. He navigated a perilous precipice throughout the war, struggling with infighting among domestic factions and threats from overseas. He managed these magnificently. He also clearly understood the relationship between military power and political ends. He held the political reins tight and saw to it that the military means were adjusted to policy ends. But this did not make him a great strategist.
>
> (Stoker, 2010: 410–11)

In fairly sharp contrast, Stoker proceeds, via reasonably generous strategic judgements on Generals Ulysses S. Grant and William Tecumseh Sherman, to deliver an uncompromisingly negative judgement on their Confederate enemy. We are advised that 'strategic thinking in the South was almost non-existent' (Stoker, 2010: 411). Although Grant and Sherman by and large stumbled and then settled upon an essentially strategic view of the war they sought to prosecute in its final year of 1864–5, their nominal successors one hundred and more years later were neither blessed similarly with strategic understanding, nor – to be fair – were they so placed in a chain of command for Vietnam, Iraq, or Afghanistan that they could compel the United States or its allies to think and behave strategically.

Theory and practice do not merely complement each other, because competent strategic performance has to rest upon a conceptual grip on that which is strategically essential. No little scale of challenge pervades this necessity for an effectiveness of military practice to depend vitally upon clear and strongly determined effort that must be guided by the light that only strategic understanding can shine. Readers should consider some wise words that flowed from the great Russian strategist and military commander, Aleksandr A. Svechin:

> [S]trategy by its very nature resists codification in field manuals. But the need for efforts to raise the level of strategic thinking is recognized everywhere.
>
> The study of strategy by just a small circle of commanders, such as the general staff, leads to the creation of a 'strategic caste', and when strategy is isolated, it becomes scholarly pedantry, divorced from practice, and it creates an undesirable gap between strategists and tacticians among commanders and destroys mutual understanding between staffs and line units. Strategy should not become a kind of Latin which separates the believers and the nonbelievers!
>
> The need for all commanders to study strategy follows from the fact that it should not be put off until the time a person is assigned to a critical leadership position. Strategy is a discipline in which success depends very little on the

memorization of precepts issued by a school or the assimilation of logical constructs contained in textbooks on strategy... In strategy the center of gravity lies in developing an independent point of view which primarily requires careful homework.

(Svechin, [1927]: 76)

Strategic competence, let alone genius, is an exceptional rather than a standard achievement for either soldiers or politicians. Even though Svechin wrote clearly and his meaning appears to have survived the rigours of translation from Russian into English, there remains a tantalizing elusiveness about the concept and practice of strategy. This intangibility, both obviously material and even intellectual, certainly contributes noticeably to the scale of challenge faced by those professionally obliged to wrestle with strategic matters. Missiles and tanks can be photographed, strategy cannot.

In this chapter we will address the nature of the challenge to sound Clausewitzian governance that the partially contrasting cultures distinctive respectively to the political and military professions must bring to the difficulties of strategy-making. We will examine both the common and the uncommon qualities that tend to be rewarded in the two professional contexts, and then explain the reasons and methods that promote cooperative behaviour. The dominant theme here has to be the relations of authority, meaning power, expressed in variably commanding terms as influence (Lasswell, 1936). Although the whole of this book is about the relations between strategy and politics, here the iron glove of a politics-led chain of command is emphasized.

Politicians and strategists: professional and cultural challenges

Alexandr A. Svechin insisted that, '[r]ules are inappropriate in strategy' ([1927] 1992: 64). This is all too true, and often has exciting, not to say adventurous, implications for decision making and subsequent practice. If there are no reliable rules for the performance of strategy, this has to mean that there must be a standard missing by which we can assess the quality of official behaviour. Because strategy requires the exercise of policy judgement concerning the probable, certainly the anticipated, political effect of selected military tasks, there can be no 'school' solution. Every strategic choice worthy of the elite adjective pertains to a unique problem in a no less historically individual context. For the rare professionals educated conceptually and by experience to think and behave strategically, fresh challenge necessarily is most likely to fuel intellectual innovation. However, education in approach to the prudent, albeit possibly bold, strategic thought can never be assumed to be the dominant characteristic of a strategy-making process. Indeed, the more thoroughly 'staffed' a strategy selection system proves to be, the less likely it is to produce a strategy suitably tolerant of unavoidable risk even including the political and military risks of failure.

The present author does not assume that all polities are substantially identical in their attitude towards risk and tolerance of some failure in strategy. Nonetheless, it is assumed here that although the cultural context for strategy-making, and particularly the character of civil–military relations, can differ markedly from polity to polity, there are major features impressively common across political and cultural boundaries. Without straining the evidence unduly, we are able to identify a distinctive set of reasons why civil–military relations should be considered a single subject for examination.

114 *Civil–military relations*

- *Ubiquity.* Not all countries have acute problems in civil–military relations, but all have some potential for such. Since it is only human for us to seek the intangible quality of security, both individual and collective, and because security can be approached only through a political process, inevitably all polities are unable to avoid a domestic context of civil–military relations. This is not an avoidable circumstance; rather is it a structural feature locked into human (political) existence. It is neither good nor bad, it simply 'is', as Nicholas John Spykman wrote of physical geography (Gray, 2015a). Problems characteristic of the professional challenges felt by politicians and soldiers will be fairly distinctive to time, place, and general culture, but in larger measure they will flow from the nature, not the particular character, of the profession in question. Politicians are always in pursuit of the authority that flows from the legitimacy of public approval, while soldiers are ever alert to the real or possible needs of an enhanced security. The character taken in the local context for politics, policy, and strategy-making does not much matter, because the nature of the deepest concerns of politics and strategy are well enough labelled respectively as legitimacy and security. The particular term of domestic argument varies widely with local details of anxiety, but these two inclusively grand sets of ideas express a phenomenon that is as near universal as makes no meaningful difference. All polities everywhere have conditions of civil–military relations, because they are unavoidable (Cimbala, 2012). There is merit in our recognizing, however, that the attitudes and behaviours we identify as distinctive to the two professions become so habitual that it is prudent to consider them significantly cultural, professional though they will be. This is not necessarily to claim a strategic cultural bias allegedly specific to place and general culture, but it is to emphasize the enculturation effect respectively of following a political or a military career.

- *Relations of power – and blame.* Because of the relative high importance of military power, it is common for soldiers and civilian policymakers to coexist in a context of some tension. When a country is at war, even if only one of strictly limited commitment, effort, and prospective consequences, such tension is likely to mar the normally even tenor of civil–military relations. For a country to fail unmistakeably in its policy and perhaps what ought to be its strategy, typically is held to require public explanation. If politician-policymakers made sensible decisions and the policy guidance was followed, why did national alliance (and largely) military guidance fail to deliver on what was agreed in planning? Similarly, if the soldiers obeyed orders and sought to follow the political guidance provided by distant national capitals, why was the resulting context on the ground in, say, Iraq and Afghanistan, close to a disaster rather than a triumph? Virtually regardless of historical accuracy concerning the course of a conflict, it is both human nature and inevitable bureaucratic politics for the participants in, and contributors to, failure to seek to place political and possibly even military responsibility upon people and institutions other than themselves. This is not prima facie evidence of malfeasance, rather is it the normal political process of governance. If events undeniably have not gone well, often it is irresistibly tempting to assign a relatively high measure of blame upon people and institutions not well equipped to defend themselves at home against intense criticism. It is a common assumption that if the course of a conflict has not advanced satisfactorily, someone(s) must be to blame and should be held accountable. We know that the American and British shift of attention and commitment to Afghanistan, largely superseding that earlier in Iraq, fell far short of comprising the British Army's finest hour. With regard to the rather strange sudden move into Helmand Province in 2008, it is now certain that too much was attempted with far too little

Civil–military relations 115

battle-ready combat strength. This major weakness of British military means should have been anticipated, if largely as the basis of prudential military planning. British policy and its political assumptions proved as flawed as British tactical methods were obliged for survival to verge upon the desperate (Elliott, 2015). The British military experience in Afghanistan (Helmand) was an embarrassing military mess that had substantial negative consequences for Anglo-American political relations. After all, the British effort in Afghanistan had very little to do with Taliban authored threats to Britain, but meant a lot for the political and military respect in which Britain was held in Washington.

Scope for the assignment of blame has been high with regard both to Afghanistan and Iraq (regarding the precipitate retreat from Basra in particular). Were policymakers to blame for asking the impossible of their armed forces, or rather did those forces fail to use the military assets at their command effectively? – Or both? Popular public sentiment naturally is likely to side with 'our boys (and girls)' in uniform who risk their lives in combat, while the political temptation for policymakers to blame the military High Command for failure to deliver 'in the field' can be irresistible. This is particularly the case if there is an acute shortage of plausibly guilty people. We have need to remember that in Britain and the United States it is both legally and culturally impossible for soldiers to criticize the High Command, most especially not the President of the United States in his isolated role as Commander in Chief (Cimbala, 2012). No matter how tense civil–military relations become, especially in the case of a losing and then a lost war, soldiers and civilian politicians are not licensed to compete in public regarding relative lack of responsibility for failure. In both countries, even when there are substantial grounds for finding fault with the conduct of the military effort, civilians who choose to hang blame largely on the military institutions of state take an enormous risk of incurring popular disapproval. This is known rather roughly as 'blowback'. Critics find that Americans love the US Marine Corps more deeply than they do a cohort of recent political appointees. This holds almost regardless of accurate assignment of responsibility for lack of political and strategic success.

Civil–military relations in the United States remain almost entirely locked into what commonly is identified as the Huntington model. Professor Samuel P. Huntington of Harvard University wrote a now long famous book in 1957, in which he drew a sharp distinction between the responsibility of civilian politician-policymakers and that of the military profession (Huntington, 1957). In Huntington's view, it is the task of civilian policymakers to make policy, and that of the military to obey orders and refrain from public political dissent about their alleged sense or otherwise. In this view, neither policy nor strategy are considered joint ventures. The polity demands policy compliance and suitable effort on the part of its soldiers; it neither strictly requires, nor even necessarily expects, political agreement between the realms of politics and military professionals. This well-established cultural norm of political compliance, possibly strategic tolerance, is all but foundational for the governance of American civil–military relations. None-theless, it is always likely to prove less than robust in the ever unexpected case of American failure 'in the field'. Culturally speaking, it is probably fair to comment that American society typically is so self-confident that failure in a foreign strategic enter-prise is close to unimaginable, until it happens, as for example occurred in Saigon, (then South) Vietnam in April 1975. Cynically, perhaps, we could argue that the British are more experienced in the politics of retreat, even ignominious retreat, than are Americans. It may well follow that truly awful British political–military ineptitude, as

116 *Civil–military relations*

over Basra in Iraq in 2008, proved less damaging to London's reputation than was merited. In best, but also worst, British official fashion, the appalling evidence of Britain's 'scuttle and run' from action in Iraq (largely Basra) in 2008 has long been covered up, though not impregnably concealed, by the skilful and greatly delaying employment of a public enquiry led by Sir John Chilcot (Elliott, 2015: 104). The Chilcot Enquiry, which supposedly should identify British names and institutions that failed in Iraq, eventually will make some public report. But, while time is not always reliable as a great healer, it does have the official benefit of imposing such extraordinary delay in its public findings that the result will be more a yawn than a source of anger. Political demand for the allegedly guilty men and women to be brought to account cannot be anticipated with confidence. The enquiry into what went wrong with the British intervention in Iraq should not obscure from notice the fact that when a foreign intervention leads to severe political and military embarrassment, competition in the assignment of relative amounts of blame should be expected. Despite the norms of hierarchy and cooperation in Huntington's model of civil–military relations, both institutional parties, civilian and military, are likely to have much to conceal from open public scrutiny. In effect, there can be a conspiracy, if not quite of silence, more of extreme reticence that requires reciprocation for mutual political protection. Although particularly policymakers may well have a great deal they would prefer to pass over in a prudent silence, it is more likely than not that the military also will have much in their recent, and even personal, records of which they are not especially proud.

• *Tribal loyalties.* The potentially immediate and close context of high personal danger has a defining authority for military behaviour and institutions that has few, if any, parallels in civilian life. Although professional soldiers typically are required to assume characteristics deemed fitting for members of particular regiments and other groupings, also quite commonly there is an outlook on the world and its challenges that is particularly military, if not entirely reliably so. The reason for this near uniformity of attitude and behaviour lies in the fundamental function of military establishments, worldwide. They exist and are supported by often reluctant taxpayers because they are understood by all interested persons to constitute the *ultima ratio regis* (the final answer of the king/sovereign). For most polities the professional soldier is a regrettably necessary cost of insurance, underpinning normal political life with its tolerable level of insecurity. Heroism is honoured and praised by soldiers, even more so by civilian by-standers. But, the military life in peace and even more in actual war is one that has to be dominated by the demands of effective teamwork. Relatively small-scale teamwork is absolutely vital in the conduct of nearly all aspects of counterinsurgency activity, combat and other (e.g. development assistance), but the context for military activity typically quite literally includes casts of tens, hundreds, perhaps thousands. The necessity for cooperative behaviour requires a clear enough chain of command for the establishment of distinctive responsibilities and for the authority behind orders. Virtually no matter how different soldiers may appear to be in distinctive clothing and with particular preferred weaponry, there are professional military characteristics that are as close to being universal as makes little difference. When examining civil–military relations it is necessary to remember that there is always a superiority in legal and political authority enjoyed by the civilian, because of the instrumental nature, not only character, of the soldier's function. It is his job to defend the polity, possibly against extreme menaces of violence largely from abroad. The political, possibly the moral, will to take military action must be based on political judgement, and the professional soldier has

Civil–military relations 117

to wait, and if necessary act, on orders from civilian authority. This is close to being a universal truth today, regardless of the individual character of regime.

The unique requirements for cooperation and control over some of the adverse consequences of fear encourage military institutions to proceed in their corporate morale-building with activities in the growth of what reasonably should be understood as 'tribal' loyalty. Understandably, smaller units typically require, and are receptive to, the transmission of characteristics broadly to be appreciated as cultural, sometimes to an extreme degree. In the United States, the US Army Rangers and also the Marine Corps each have quite distinctively characteristic material and physical appearances, and the facility of communicating under pressure in a distinctive specialized language that rapidly becomes thoroughly habitual (Johnson, J. forthcoming). To some degree such acquired characteristics can be taught, but more commonly they simply are the result of a process of enculturation. This transformation of young American (generally) males from ordinary teenagers into reliably disciplined, honourable, and if necessary even heroic Rangers and Marines is the product of a process of cultural conditioning; it is unavoidable and inevitably successful if a person's enlistment is to prove satisfactory. Genuinely eccentric characteristics are not tolerated by non-commissioned officers or by fellow enlisters.

Such near uniformity in culture, flowing as it must from the dangers and demands of the anticipated duty with its instrumentality in needed obedience to civilian policy, inevitably does not leave the more active intellectual assets of people entirely uninfluenced. Of course, there are always a few individual soldiers inclined to speculate on strategy and operations for the world beyond tactics today. However, the practical demands of the tactical realm of fighting leave little room for conceptual leisure that is likely to prove only idle. I do not intend this part of the analysis to sound at all patronizing or demeaning to the professional solder and his tactical behaviour. What I am trying to convey is a clear sense of the soldier's necessarily subordinate role to civilian policy that is born of inevitable politics. The real challenge in civil–military relations is when the different contexts comprising the military and political worlds meet on and from the strategy bridge. Self-evidently, smooth cooperation between military knowledge and some understanding, and the variable velocity of political will behind policy decision, cannot prudently be assumed to be near automatic, let alone inevitable. From time to time, often on little notice, a polity will demand that its military instrument must do what the domestic taxpayers expect and require by way of the infliction of hurt on foreign wrongdoers (of course). Since individual military careers are rarely advanced as a consequence of the delivery of unwelcome negative judgement on the schemes of politicians, inevitably there is a professional military bias in favour of saying 'yes, sir/ma'am'! Even if the military suspects that policy is requiring strategic delivery beyond its capability to produce, who really can be sure until one tries? Perhaps the much favoured Clausewitzian quality of luck will intervene by some surprise to improve our strategic prospects (Clausewitz, 1976: 85).

Inevitably, and almost certainly deservedly – though not by the squaddies on the sharp end of war – ill-considered and clearly imprudent military adventure are punished by inevitable political evidence of failure, great and small. This is always embarrassing and it results in the encouragement of a search for those people and institutions who allegedly failed in the needed military action. The blame game is played unavoidably in all polities. Tribal military loyalty serves to suppress public knowledge and comprehension of some, at least, of the evidence of apparent blame, but usually there is more than a

118 *Civil–military relations*

sufficient appearance of incompetence for some mud to stick beyond possibility of easy cleansing... (Bailey, Iron and Strachan, 2013). When politician-policymakers point the finger of accusation at their military instrument, often they will have high hopes that the norm of quiet obedience, even loyalty to the authority of the political up the chain of command, will hold firmly enough (e.g. not entirely beyond plausible disproof) to outlast the persistence and patience of critics. Strategic, for eventual political, success has no difficulty identifying policy parenthood, both real and possibly fanciful.

• *Politics and human nature.* Seductive though it can prove to be to an analyst to attempt to seek and almost certainly discover cultural differences between civil and military power on both banks that ought to be connected by a strategy bridge, it would be a serious error to pursue that line of thought too assiduously. Indeed, it would be the same mistake that is made when changes, in contrast to continuities, are privileged in overviews of strategic history. What would be lacking would be sufficient recognition of the reality of our common humanity across cultures and choice of styles in governance. The point of most importance is that there is a universality of the context of civil–military relations for the conduct of politics everywhere and at all times. Crises in relations between professional politicians and professional soldiers may well be rare, though certainly a condition characterized by some tension is far from unusual. What needs emphasis is the enduring nature of the principal sources of strain in civil–military relations and the leading reasons for such conflict, ever potential, if not necessarily extant.

We can seek to explain conflict in civil–military relations largely in terms of occasional clashes of personality and contrasting responsibilities. However, it would be an error to analyse tension and worse in civil–military relations primarily in such terms. Although societal political choices concerning style of governance and policy will be more or less likely to lead to civil–military tension, behind the rich detail of strategic historical experience lies an abiding reality of potential for conflict that does not, indeed truly cannot, go away. All polities strive to achieve an acceptable estimate of the condition of their security. Because there are always permanently established political and military cohorts tasked to answer political and military issues of policy about public safety, there is a perishing dialogue underway that we refer to as civil–military relations; this dialogue is institutionalized. Since societal resources inevitably will be somewhat limited in regard to rival claims concerning public needs, conflict over allocation is unavoidable. Rephrased, there will be competing demands for some of the same pot of money. Every decade in many countries has produced the experience of more or less acute crises in civil–military relations, as competing priorities for public expenditure join political battle. There is a widespread, though not universal, conviction that it is not fitting for professional soldiers to wade actively and openly into the often odorous mud of domestic politics. In part as a consequence much of the dark and possibly dirty detail of defence budgeting is left expediently by soldiers to the political machinations of their functional allies in defence industry.

There is little that should be condemned about an enduring structure of civil–military relations certain to persist in domestic, possibly also inter-allied, conflict. Our principal human security structures, the state and the international system of states, all but guarantees an enduring if variable reality of permanent tension. Given that a polity's defence planners can never be certain as to what menaces will approach their society in years to come, there is always going to be ample scope to endorse and even urge investment in preferred defence programmes. Though schemes entailing major reductions in a defence budget are carried through, certainly are attempted from time to time, as for example under President Barack Obama, civil–military relations can be tense, even intense, regardless of whether societal allocation for defence is rising or failing. The reason lies in the nature of the political challenge. Defence planning cannot help but be an exercise in guesswork, no matter how long explanatory and excusatory briefings may be (Gray, 2014b). Because we can obtain no reliable detailed knowledge about our security needs in the future from the future, we are condemned to rely largely on political judgement. This judgement, meaning guesswork, always is reached, frequently changed indeed, as the often disturbingly uncertain product of political process. The competing strengths of particularly (self-)interested domestic parties who have economic and political stakes in the shape and character of defence budget decisions determine who wins and who loses. Economic well-being and votes are both likely to be at hazard in the near constant political conflict over the allocation of scarce resources.

Although there is need to be careful in offering generalization concerning politicians and civil servants on the one hand, and professional soldiers on the other, there are undoubtedly cultural, indeed plausibly 'tribal' differences between the two or three careers that are substantially contextual. For the soldier there is often some menace, just discernible, if not reliably predictable, on or over the time horizon for tomorrow; a danger that he is required to be ready to meet at any and potentially every risk to his personal life. For the politician-policymaker, the hazard rarely exceeds the temporary embarrassment of unemployment. Whereas the soldier may be required to commit himself to battle to the point of ultimate personal risk, the average politician most likely would scarcely be discomforted by a period out of public office. Clearly, there is an unavoidable asymmetry in obligation between the soldier's and the politician's 'tribes'. This contrast is stark and lends itself to plausible explanation in blunt terms. Expressed thus, soldiers may contribute to strategy, but if they find themselves in serious trouble, most likely it will be because of the policy choice made by a domestic political process in which commonly they have eschewed active, near certainly any public, participation.

Context of strategy

Strategy provides essential context for all civil–military relations, whether they are conducted well or poorly. Senior military professionals may not reason competently in a manner calculated to elicit strategic sense from military power, but such meaning can be found in every hierarchical order of relative power. It has to follow that a real, if not necessarily recognized, strategic context accompanies the mixed process of conflict and cooperation we have learnt to label as civil–military relations. Given the frequency of credible lament over the weakness of strategy in Britain and the United States, for leading national examples, it may seem strange to appear to notice, certainly not celebrate or excuse, the near absence of strategic design as a policy enabler. To the contrary, what requires recognition is not so much an absence of strategy, but rather a strategy chosen by default. The choice will have been predetermined by a prior lack of what might have been more suitable strategic ideas. Just as all tactical military behaviour has some net strategic value, positive or negative, so all episodes in civil–military relations cannot avoid being conducted in the mixed light and shadow created by particular conditions of strategic context. From time to time this context itself can be the subject of acute

120 *Civil–military relations*

controversy, as political meaning is imputed, which is to say probably assumed, to rival positions concerning alleged needs in national defence. However, what is more important is that the commonality of a strategy context should be noticed and understood. Because there is always a context of strategy for polities' defence planning and preparation, security communities are not at liberty to remove themselves by political determination from a condition coloured by strategic hazard, which does not mean that some usually attempt to do so.

Some readers of this book may be a little puzzled that it insists so firmly upon there being permanently extant a pragmatic authority to strategy. Surely, it might be objected, not infrequently it is argued, apparently credibly, that defence and perhaps other strategy is nowhere to be found. Germany in 1918, and 1944–5, or the United States in the 1960s and 2000s, seem to have functioned in what is characterizable as a strategy-free, certainly light, zone. Contrary to the worth of appearances, however, a national security condition noticeably short of strategic direction is not, ipso facto, one that has to be bereft of strategy as a deserved consequence. Regardless of the near heroic level of ignorance within which they were fairly contentedly engulfed, the Wehrmacht's organization, deployment, and operational intentions on 10 May 1940 constituted a potentially deadly menace that could, and duly did, unhinge the entire Anglo-French system of defence in the West (Frieser, 2005). The German offensive had not been expected by its authors to defeat France in a single campaign, but that was the military strategic reality and opportunity at the time. Often it is not clear just what the strategic context for a polity's civil–military relations should be understood to be, but appreciation of that familiar and inevitable relative ignorance does not weaken the force of our argument. Truly what matters is full recognition of the material and conceptual reality of the then current strategic context. Of course, these elements of central importance do not exhaust what needs understanding in order to examine a 'strategic balance', but their emphasis remind us of a significant ordering reality about power relations, no matter how the content of domestic debate in civil–military relations ebbs and flows. There is always and unavoidably a strategic context behind, sometimes stimulating, polities' debates on defence, including those that engage the political and military institutions of state more, or as much, on economic issues as those about relative weight of political influence.

Cooperation, competition, and conflict

Civil–military relations everywhere and at all times are conducted by individuals who have both personal and institutional interests, as well as personal characteristics. The latter may well not lend themselves readily to a habit of cooperation, let alone accommodation, with the orders and other demands from the world of policy with its often intense political controversy. There should be no room for serious doubt about the steps on a hierarchy of legal and political authority. Nonetheless, the scope and occasion for civil–military antagonism and conflict is present in the enduring structure of somewhat contending responsibilities that separate the policymaker from the soldier. We can go further and note that far from tension in civil–military relations necessarily meaning any dysfunctionality of process, such disagreement usually is as necessary for prudent governance as it may well be unavoidable, given the probably forceful characters most directly engaged. While Eliot A. Cohen's 'unequal dialogue' has to privilege the authority of civil power, nonetheless there are times in many countries' experiences of statecraft when that civil authority ought to be advised and warned to the effect that its current policy wishes are unwise and possibly impracticable. By no means is it the sole responsibility of the military establishment to tell the government when it seems likely to make a serious error, but it has to be (just) within the military domain for its leaders to inform politicians of their reasons for disagreement with current or emerging policy choice. This is not improper, let alone illegal. Nonetheless, it may be politically unwise, given the frequency and occasional intensity with which political decision-makers can endorse dubious solutions to burgeoning challenges. Chief executives typically have a habit of selecting for the principal military roles in advice to government soldiers trusted to be loyal, discrete, and broadly on board with the policy choice made by the Prime Minister or President. The role of loyal military opponent is not one that can endure in the rough and tumble of often brutal domestic politics. A president can tolerate, even welcome an in-house friendly critic, as was George Ball to President John F. Kennedy over American policy and strategy towards South Vietnam, but there will be limits to the permitted dissent. The political pressure that accumulates and gathers about a controversial policy is likely to prove strain enough on the individual decision-maker, without any additional tolerance of, as it were officially licensed, disagreement. No chief executive can be expected to tolerate, let alone encourage, political and strategic dissent very far beyond a near ritualistic level of repeated expression. It is one thing to dissent on strategic ways and military means, it is quite another to challenge the legal, moral, and political basis of what is proposed by the highest level of government.

Pragmatically, it can be difficult for the soldier to know how far he is allowed to proceed with dissent over strategy, because our subject in this work entails an attempt to understand where enough dissent for the responsibly prudent provision of expert advice becomes more or less direct disagreement with the political desires of the government. Since the political legitimacy of democratically elected politicians cannot be questioned sceptically by the military, inevitably there will be occasions when senior soldiers are convinced that the White House or No. 10 Downing Street are bound on a policy voyage to either a small or a major disaster. In that anticipated policy context, the professional soldier may have to face up to an uncomfortably stark choice. On the one hand, he can attempt to speak the truth as he knows it to political power; on the other hand, he could decide that explicit public criticism most likely would result in his closing whatever potential for constructive influence he still retains. Rather than risk being tainted by more or less plainly unwise policy, the soldier may choose to retire and most probably as a consequence lose any possibility of promoting some influence for political and strategic good as he sees it.

Operational consumption of strategy?

The primary role of a strategy bridge must be the enabling and sustainment of the necessarily unequal dialogue connecting the worlds of policy-politics with that of military capability. In practice, however, time after time in the twentieth century the vital connection not made at all adequately was that between strategy and its supposed major instrumental servant, military operations. For conspicuous examples of this lacuna, consider briefly the American experience in the Civil War and fast-forwarding nearly 150 years, the frustrating experiences in Iraq and Afghanistan. The same deficiency in American strategy (Union and Confederate) was evident in all these historical cases. Moreover, the repeated problem was not, indeed could not simply be a poor strategy, because there scarcely was one worth citing. Admittedly, this is somewhat unfair to

122 *Civil–military relations*

President Lincoln and also to General Grant, who did think and endeavour to perform strategically at least for a few days, if irregularly each week. It is tempting to home in on the real and alleged weakness in American strategy provision for the wars at issue here. But there was and remains today a more deadly malady than that which obviously assails the American strategy-making process, with its difficult, even painful, devouring of scant Presidential time and effort in Washington, DC. Repeatedly, the United States has demonstrated ultimately, through political failure on the field of military action in theatre, that it fails to understand what is required of operational artistry on the part of its senior commanding generals (Kelly and Brennan, 2009). The American weakness deadly to the enterprise in Vietnam, Iraq, and Afghanistan, as it was in 1861–5 also, was a lethal inability to show and perform with strategic sense in the conduct of the operational level of warfare. The operational level is anticipated to be hierarchically the most senior zone of action wherein politicians and their issues play, at most, just occasionally visibly in brief and token visits to the 'front' in theatre, but safely enough protected. After a day or two of mess-tent visits and seemingly endless PowerPoint presentations, the country's elected political leader-policymaker jets off with job done; he has shown that he cares! But, more often than not he will fail to pose the brutal sounding challenge that a strategist should insist be posed, 'so what?' – of course.

At least two considerable problems serve to cause difficulty for the challenge of translation from an operational level of advantage to one worth calling strategic. First, both the strategic and the operational levels of command need to understand the nature and locally specific character of the challenge. The operational level of command should be guided by a strategic sense with a compass able to guide the primary direction of military effort. Similarly, the theatre level of high military command has to comprehend the kind of strategic guidance that his operational level generals must have indispensably. It is not adequate for a General Robert E. Lee to have no carefully prepared intention should he be obliged to confront General Meade at Gettysburg. Expedient hope is not strategic sense, and Lee did not demonstrate much of it as he scurried with great relief, given his desperately familiar logistical weakness, back over the Potomac following the defeat of his Army of Northern Virginia early in July 1863. He was saved primarily by the undeniable fallibility of George Meade, whose battle-roused victorious army was eager to try to ensure that Lee was not able to recross the river at Harper's Ferry. Although Meade showed scant strategic sense, Lincoln's was acute and timely in the summer of that year. But, Lincoln found that general after general in the Union Army did not succeed in proceeding intellectually, let alone in demonstrable performance, up the hierarchy of conceptual understanding and grip, from the operational to the strategic, ultimately for the political consequence level that was owned legally and politically by the President alone.

The second problem with the translation of operational level military effort into strategic coin lies in the frequent absence of content in the country's strategy basket for a particular challenge. In this familiar situation, where there is no meaningfully specific strategic context, one is left with the frustrating truth that, to paraphrase, 'it is not usually feasible to attempt to put in what God (or the White House) has failed to provide already'! No matter how tactically skilful American and British Special Operations Forces (SOF) proved themselves to be in Iraq and Afghanistan, 'so what' difference could it make when there was no plausible strategic grand design for excellent local efforts? (Finlan, 2008; Elliott, 2015). Our SOF in effect were doing what Americans call tactical 'whack-a-mole' and the Israelis refer to reluctantly as an endless unavoidable 'grass-mowing'. The deadly small and precise actions called 'targeted killings' certainly are not pointless, but the points in question are really only tactical; they cannot count favourably towards operational, let alone strategic or ultimately political advantage.

Tactical expediency by flexible and adaptive troops is highly advantageous; it characterized the performances of the German assault divisions in the great Michael Offensive of late March 1918, but it tends to come at a heavy cost in elite troops; this means it cannot prudently be considered the basis for war (even reliably on the operational level) winning military effort (Zabecki, 2006). However, when strategy in any sensible meaning of the concept is not present for guidance in-theatre, which was the persisting context for Allied endeavours both in Iraq and Afghanistan, the operational level of command virtually is condemned, as it were by default, to demote itself to the level of grand tactics. During the later years in Central Asia, for example, it was quite common to find both American and British military commentators asking the following uncomfortable question: 'can we simply kill our way to some facsimile of victory?' How many 'moles', and how often, do we need to 'whack', how often does the grass need to be trimmed literally, and to what end? In practice, repeatedly in wars what can be found is a gaping void where strategy should be for the sensible, ultimately political, guidance of operational level military commanders. This space cannot be filled at all adequately through tactical or even operational excellence. When strategy is missing, who or what is the enemy's king to be checkmated? When this void appears to be unfillable by intervening foreign forces at acceptable political, moral, and military costs, it is time to withdraw from the adventure, admitting that although our national and allied motives may have been impeccable, the job was not practicably doable. It is probably needless for this book to record with crystal clarity the empirical point that it is desperately rare for any government to admit to past major error. Probably the most egregious protracted example of demonstrated failure was provided by the United States in South Vietnam, 1965–73 (or 1975, for the awful roof-top denouement).

Military command has not proved courageous in modern times in telling the political bank to the strategy bridge that the military job is not doable at tolerable cost. Anglo-American military commanders did not register glittering records in Iraq and Afghanistan, as the persisting contexts of high-level insecurity attest. Visiting politicians were fed on hope, rather than well evidenced expectations of success. Typically, one- and two-star generals scurried out of the local scene with almost indecent haste, job done! The job most in question was the adding of a vital operational command notch to their resumes. We are compelled to find fault with process for civil–military relations that persistently seemed either unwilling or unable to develop and implement even a plausible facsimile of strategy that might have been effective, eventually, in the undeniably very different contexts of Iraq and Afghanistan. However, notwithstanding the major differences between those theatres, it was the same army from America and from Britain that sought to function there to benign effect in and for both. An especially galling historical detail of this should-be strategic tale is that the British Expeditionary Force (BEF) that Guderian and Rommel expelled back across the Channel from Dunkirk in late May 1940 by and large fought courageously. It resisted in operationally hopeless circumstances, holding the long perimeter to avoid losing the intended departure port. By contrast, the British exit from Basra was a humiliating historical example of 'scuttle and run'. It may have been on balance advisable to depart in prudent haste, but it both appeared to be, and it was, cowardly and more than slightly incompetent when regarded in operational, let alone strategic, context.

Conclusions: who is in charge?

Whether it was the immortal but fallible Harold Godwinsson of Wessex and England in 1066, or the Duke of Marlborough in the 1700s, there was no doubt in those six centuries that if the monarch or his, or her (thinking of Marlborough and Queen Anne) clearly deputed Military Commander-in-Chief was present to direct and especially to fight personally in battle, most issues of choice and responsibility for success or failure were settled thereby. Modern communication technologies, however, inevitably have opened the possibility for civilian politicians and civil servants, usually poorly informed about military practicalities, to attempt to interfere with lethally inappropriate military advice for the local commanders in theatres of war they happen to visit. Even when visiting politicians are quite well educated by locally knowledgeable critics of the official, usually upbeat, military line conveyed by the unavoidable 'bells and whistles' of Power-Point, the visiting civilians are unlikely to be exposed perilously to 'other' points of view. This is a context wherein military teamwork is expected, not for theorizing frankly about alternatives in critical review. Since our politicians and most senior civil servants appear to exist in a political-policy 'bubble', albeit devoid of meaningful foreign content bearing upon our sundry military interventions far abroad, this is scarcely surprising. For a personal example, this author recently endured listening and partici-pating in a hard fought British general election campaign, but I did not hear anything more than rare and swiftly passing reference made to the recent national military humiliations that were the result of the failed interventions in Iraq and Afghanistan, both. The major domestic changes that resulted in a historic Conservative–Liberal coalition government in Britain, the first such since the late 1930s, and the remarkable election as President of a highly talented Black leader in Barack Obama, in both cases failed to make a near-term seismic shift for the better in policy or strategy on military intervention. The British scuttled or ran out of Iraq, and landed in even deeper astrategic water that they could not navigate in Helmand Province in Afghanistan. The United States Army, despite the failing efforts of the over-praised General David Petraeus, fared little better when the consequences of his initiative were considered coolly. It is made clear in the memoirs of the tactically, just possibly operationally, talented American theatre Commander-in-Chief, General Stanley McChrystal, that whatever it was that attracted American voters to Barack Obama, it certainly was not evidence of strategic understanding or special executive competence (McChrystal, 2015).

Strategy is hard to find as a flexible and adaptable product of civil–military relations in the United States and Britain. Moreover, even when there are societal and beyond (e.g. tribal, domestic political, allied) reasons why strategy comes to be recognized as practicably impossible (e.g. for Germany in 1943–5), there will be reasons of career, duty, loyalty to troops, habit perhaps, why commanders deprived of the higher guidance by strategy will continue to direct the fight even when hope of sudden advantage is lost. A true strategy deficit is nearly always fatal for national and allied interventions, and for the attempted conduct of wars and warfare of all character.

Key points

1   Extraordinary strategic talent is exactly that, extraordinary, not unusual.
2   'Rules' are not appropriate in strategy.
3   All countries typically have some difficult issues in civil–military relations.

4   The 'Huntington model' of civil–military relations identifies and prescribes a very clear dividing line separating the world of professional military expertise from that of political choice.
5   'Tribal' loyalty is a common feature of military organizations. At root, it is a reflection of the unusual personal risks in soldiers' lives and the necessity for strict discipline.
6   Both competition and cooperation are required for an effective strategy-making process.

Further reading

Bailey, J., Iron, R. and Strachan, H. (eds) (2013) *British Generals in Blair's Wars*, Farnham: Ashgate.

Cimbala, S. (ed.) (2012) *Civil–Military Relations in Perspective: Strategy, Structure and Policy*, Farnham: Ashgate.

Clausewitz, C. von (1976) *On War*, ed. and trans. Howard, M. and Paret, P., Princeton, NJ: Princeton University Press.

Cohen, E. A. (2002) *Supreme Command: Soldiers, Statesmen, and Leadership in Wartime*, New York: Free Press.

Elliott, C. L. (2015) *High Command: British Military Leadership in the Iraq and Afghanistan Wars*, London: C. Hurst.

Gray, C. S. (2010a) *The Strategy Bridge: Theory for Practice*, Oxford: Oxford University Press.

Howard, M. (1991) *The Lessons of History*, New Haven, CT: Yale University Press.

Murray, W., Sinnreich, R. H. and Lacey, J. (eds) (2011) *The Shaping of Grand Strategy: Policy, Diplomacy, and War*, Cambridge: Cambridge University Press.

Murray, W. and Sinnreich, R. H. (eds) (2014) *Successful Strategies: Triumphing in War and Peace from Antiquity to the Present*, Cambridge: Cambridge University Press.

Ricks, T. E. (2009) *The Gamble: General Petraeus and the Untold Story of the American Surge in Iraq, 2006–2008*, London: Penguin Books.

Simpson, E. (2012) *War from the Ground Up: Twenty-First-Century Combat as Politics*, London: C. Hurst.

Stoker, D. (2010) *The Grand Design: Strategy and the U.S. Civil War*, Oxford: Oxford University Press.

Stoker, D. (2014) *Clausewitz: His Life and Work*, Oxford: Oxford University Press.

Strachan, H. (2013) *The Direction of War: Contemporary Strategy in Historical Perspective*, Cambridge: Cambridge University Press.

9 Politics and defence planning

> *Reader's guide:* The meaning and character of uncertainty. An unforeseeable future. 'Moral force' and fighting power. Failure to achieve the impossible. Is surprise avoidable?

Introduction: what is uncertain?

It is arguably paradoxical that although we can know nothing about the future based on any direct evidence, nonetheless we are able to assume with high confidence that we are well enough informed about the nature of that future. However, in order to believe this argument one needs to endorse the kind of reasoning being promoted in this book. Specifically, here we advance the proposition that the course of strategic history shows a complex mix of both certainty and change. In its enduring nature, this history does not alter in significant ways and means, while in its ever dynamic character change is either permanent or threatening to be so. The argument just stated may well appear implausible to readers who believe that the strategy and politics of, say, the Roman Empire in the first century of the Christian era was a period unique to itself, with generically similar logic possibly applying to any and perhaps all other historical episodes also. Admittedly, it can be a challenge to trans-historical understanding to identify themes in strategic history that endure, despite the more obvious reasons for finding them so altered in specific character as to call into serious question the suggestion of a fundamental commonality across time, space, and circumstance. Notwithstanding such occasional difficulty, this text finds more, and more fundamental, sources making for continuity than evidence of lasting significance for change. It may be recalled that the view taken here of strategic history is an holistic one. We find clear enough evidence of functionally strategic, certainly of political, thought and behaviour in all climes and periods, regardless of the superficial changes that may be noticed in order to flag possibly significant alterations in style and means. The sometimes deadly game of politics is played for personal and institutional stakes in an effort to advance interests in any and every context that lends itself to opportunity.

It is my contention that the function of defence planning, inter alia for strategy, effectively has proved to be needed permanently throughout strategic history. Unavoidably, this means that the uncertainties of such activity also persist across time and space. Such persistence will not impress us if we choose to believe that major alterations in our context of security have been effected from time to time. For example, changes that would transcend mere shifts in the character of potentially violent inter-state competition, and have notable meaning for the nature of war and its warfare. I am not persuaded that the nature of inter-state political relations has shifted significantly, let alone definitively, away from a war-prone context. However, the relative shortage of evidence of great-power warfare over the past 200 years is possibly noteworthy, though the reality of armed conflict has been so grisly, and continues to be so awesomely potentially grim, that I am disinclined to join Professor Pinker in his analysis that believes war largely to be yesterday's problem for the human race (Pinker, 2011).

This ninth chapter comprises a study of the politics of strategy-making, principally in this new twenty-first century. However, it matters scarcely at all which politics or political context we choose to highlight in the text because our subject provides an essential unity of largely common relevant experience. In all periods, politics had to work with the basic structure of the interdependent logic in the theory of strategy; it did not much matter who they were, who their foes might be, or how they were armed. They all needed to settle politically upon their policy goals, decide on their preferred strategic methods, and identify their disposable military means. The whole venture on behalf of community security was shaped and possibly driven by reigning contemporary assumptions concerning the future.

It is difficult to convey the true depth of our unavoidable ignorance about the future. Planning for the future is a near universal behaviour, one that is as unavoidable as it is resistant to confidence and reliability in prediction. The strategist as defence planner is obliged to step beyond the empirical evidence on security context in order to prepare prudently for dangers that may emerge over time in the future. However, because the future is a temporal step impenetrable by our physics, we are compelled to pretend that we are, nonetheless, able to be prudent in preparing for and against that which we cannot know reliably (Gray, 2014a: Ch. 3). Although this fundamental problem is well enough appreciated, we cannot say that it is understood. In the practice of governance, soldiers, politicians, and civil servants seek to act and behave as if they did know why they did so. There is a pretence of foreknowledge of the relevant future that is an affront to a physics class. In my careers in the United States and Britain as an adviser on defence, I have tired of wasting my breath objecting to the often deadly inaccurate throw-away phrase, 'the foreseeable future'. The future may prove to have been foreseeable in some great matter, though certainly not in many small ones, but in the main the concept of a foreseeable, even simply an anticipatable, future, is always liable to prove ridiculous and politically embarrassing. Considered coolly in long retrospect, some trends, themes, even patterns tend to appear to emerge from the disorderly chaos of international political and strategic relations. However, such perceptive insights tend not to be available to those most in need of their guidance at times when such appreciation might have been of practical utility. Looking back over the course of the last 200 years of great-power relations, we are compelled to admit that the political and strategic future most definitely has not been foreseeable (Gray, 2012). Given this persisting reality of misunderstanding on the part of supposedly expert experienced professionals, how great is the challenge to find adequate prudence in defence planning?

Future foreseeable?

The near constant universal effort that we humans feel and indeed are compelled to make in an effort to peer into the future of interest for our security is all but rarely condemned to failure, notwithstanding the naïve or deliberately deceptive casual

128   *Politics and defence planning*

imaginative employment of the concept of a future that is wonderfully foreseeable. Most emphatically the future is not foreseeable. It should be conceivable with broad brush strokes to those bold enough to examine our history somewhat in strategic terms, but it can never be a source for a predictive quality of advice. The trouble lies not so much in an unwillingness of an inanimate and currently inactive strategic history to play a key agency role for us. Rather is the challenge the inconvenient and unalterable fact that our human grasp of the principal causes of historical happenings is nearly always pathetically weak. Rephrased for greater clarity, while we should be able to spot some likely, perhaps very likely, causes of future conflict and war, the entire cause-to-consequence chain is permanently in significant measure problematic. The leading reason is not hard to find. There are too many agents and agencies able to move in ways that will affect the relevant international order for us to be confident we can find and perhaps treat the causal chain that will, or even could lead to war. Even if we feel able to foresee with high confidence that a much feared or desired trail of consequences is likely to follow on our deliberate moves, we can never be sufficiently certain as to warrant the relevant prognosis thoroughly reliable. This is not particularly only a modern deficiency, let alone a contemporary or anticipated future one. The human race has never been able to chart its future course in helpful detail. Although we have usually, though not invariably (surprise does happen!) understood and even anticipated the occurrence of large-scale tragedy, it has been rare, indeed usually impossible, for us to be able to anticipate great occurrences with anything resembling total reliability. If that is what commonly is meant by the inaccurately worded concept of a foreseeable future, the sooner this awful impossibility is given its necessary burial the better.

Despite the negative view taken here on standard futurology, some of that rather strong and scientifically impossible quality is needed, certainly is wasted, permanently by policymakers and their military strategists as they strive to part the impossible seeming curtain of time that persists in hiding the future from view. The general truth inseparable from the argument here is the inconvenient one that demands we strive functionally to look ahead in time. Obviously, future defence planning is about the future, though not entirely so. After all, how we perform in the future, and exactly when we are able to do so, must depend critically upon the current state of our preparations for deterrence and warfare; lead-time often is the essential constraining idea. It covers, for example, the several reasons why the United States could enter the First World War on 17 April 1917, but not be ready to face the German Army on the Western Front until its forces launched the extravagantly costly Meuse–Argonne Offensive in September 1918.

Given the burgeoning unrest internal to the Central Powers in the summer of 1918, following the disappointments of the great *Kaiserschlacht* launched initially against Britain's British Expeditionary Force (BEF) on 21 March 1918, it is perhaps surprising that the German Army was willing and just about able to fight on through the summer of 1918. But, there were so many different and politically potent reasons for a near-term German military collapse that it was a considerable exercise of the Allied imagination to be willing and able to behave in the continuation of the Great War that then appeared credibly to be reaching, or even beyond, its culminating point. Simply put, there are just too many variables, some likely to act quite independent of many of the rest, for people to be confident that they could plot and plan even for a very near-term future. Of course, an ongoing Great War provides a certainty of dominant context that mercifully is wholly absent early in this new century. While this is a blessing on nearly

Politics and defence planning 129

all counts, it cannot be denied that the absence of violent action on a large scale does threaten to complicate and frustrate the professional lives of strategists. This agreeable condition of non-war – to discount somewhat the minor troubles and entanglements in Iraq and Afghanistan from 2001 until 2014 – brings to the fore all manner of domestic political pressure within the state that had been intervening far abroad. Inevitably, following a distinctly spendthrift decade of expenditure on warfare, even the United States under President Barack Obama, principally with the highly competent if strategically unimaginative Robert Gates as his Secretary of Defense, were moved to effect relatively large reductions in the defence, and more broadly the national security, budgets.

Time and again, this has recognized the need to emphasize the permanently operating factors (wording borrowed from Joseph Stalin) that all but command a notably domestic reaction to a context that may well appear to be principally foreign. The politics that shape and size defence spending typically are dominated, certainly are influenced notably and everywhere, by domestic considerations. Defence policy is made at home. It follows necessarily, unavoidably, that professional politicians have no practical choice other than to be responsive, possibly in a prudently anticipatory way, to expected pressures from domestic interests that may or may not, depending on regime types, have serious political (and electoral?) clout. The meaning of this near universal reality has to be that the politics, the ever active pursuit of greater influence on controversial decisions, of defence planning and its possible strategy, is unlikely to be a matter strictly aligned with recognizable international strategic reasoning. Rather, most strategic decisions reflect to a greater or lesser extent the interests of those individuals whose careers and the prosperity of institutions that are the agencies for their advancement; commonly these are bound indissolubly as one. Politics in the making of strategy therefore is not and cannot require only episodic interventions in the general affairs of the polity. Instead, calendar certainties attend every stage in the process of defence budget making, especially in the extremely bureaucratic and also politicized United States government with its constitutionally mandated separation of powers. It is scarcely surprising to be compelled to appreciate that the politics of national security never stops, or even is placeable on temporary hold in that country.

Admittedly, it is often challenging, beyond a reasonable point of plausible guesswork and working assumption making, to be at all certain what the more accurate path of cause and consequential effect has been. Why did the United States intervene on the ground massively in Vietnam, and fortunately less heavily in Afghanistan and Iraq (though at some notable cost in probable local effectiveness)? Why is President Vladimir Putin probing for new vulnerabilities in Ukraine, instead of accepting with gratitude the genuine hand of assistance that the NATO countries believed naïvely and wrongly he had accepted broadly on the terms with which they were offered? The most direct answer, of course, was that considerations bearing directly on the European International Order were assigned a much lower priority in Moscow than were those calculated and felt by Putin to have positive political resonance for the likely stability of his role in Russia. Stability of domestic and international order plainly were placed deliberately in a state of high tension, one with the other, and domestic Russian politics was the winner.

Over the horizon

Argument frequently is advanced that the quality, perhaps the quantity also, of weapons is not a reliable indicator of probable fighting power. In other words, while the weight

130 *Politics and defence planning*

and structure of a military posture should be capable of serving as a fair indicator of the leading security concern of its owner, these empirically checkable details may not serve most usefully as a guide to future strategic behaviour. It is important to remember that weapons lack all autonomous agency, rather are they only the mechanical and electronic slaves of the political will of human policymakers and strategists (Gray, 1993). Appreciation of this point provides a caveat against leaping to judgement with undue haste when new military programmes are announced or actually unveiled and revealed visually. There is excellent reason why a standard form in which to characterize threat is expressed simply in the following way: threat = capability x intention. It matters less what is in a neighbour's tank park, but a great deal more in how seriously he considers using it. The translation of meaning from inert metal into moving vehicles and machine parts needs purposeful human intervention.

A desire to peer into the future is not only an ages' old vanity project, in vital addition it is an inescapable duty of defence planners. Neither defence planning nor strategic analysis can be scientific activities, because reliably correct answers cannot be provided in answer to pressing questions. Certain knowledge in which we can place confidence is not obtainable. Quite literally, it is not possible to study a country's apparent challenges in defence planning intentions and settle with high confidence upon some metrically expressed certain solution. Although careful study, eschewing a leap to hasty conclusions, is always to be welcomed, this is a case wherein the nature of the subject thwarts us. Notwithstanding the superficially obvious logic in the simple threat formula provided above, a little reflection reveals that actually it has little, if any, utility. The reason is that each of the vital concepts specified inherently is unstable and therefore lacks meaning for the purposes of defence planning. As a purported guide to the future for the education of defence planners, the austere formula is close to useless, though it may serve potentially to sound a warning for those willing and able to look beyond what is entirely obvious. Military professional defence planners should find a common sense logic in the elementary idea that threats in the future must comprise a malign marriage between military capability and political intention, but little of strategic value can follow in the absence of much deeper understanding.

What tends to be missing from analyses of future strategic history is a sophisticated grasp of both the political and the military nature of the subject. The future will have a single and unique course, but that path can be discerned only in some retrospect, if even then. In other words, future history is constantly in a dynamic condition, never complete, but always is in a process of becoming whatever the abundance of relevant influences makes of it and with it. Also, the course of history, conveyed in the great stream of time, has no independent purpose beyond that of those which we choose to assign (Howard, 1991). Human agency is a permanent challenge for the understanding of defence planners, because they are condemned to attempt an impossible mission, to foresee that which cannot be foreseen at all reliably. If we consider the basic elements in the notional threat formula as outlined tersely above, we find what may appear misleadingly to be some helpful conceptual guidance. Unfortunately, concepts that can appear to have utility as keys to understanding often prove to be insubstantially hollow of meaning. Bearing in mind that defence planners have need to know what military capabilities in support of which political choices are possible or probable in the near-term strategic future, they soon discover that elementary formulae can only serve the most basic of educational needs in overly austere PowerPoint fashion. The difficulties for the defence planner are twofold and permanent. First, the military capabilities of possible

Politics and defence planning   131

foes will not be constant, but rather most likely will mature dynamically, and even in an important sense interactively, with our own, though hopefully not in the actual clash of battle. Military historians tell us that fighting power cannot be calculated with reliability metrically from the apparent balance of weapons and their support systems. Clausewitz alerts us to the potency of what he terms the 'moral element', as contrasted with 'physical force'. We strive to understand how determined an enemy will prove to be in his determination to fight. Very few fights have to be conducted in order to effect the complete destruction of enemy forces. Clausewitz noted speculatively that:

> Not every war need be fought until one side collapses. When the motives and tensions of war are slight we can imagine that the faintest prospect of defeat might be enough to cause one side to yield. If from the very start the other side feels that this is probable, it will obviously concentrate on bringing about *this probability* rather than taking the long way round and totally defeat the enemy.
>
> (Clausewitz, 1976: 91)

What is most significant about this highly conditional reasoning is Clausewitz's endorsement of a conflictual context of limitation of military effort. Even more to the point for relevance here is the predictable likelihood of our not being at all certain ahead of the outbreak of warfare just how determined an enemy will prove to be. This is not at all a small, even trivial matter of detail, because our defence planning really has need to know how hard the enemy will or plausibly may choose to fight. So high is the relative importance of this issue that one should extend the reach of its logic so as to accommodate what may well be the most important of Clausewitz's nuggets of prudent advice in *On War*. He insisted plausibly that:

> The first, the most far-reaching act of judgement that the statesman and commander have to make is to establish by that test [of wars varying with the nature of their motives and of the situations which give rise to them] the kind of war on which they are embarking; neither mistaking it for, nor trying to turn it into, something that is alien to its nature. This is the first of all strategic questions and the most comprehensive.
>
> (Clausewitz, 1976: 88–9)

A difficulty for the defence planner is that he may well not know, either ahead of the event or in the early stages of a war just what it is that he signed on for his country's armed forces to conduct. This difficulty often has depths that a foreign intervening military force has difficulty appreciating. The warfare in question may not so much spring from elements well understood by us, but rather from societal, often literally tribal antagonisms that grow alarmingly in conditions of acute tension. But, severe though the surprise may prove to be as military and para-military resistance to our efforts is made manifest, it is sobering to recognize that local armed resistance to our endeavours to establish stable governance most likely has not been organized with strategic, or even operational purpose. When Western military forces intervene in traditional, largely still tribal, areas, in cultural ignorance they can hardly help but function unintentionally as protagonists for some local interests, and in action opposition to others (consider the Allied role vis à vis poppy eradication in Helmand Province, Afghanistan). The Western forces are more than likely to find themselves out of their

132 *Politics and defence planning*

depth both militarily and politically, as they strive to function in a local cultural context for which they are almost entirely unprepared (Johnson, 2011).

Most wars and their warfare do not have a permanent stable nature or character. This vital aspect of strategic historical reality is not one that is sufficiently well recognized. Contemporary and quite probably future warfare most probably will not have a fixed enduring character. I am not suggesting necessarily that belligerents intend and then, as it were, orchestrate a variable character of armed conflict. It is necessary to appreciate the likelihood of strategic history betraying far more creative and responsive opportunities than that. We should take more seriously than usually we find convenient the likely operations of a process of competitive invention, meaning that the defence planners on both, perhaps all, sides quite literally will find themselves embarked on forms of combat substantially unknown and unknowable. The belligerents will be inventing, perhaps discovering, the character, possibly the nature also, of a particular war in the all too live course of participation in real-time events. While speculative anticipation might aid strategic comprehension, it is probably more helpful to consider such a process as being significantly unique. Although all wars have important, indeed defining, features in common, in addition each one is different to some lesser or greater degree.

The problem for Western defence planners is unmistakeable. They are obliged to seek to follow Clausewitz and understand the kind of warfare to which their country's policymakers seek to commit them. But, it will be as close to a certainty as makes no difference that intimate understanding of the pertinent detail concerning conflict in substantially tribal society cannot be grasped reliably in a hurry. It follows, indeed it has to follow, that when Western forces intervene far abroad they will not enjoy deep appreciation of the local context, especially concerning the historical processes responsible for creation of that context. That condition of ignorance is a light year removed from Clausewitz's comprehension of the forces and competitive processes judged ever likely to be dominant in his period for European statecraft and strategy in the 1810s and 1820s. The Western defence planner today must strive to grapple effectively with a short-list of major interacting uncertainties that he cannot be well enough prepared to understand and counter. Specifically, he will not know for certain:

1   The kind of warfare that he must wage: while the nature of war does not alter in its basic nature from context to context, so much can never be said for its character. War and its warfare can grow seemingly organically as a consequence of its real-time course (Porter, 2009). What happens is that belligerents effectively can find themselves compelled to wage a character of combat that is more the product of the military logic of events than of superior political direction. Clausewitz himself noted this phenomenon when he drew a distinction between the 'grammar' of war and its 'logic' (1976: 605). This 'grammar' is unlikely to be strategically instructive for the guidance of military effort; it is far more probable that its notably compelling logic will be confined to the tactical and operational levels of warfare. In a vital sense, to summarize, the combatants will proceed in their fighting whither the course of combat appears to lead them. For defence planners, this familiar context is one wherein loss of control of the course of warfare becomes a source of major anxiety, even alarm. The reasons for loss of unilateral control are all too obvious; they can be summarized as the enemy's determination, ability to innovate, and potency as an active game-changer. Given that war is not exactly an unknown phenomenon in strategic history, it is quite startling to appreciate how often and

Politics and defence planning 133

how seriously polities fail to understand the combat event as an interactive system. Moreover, the interactivity of actual warfare is likely to produce a character of combat that neither belligerent previously had anticipated.

2 It is rarely prudent to assume that the political future for defence planning is well settled and can be treated as being well enough known to allow for orderly planning activity and consequential deployment. Politicians tend to dislike fixed positions on high policy, because the more effective among them understand that theirs needs to be a context wherein compromise and occasional exceptions to principle are tolerated and indeed are recognized as necessary. The professional politician-policymaker need not be wholly unprincipled, let alone deaf to ethical consideration, but he does require the ability to be flexible and occasionally to concede some partial legitimacy regarding the political claims of rival politicians abroad. He may not need to yield too obviously on points of principle, but he makes high policy 'in the round', and he has to be particularly attentive to foreign demands that appear not incredibly to be backed by the threat of military force. There may well be occasions and circumstances wherein the statesman-policymaker can find no room for politically tolerable compromise. This was the British situation on 4 August 1914 and again on 3 September 1939, but it is unusual for policy choice to be choked off entirely. Always assuming that a politician does not welcome the onset of war for domestic reasons, it is rare for him to prefer the path of combat with all its unknown major risks, compared with the advantages to be gleaned from a tough looking political stand on most of the apparently pertinent principles.

It is not sufficiently well recognized that little of what is most relevant to defence planning lends itself to reliable prediction. On the one hand there is the rich uncertainty of events and their consequences. No matter how skilled our defence planning staffs, the extraordinary high costs of defence preparation today have to mean that only a selected few of the material and human military assets we might be able to buy will be afforded. A compelling logical consequence of that fact about highly selective procurement is that our purchases need to be suitable for multi-tasking. As a general rule, specialization of utility will be an anathema; it is unaffordably expensive.

There is a solution of sorts to the dilemma of unavoidable ignorance concerning the future. A dominant solution to the challenge of uncertainty simply can be to plan to employ the more useful looking character of rapidly deployable military forces, and hope they can create the military effectiveness that may be required in order to shift recalcitrant minds, if not hearts. Because case-perfect marriage between planned and provided military forces is unlikely to fit more than a very occasional revealed need, for want of anything better we choose to deploy and employ the forces we have. The hope, if not expectation, is for a good enough military for a tolerable political outcome. Many military units are capable of fulfilling a range of tasks that ought to be strategically meaningful and relevant to a case in point. As Williamson Murray has emphasized, the ability of military forces to innovate and adapt in the event of demonstrated need is essential (Murray, 2011). If anything, there is probably undue specialization of pre-planned military function today, particularly as somewhat elite units seek to maintain and assert their 'special-ness' (Finlan, 2008).

If defence planning strives too hard to cover a range of disparate duties, it is likely to find itself the master of military capabilities that are relatively poor performers of almost every kind of task they are assigned. There is some security in numbers as well

134 *Politics and defence planning*

as in quality, and defence planning has to be careful it does not trim unduly the security that is to be found in mass as well as quality.

By far the most important strategic truth about defence planning is frank recognition of the certainty of uncertainty. Unfortunately, little satisfaction can attend this recognition, because ignorant of the future or not, the planning task has to be conducted; it is not discretionary. Two inconvenient persisting realities exist prospectively to blight the professional lives of politician-policymakers and of defence planners seeking to be strategic. Specifically, neither policy and its politics, nor any particular case of military use will have reliably settled characteristics: policy and its undergirding politics always shift over time and with circumstance, and so also, though probably to a lesser extent, does the character of relevant armed combat.

Mission impossible? Why sometimes we fail

From time to time defence planners in nearly all countries and alliances fail to achieve what they previously had believed were reasonable and attainable objectives. It is in the very nature of strategy to pose an extraordinary array of difficulties for the potential frustration even of notably apparently gifted and somewhat trained, well, experienced at least, strategists (Gray, 2010a, 2014c). There simply is more that can go wrong with strategy than with any other particular field of like endeavour. Most probably it is true to hold that really there is no usefully comparable field of human effort. The likelihood of this being true is not difficult to grasp once one has reflected upon the meaning and requirements of literally every element in the austere basic logic that governs the topic. *Political decisions* – some irrecoverable, others probably amendable, *strategic ways* – methods and instrumental goals to many military means in action to achieve desired political consequences, *military means* – hopefully prepared in number and quality suitable for the tasks that may appear with scant notice, and the *assumptions* that legitimize, if they do not actually guide, the entire venture of the ship(s) of state and alliances to the brink or into war. The present author is able to speak with some useful experience about the challenge in seeking helpfully to identify the difficulties that the strategist as defence planner cannot evade prudently. Of course, the planner may be fortunate in being able to postpone some critical decisions that bear upon strategy, confident in the hope, if not the expectation, that much will be revealed by virtue of patience and waiting. This is not to deny that much prudence in delay of decision is offset if the enemy uses the time he is gifted by our (prudent) delay to steal a march or two with consequences on the ground from which we are unable to recover. For example, Heinz Guderian and Erwin Rommel's rather imprudent crossing of the Rivers Meuse and Sambre in May 1940 stole a march that had lethal operational, indeed potentially strategic and also political, possible if not probable consequence for the Anglo-French and Belgian deployments in Flanders in May–June of that year. Admittedly, the catastrophically poor consequences of the Allied introduction to the Wehrmacht's demonstration of the great virtues of a maneuverist style in operational warfare was an exception in military skill – and good German fortune – in the Second World War. It serves helpfully to remind readers that in campaigns and indeed whole wars beyond ready number, timing has been proved to be the least forgiving of errors with which to err, regardless of historical period and strategic context.

In conflict and war of every character, it is appropriate and necessary for us to pass judgement upon the quality of the political process that employs professional defence planners with regard to its ability to decide upon a launch point for warfare that subsequent happenings suggest was 'good enough'. The 'good enough' criterion is not one that has much appeal to those trained in a hopeful ability to identify what is sufficient in the procurement of relatively scarce physical assets (Gray, 2010b). However, some reflection on the true scope and intensity of residual uncertainty soon alerts people to the wisdom in frank recognition of the unattainability of some kinds of understanding. For example, if we assume, as in practice we do and indeed must, that Vladimir Putin is deterrable over his ambition to restore some or all of Ukraine to its historically quite recent place within the great Russian empire, just how can NATO prudently, though not dangerously, seek to optimize the high likelihood that he will reconsider his policy and strategy? Bluntly, are there demonstrably correct solutions to deterrence puzzles? If the US, British, and general NATO military postures cannot be fine-tuned for truly assured compliance with a good enough criterion, what may be done by way of a practicable alternative, if there is such, of course? This may appear to read as a rather brutal thought given the somewhat respectful tones in which defence planning typically is discussed, but senior officials, political and bureaucratic, would merit high marks for honesty were they to sport a tie that declared to interested electors that 'we do not and cannot know what our country should purchase and maintain in the hope of sustaining deterrence, but we are honestly convinced that what our political process has decided to acquire and maintain militarily will prove "good enough" for its primary deterrent purpose'. Needless to say, such a startling admission would be taken as meaning, certainly implying, that our Ministry of Defence and the US Department of Defense do not know what they need to be doing; ipso facto, why they are doing it. One should not hold one's breath waiting for a completely honest strategic admission of such guilty ignorance. Or, should it not be dismissed as such? Are the strategic needs of the country and Alliance determinable soundly with any precision?

Defence planning needs to rest upon some useful particular ideas concerning the size and quality of national and alliance military posture. In short, most people have little trouble recognizing the high validity of the 'good enough' rule. However, it can startle a professional audience of defence planners and their political masters if we introduce the rather roguish and notably illegitimate thought into the briefing that really, most probably, there is no 'good enough' level and quality of military preparation determinable, let alone plausibly briefable to an already sceptical audience. This is close to considering an alien notion. It is to suggest that I can study my country's possible defence needs, and yet be frustrated by an honest inability to decide what is, or ought to be, 'good enough'. For defence planning, as for so much else in governance, the truly golden key to right enough answers is prior selection of suitable political assumptions as a substantial basis for subsequent policy. It matters greatly not to forget that the most important basis for strategy is choice, but nearly always should be prudence. The entire venture of strategy, grand and military both, is instrumentality for desired political consequences. Clausewitz did not employ these particular words, but plainly it is what he was arguing convincingly. Failure of strategy is not remarkable. To fail in a competently conceived assault upon a target that proved to be impossible to take, despite the issuance of due professional warnings to policymakers, are not grounds for military disgrace. It could be claimed that when a defence planner as general finds himself heading down a strategy road that appears to be impossible, and from which the only personal recourse is a timely retirement, then the prudent personal route for duty may well be abdication from the scene of the strategy crisis. Senior soldiers in many countries,

136 *Politics and defence planning*

who have lost much of whatever faith they may once have reposed in the overall political and strategic wisdom behind and in their orders, have chosen not to participate in a galloping and apparently unstoppable disaster. The alternative may be to stay on and seek to save what, if anything, they are able of their professional reputation. Unsurprisingly in this study of strategy and politics, and taking appropriate argument in guidance from Clausewitz as usual, we discover that Eliot A. Cohen is thoroughly vindicated in his privileging of the weight of role he assigns to politicians and their politics in the intimate relationship that they play with the making and performance of strategy. It is an 'unequal dialogue' between the two pathways (Cohen, 2002).

The argument advanced, indeed necessarily repeated, above is so empirically compelling and familiar that one can only wonder at the fact of its being so ill comprehended. Once one has grasped fully that war and its warfare inherently are political and can be nothing else, even if they masquerade as an armed morality, one should be well enough prepared for the master claim that policy, driven and ever shaped by politics, is what armed conflict is all about. From land and honour-hungry Crusaders in the eleventh and twelfth centuries to deluded Jihadists today, it is politics and its intended meaning that is in the directing seat for war and its warfare. This insight, admittedly pressing against categorization simply as banal, only escapes dismissal as trivially self-evident because it continues to escape due attention because it is not reasoned through rigorously.

Everything about defence planning and its selected strategy(ies) is the product of political process. This thought can be upsetting to those more analytical scholars who endeavour to believe that some close approximation to correct answers is precisely calculable, provided only that the right theoretical treatment is applied. As Jakub Grygiel has argued, notwithstanding the high ranking that Western societies assign to the sciences, both physical and even social, as a careful matter of disciplined scholarly definition, there is and can be nothing of note achievable in the scholarly region of science with respect to future national security (Grygiel, 2013). For an endeavour to merit the ascription 'scientific' it has to be capable of, even only *en route* towards, achieving reliably correct research results. To secure such, the scientist, physical or social (or mathematical), needs to have the ability to conduct or observe truthfully controlled empirical experiments for the purpose of demonstration of validity of claimed results in theory: that is it! Because of the pragmatic authority of the temporal dimension to politics and strategy, it is entirely impossible for people today to be capable of deploying for our research convenience any evidence from the future about that future; evidence that may have a lasting resonance to which future policymakers and strategists are in some degree respectful, perhaps, indeed very likely. But that important probable fact does not suffice to cover the case of need specified here.

The politicians and the defence planners are both fearfully troubled by a severe problem of absent evidence. Given the enormity of the uncertainty and sometimes revealed problems concerning polities' security in the future, this is not a minor matter. Neither is it one that the electorate, any electorate, is inclined to condone simply on the grounds that it is impossible to fulfil. After all, defence and foreign policy officials, both professional and only temporary, talk and attempt to behave as if they knew what they were doing and had some highly privileged understanding concerning why they sought to do it. Politician-policymakers tend not to prosper if they are caught out on the hustings, embarrassed by some foreign challenge for which they have no answer and, more likely, towards which probably they did not even have relevant questions. What

Politics and defence planning 137

tends to be seriously absent on all sides of policy and strategy-making is honest recognition of the outer limits to knowledge; some understanding is probable, but the future is stranded in a fog of uncertainty. The absence of this knowledge feeds the appetite for political controversy. An acute shortage of certainty of comprehension is the usual context for political process, which almost by definition targets the future, or perhaps the promise of a better future. Politicians or policymakers are locked permanently into the promise of a brighter tomorrow because of the power of hope. This is not unreasonable; electors do not usually follow parties that seek to privilege a yet grimmer tomorrow.

Conclusion: need we be surprised?

Genuine surprises occur and Black Swans, of previously unknown genus, do appear to the honest and innocent or naïve amazement even of supposed subject professionals (Taleb, 2007). Having discarded the tyrannical authority of the absurdly old fashioned ideology of communism, though more honestly expressed as brutalist state capitalism, Russia should have surprised no one by returning to quasi-tsarist rule and the quest for more security where it matters most, with the empire that is the homeland. We do not and cannot know, save possibly, but only possibly through defections and espionage, exactly where and how Vladimir Putin will choose next to apply irredentist pressure on the Eastern tier of new NATO members; nonetheless we can be certain that political pressure exerted noticeably by means of military menace is coming our way. It is more likely than not that Putin himself does not know how bold and perhaps dangerous to be or appear, so most probably his unpredictability is a mystery to all concerned. Opportunists are like that. The path of the opportunist who flirts with high risk, however, is especially perilous, given its uncertain course and likely inaccessibility to calculated efforts to achieve adequate deterrent effect.

Little about the ever emerging context of global strategic history is seriously novel to the point where it makes sense to claim that all, even much, is changing. However, that context for the conduct of civil–military relations very largely is stable, though probably alas with but one highly significant change in the repertoire, and arsenals principally of the great power. Specifically, the nuclear character of some acute international crises, let alone the scarily robust way in which Putin advertises Russia's ample nuclear armament, reminds us of nuclear danger. This peril may merit lonely characterization as being so substantial an alternative in the nature of feasible, plausible warfare as to warrant its recategorization as a change in the nature of armed conflict. Not least must this extreme expansion of the risks inherent in some conflict warrant upward scaling in the potential importance of the dangerous military events. Of course, inevitably there has mushroomed into existence an all but explosive growth of study groups as well as official, semi-official, and of thoroughly non-official study and advice groupings, motivated by various levels of nuclear concern, headed by near panic.

Notwithstanding two and a half thousand years of scholarship, our grip and grasp of understanding upon the principal causes of war and its warfare is almost pathetically weak. It is even more sobering for us to consider the plausible hypothesis that war does not lend itself to scholarly, popular political, or expert professional strategic assault. Primarily this opaqueness is the result of war being so variegated in forms when it emerges from the ever rich mix of causation provided by international and domestic political contexts. It is tempting to suggest that war does not happen as a great

138 *Politics and defence planning*

abstraction; it is always particular in its causes, course, and consequences. This means that scholarly assault on the phenomenon of war cannot target particular viruses for war, because there are none such. As best one can tell, there are always likely to be popular leaders who wish to preside over polities that are greater still, and rarely will be short of policy issues that can be exploited expediently to serve as convenient reasons for armed conflict. But, nuclear armament raises the risks strategically in a quite unprecedented way to our political conduct of future security. It is a supreme irony of our strategic history that what appears to be the most robust barrier against strategic adventure also happens to be prudentially unusable. Naturally, indeed logically, policy-makers cannot abandon the possible, but highly plausible, benefits for national and international security that may flow from possession of nuclear weapons. This flawed blessing rests both upon the anticipated 'grammar' of warfare in a nuclear age, and no less significantly upon the definitional truth that 'war is nothing but a duel on a larger scale' (Clausewitz, 1976: 75). What has changed is that the risks in warfare have far outstripped the potential benefits, except, of course, when and where an unusually bold political leader can exploit the fear factor. This factor has proven irresistible as a strategic prop with attractive benefits for any, prospectively many, to exploit in the hope of political gain, offensive though primarily defensive.

In this chapter, we have sought to privilege the concept of uncertainty. Defence planners, many of them highly competent analysts, simply do not and cannot know what they need to understand about this particular episode in the great stream of time (Neustadt and May, 1986). The primary challenge is to attempt to identify some familiar reliable source(s) of evidence that might stand and hold usefully as practicable guidance for the choice of future strategy. As Clausewitz insisted so firmly:

> [t]he political object – the original motive for the war – will thus determine both the military objective to be reached and the amount of effort it requires. The political object cannot, however, *in itself* provide the standard of measurement. Since we are dealing with realities, not with abstractions it can do so only in the context of the two states at war.
>
> (Clausewitz, 1976: 81)

He went on to describe and define the character of a condition in the relevant political (and possibly cultural) context of a particular adversarial relationship. This adversarial nexus falls scarcely short of alarming, given the contemporary presence of nuclear danger. The peril is not likely to diminish noticeably in an anticipatable future.

Our lack of knowledge about the future creates a condition of permanent ignorance. We need to stop worrying about a lack of knowledge that must be permanent. However, we are able to identify a range of plausible answers based on the more general historical evidence that can be understood by strategic categorization of historical experience. Instead of striving hopelessly against scientific feasibility, defence planners could employ their knowledge of past behaviour and misbehaviour in statecraft and strategy in order to seek some useful, we cannot honestly say accurate, guide to a range for the probable. The evidential basis for this relaxed approach to analytical rigour in scholarship is, of course, my belief that there are many essential continuities in behaviour between and among all the periods into which we decide particular options in strategic history can be fitted well enough. Naturally, there is scholarly peril here. Social 'scientific' analysis, no matter how skilfully conducted with the methodological assistance of impressive looking formulae and tools for cunning metrication, remains potentially fatally lacking in even the possibility of acquisition of certain knowledge about the future. There can be only one valid source of evidence, the future itself, which literally can never arrive, at least not until we are able honestly to redraft physics text books. However, there is much to be said in favour of our education by a method that I understand for learning by apparent type of example. We cannot spot the certain winner, nor perhaps even the probable one, but we ought to be able to identify the choices and particular doubts the defence planners among our predecessors (understood in functional terms) decided to pursue, and why they chose to follow the paths that they did.

What I have just described is not so much a methodological option for defence planners and their political policymaker masters, as rather an approach to suitable education that is feasible, though certainly not immune to the effect of bias and undue exclusivity of choice (Gray, 2014a). My most favoured approach to the impossibility of future defence planning owing to the complete permanent absence of authoritative evidence is seriously problematic. It requires many analysts to park some of their prejudices about personally unfavoured futures and allow honest tolerance of enquiry to reign.

My endorsement of strategic historical education can only serve as a general guide to, and guard against, perilous exclusivity in analysis and subsequent policy misjudgement. Such tough problems as the necessary timescale for generational scale replacement, or suitable substitution of whole classes of weaponry, will remain for political process as well as careful analysis to resolve. Moreover, unless appropriate political and strategic education for nation alliance security is made, it may not much matter how we decide upon defence challenges, or with what. Two concepts employed extensively here already all but demand to conclude this treatment of an approach to defence planning with modest inclusivity. I have a pressing concern that whatever the many errors that undoubtedly we will make in the political process that results in the policy choices we will enable with our future strategy, we do need to be correctably right enough on the major international strategic duties our polity has chosen to perform. The inclusive approach endorsed here does not carry claims for certainty, but it does identify ranges of state and alliance behaviour that are near certain to contain vitally important kernels of lasting truth. This, it must be admitted, is not to deny the admitted absence of evidence that would pass a rigorous test for freely replicable scientific certainty of knowledge. Readers may recall that much earlier in this chapter we discussed the 'good enough' rule for defence planning and the political process on which it has to be based permanently. Political process of whatever kind locally favoured is the enduring foundation for the making and implementation of strategy. Also, this persisting political process needs to be capable of ordering change to a policy course. In their rightfully privileged superior turn, the political process has to be both capable and willing to pull the plug on gross imprudence, when such a malady occurs.

The second idea endorsed here in the strongest of terms is the high concept of prudence (Aron, 1966). Unfortunately there is no sure way to generate certainty of knowledge concerning what would prove prudent and what imprudent until it may well be impracticable or even impossible to take timely corrective policy action. Furthermore, I am aware that disturbingly often the course of national strategy may be corrected or even aborted should inadequate supervision of senior military officers permit unwise tactical and operational choices to be made. The possibility of an outbreak of bilateral nuclear conflict seems almost tailor-made for imprudent, if honest and in a vital sense

140 *Politics and defence planning*

possibly responsible seeming, professional military choice. This could occur should political direction, strategic guidance, and discipline by the troops not be demanded and made. We need to remember that we have zero strategic historical experience of nuclear warfare, but also we understand that the path of imprudence may be unduly easy to take mistakenly.

Key points

1 Major identifiable themes have persisted throughout the whole course of strategic history.
2 Future history in any detail can only be guesswork, because we do not and cannot acquire direct empirical knowledge about the future from the future.
3 Fighting power is not reliably calculable or likely to be constant.
4 The character of a particular war will be revealed only by its course and detailed content.
5 Combat and therefore all war and its warfare are adversarial and interactive.
6 Because the course of a war often proves to be surprising to the belligerents, the ability to innovate and adapt is vital for professional soldiers.

Further reading

Arbella, A. (2008) *Soldiers of Reason: The RAND Corporation and the Rise of the American Empire*, Orlando, FL: Harcourt.
Brodie, B. (1973) *War and Politics*, New York: Macmillan.
Davis, P. K. (ed.) (1994) *New Challenges for Defense Planning: Rethinking How Much is Enough*, MR–4–RC, Santa Monica, CA: RAND.
Enthoven, A. C. and Smith, K. W. (2005) *How Much Is Enough? Shaping the Defense Programs, 1961–1969*, Santa Monica, CA: RAND.
Gray, C. S. (2012) *War, Peace and International Relations: An Introduction to Strategic History*, 2nd edn, Abingdon: Routledge.
Gray, C. S. (2014c) *Strategy and Defence Planning: Meeting the Challenge of Uncertainty*, Oxford: Oxford University Press.
Hamilton, R. F. and Herwig, H. H. (eds) (2010) *War Planning 1914*, Cambridge: Cambridge University Press.
Herbig, K. L. (1986) 'Chance and Uncertainty in *On War*', in Handel, M. (ed.) *Clausewitz and Modern Strategy*, London: Frank Cass, pp. 95–116.
Kent, G. A. (2008) *Thinking About America's Defense: An Analytical Memoir*, Santa Monica, CA: RAND.
Krepinevich, A. F., Jr (2009) *7 Deadly Scenarios: A Military Futurist Explores War in the 21st Century*, New York: Bantam Books.
Quade, E. S. and Boucher, W. I. (eds) (1964) *Analysis for Military Decisions: The RAND Lectures on Systems Analysis*, New York: RAND McNully.
Stevenson, D. (2006) 'Strategic and Military Planning, 1871–1914', in Imlay, T. C. and Toft, D. (eds) *The Fog of Peace and War Planning: Military and Strategic Planning under Uncertainty*, Abingdon: Routledge, pp. 75–99.

10 Morality and its ethics in politics and strategy

> *Reader's guide:* Three is a shaky marriage: morality, ethics, and strategy. Moral standards and the importance of ethical guidance. Political complications: not a moral tale. The high significance of the concept of security. Ethics and security.

Introduction: three in a shaky marriage

Strategy and the political judgements that enable it are capable of effecting literally anything. The permissive approach is not usually the method preferred, because almost invariably it could have most unwelcome consequences in kind. For the moment, it suffices to consider the moral and consequential ethical aspects of strategic history. Some readers may have noticed that we have devoted next to no attention in this book so far to what broadly can be understood as moral issues. However, in order to be unmistakeable beyond possibility of noteworthy doubt, it must be made clear the attitude taken here in regard to the morality and ethics of politically motivated military violence. I am not at all dismissive of the potential importance of moral principles, or of the ways in which such standards occasionally are employed in active international political relations. Nonetheless, in the course of many decades of professional and sometimes public strategic argument, I can count on one hand the occasions when I have been obliged either by circumstance or by strong personal desire to cast strategic argument in some explicitly ethical content. Although I have debated most of the more alarming actual and especially potential strategic terrors of our age, I have attracted surprisingly little criticism on moral grounds. Of course, a rather cynical comment in response to that claim might just be that those commentators who do or certainly could and would have raised potent moral objections to my arguments, saved themselves the trouble by not reading it. There is a genuine problem here. From time to time, it is desirable for students and young scholars to be confronted with the necessity of justifying their study of strategy in moral terms. Humans are incontrovertibly moralizing animals and we always take an ethical view of strategic history, past, present, and anticipated to be future. This does not mean that our political and strategic preferences and choices necessarily should be considered usual ones conducted in practice in ethically enlightened ways. But, it does mean that most public policy decisions, in many polities virtually regardless of regime type, are obliged to offer some justification of morally righteous intention in explanation of their decisions. Often the overwhelming problem for order in international politics is not an absence or even a weakness of ethical concern abroad (of course!), but rather the content of foreign decisions and their expected and

142 *Morality and its ethics*

especially their unexpected consequences for our policy and strategy. We must never forget, let alone knowingly put aside, Clausewitz's insistence upon the permanently adversarial nature, not merely character, of all strategy (Clausewitz, 1976: 75).

In minor key because of the relative poverty of treatment of morality and ethics in this book so far, but in major key because of their permanent presence in and about the counsels of governance, this chapter opens by examining the function and role of moral principles and their ethical enablers for politics and strategy. We proceed next to note the empirical challenges that political context of all kinds has strewn in the path of would-be moralizers through the ages. The nature of politics all but commands an expediency in pragmatic choice of method that can reduce the status of ethical compliance to that of a disposable burden for statecraft and strategy. This text has sought to insist that the policy directing strategy is always the product of active politics, regardless of the character of the political regime. This naïve sounding truism is so well understood that it tends to pass understanding by less notice than it deserves in the grand explanation that we have to apply to make sense of strategic history. The chapter concludes by offering pertinent reflections on the moral choices revealed particularly in the more exciting years of the twentieth century.

Moral standards and their ethical guidance

All claims alleging an irrelevance of moral standards in and for strategy need to be dismissed outright as fundamentally mistaken. Books and reports that might employ, even if they choose not to highlight, topics in moral and ethical terms do not in fact do so. In fact, it is little short of surprising to find just how limited typically is the explicit treatment of moral topics in the literature and public professional discussion of national strategy. Long personal reflection about the reasons for this near scholarly silence proves almost to reveal truths close to being so obvious that typically they evade notice. This may be acceptable among and between consenting adult strategists, but it is certainly far less tolerable if it comes to reflect an attitude of disinterest, even dismissive disdain among students. An important purpose of the argument being made here is to clarify how political communities cope with moral demands partially of their own cultural making. It is important to the process of strategic education that students should understand fully why our human history always has been blighted by a strategic theme. Particularly is this essential if the history that is taught fails to unravel the reasons and context that compel attitudes and behaviour we must label strategic.

Morality and its local ethics have not troubled this text very much up to the current point. The principal reason is because empirically there has been no necessity for them doing so. Very occasionally, probably rather less frequently than would have been desirable, I was obliged to defend, at least to debate in a public forum, the probable actuality of nuclear danger, and as a logical consequence the moral acceptability of the scale of risk thereby entailed. Whether or not the danger in the easily identified risks is deemed tolerable, such public discussion as ensued was conducted almost entirely in political, not ethical, terms. I do not pass conclusive judgement on this rather strange fact, largely being personally content simply to register its existentiality.

It is arguably ironic that moral standards and ethical practices plainly are practiced in the irregular warfare currently waged against the Islamic state known as ISIS. For example, drone strikes are not sanctioned when and where there would be a severe risk of inflicting unacceptable damage upon civilians assumed to be innocent of giving us offence. Also, recreational and other violence against civilians is deeply condemned amongst all Western armed forces. This prohibition on the misuse of armed force is sincere and fairly deep, even though undoubtedly it needs to overcome the emotional and psychological urges of young men placed in situations that could have been calculated as certain to produce and elicit near visceral survival reactions. Ethically compliant behaviour is regarded normatively as standard military practice today, and it is enforced as far as proves possible both at the small unit level of warfare and in the formal legal attitudes adopted and enforced by military institutions as a whole. This is not to say that all warfare today is in fact conducted strictly according to morally high ethical standards, but it is to claim on the basis of potential evidence that if and when force is employed unmistakeably abusively, there can be severe negative consequences for the abusers, whomever they happen to be. What is being described does not amount to a transformation in the nature, or even just possibly in the frequent and changeable character of warfare. Arguably with the grim exception that nuclear dangers continue to provide, the international political context today yields considerable opportunity for morally founded constraints to play a noisy role in commentary and legal judgement about the ethically dubious uses of force.

Nonetheless, one feels too compelled to ask, of course, 'so what?'! How much does it really matter that an International Court of Justice sits and operates from The Hague? Rarely are exceptionally brutal dictators tried and found inexcusably guilty. However, this is a book about strategy and the politics that are policy, not the high temperature of moral outrage that (most typically) African and Asian dictators can stir almost into flame. We have to ask, as usual, 'so what?' Is it plausible to argue that warfare is evolving into a variant of 'lawfare', and that violence will be so well regulated that typically it will more resemble police action rather than raw political ambition? In other words, is it even remotely possible that war and its warfare will alter their natures in favour of ethically compliant threats and actions? Such a benign transformation is beyond the realm of possibility, it is not merely unlikely. The reason, as explained elsewhere in this text, is because the causes of war comprise a complex entanglement that must entail, indeed has always entailed, malign reciprocal interactions among three leading elements: human nature, politics, and strategy – each depends crucially upon the others and each appears to have a lifeform eternal in nature, though certainly not in changeable character. In summary:

- Human nature obliges us to seek physical and psychological security.
- In all of history the creation of political community has been found superior to alternative approaches to the quest for security.
- In order for the state to provide the needed security, political process has been essential in the continuous and frequently changeable ways adopted and adapted for sufficiently sound governance (i.e. does it work well enough?)

All three interconnecting steps have been indispensable. The alien and sometimes exotic practices found abroad have mattered scarcely at all for the basic mutual logic of reciprocate complex inter-dependence. We can claim with confidence that strategy, which is to say the direction and actual use of armed force for the ends of policy as decided by politics, is the consequence of an unchanging human nature, with particular reference to its universal and eternal recognition of the need for security. Claims in favour of a biological or possible political transformation with human strategic context

144 *Morality and its ethics*

are foolishly laughable; they are desirable and sometimes admirable, but they tend to be distracting from more urgent needs that have much more to do with the ever present quest for security.

Lest I appear to be casting unduly pessimistic commentary on a subject as significant as security, I will register a positive thought that may serve to balance the books noticeably in argument. Specifically, although there is no worthwhile evidence to suggest that the human race is likely to change its ways in regard to security, it is noticeable just how tenacious the concepts about the waging of just war have proved to be (Coker, 2008). It is probably safe to argue that any and every threat of actual use of military force today and in the future is in political need of some moral covering fire.

When we refer to moral force, usually we claim, or perhaps just imply, that a standard expected for right conduct can be applied to the realm of political and strategic practice. The theory and the practice of politics is all but free of inhibitions that can be understood as moral. The grim historically attested truth is that there are no rules suitable for the problems that strategy and strategists have to face (Svechin, [1927]: 64). This is such an extreme sounding position to hold that not infrequently it is rejected as implausible, which it ought to be and almost certainly is most of the time on most issues that divide political communities. Unfortunately, severe difficulties arise when a polity chooses to behave in ways and for policy ends that transcend a standard regarded as normal at the time. It is ironic that there is no morally impressive argument, resting empirically upon reliable evidence that can justify the taking of substantially unknowable risks in contexts of nuclear danger. Moral values and their ethical guidance are thwarted comprehensively by an absence of practicable alternatives for national defence. To argue somewhat in moral terms, we can claim to threaten or even do what unforgiving circumstances indicate that we must, hoping that a claim stated in that way might excuse morally dubious practice. Our political culture prescribes, indeed all but commands, a standard of individual and institutional behaviour that should be flagged in moral terms. Whatever the letter of the law might be explained as saying, there is in culture expressed in narrative terms an explanation familiar to most members of our society. Of course there is always a small rogue element of individuals and probably the organizations they drive that will think and behave in a manner innocent of rules or indeed any influence by formal legal or informal cultural prohibition.

No rules for strategy

It is important to register fully the insightful judgement of the great Russian strategic theorist Alexandr Svechin, when he advised that there are not, and by plain logical implication should not be, any rules for strategy or strategists (Svechin, [1927]). Admittedly this is an extreme point of view, but nonetheless it is fundamentally correct. Whereas the tactician and the operational artist can seek professional guidance from practical authorities in their efforts to behave in technically correct ways to solve their difficulties, the strategist cannot usually seek inspiration from any expert beyond his particular case of need. The strategist so often is required to face and cope uniquely with issues that assistance prudently cannot be anticipated from historical context or, indeed, anywhere else. The difficulty for the strategist can be illustrated clearly enough by an example.

As a general rule, the scale and intensity of risk in world politics cannot be known. To explain: most probably it will not be possible to make a judgement in moral terms, because there will be no way in which we can estimate reliably the intensity of danger we may need to face. If a Russian political leader chooses to behave provocatively towards one or more of NATO's new Baltic tier of member states, the novelty of the context places a burgeoning crisis in a category of deep uncertainty that transcends calculation. It will be more likely than not that the Russian leader himself would not know, indeed could not know, just how far he dares to press NATO before the risks of nuclear confrontation should be regarded as foreclosing of further risks. All too obviously, in a crisis both sides must proceed both opportunistically yet somehow with minimal prudence. In fact, everywhere one probes for some strategic guidance concerning noticeably unique international political developments, one finds some critical measure of irresolvable uncertainty.

Accepting the risk of danger of genuine moral incalculability, statesmen and strategists often cannot know how heavily they should weigh what they believe probably to be at stake. Because our understanding of the future consequences of contemporary behaviour is unknown and unknowable in any reliable detail, often we are obliged to make choices with moral content based on little more than guesswork and hope. In significant addition, frequently we are obliged to act, or not, in the world on the basis of no reliable calculation of cost and benefit. Behind these comments lies what historical evidence suggests strongly has been an eternal and ubiquitous human need for the making of moral judgement. Whatever the severe limitations upon detailed knowledge and understanding, there is an urge to frame and pass judgement in moral terms. Politicians and the strategists they need to guide from time to time can never afford to ignore and neglect the moral elements in state behaviour. People often will be woefully ignorant of why and how international crises occur, but they are unlikely to be beyond emotional mobilization as a result of their being exposed to selected alleged evidence of foreign misdeeds. People argue, though do not necessarily reason, in moral terms, and the feelings of narrative outrage can be expressed as a political anger that is dangerous for international security and order. When considered in a nuclear context, public hostility to some alleged peril from abroad is likely to require careful official handling. Vladimir Putin needs to be careful he does not fuel domestic demand for bold action that cannot prudently be satisfied.

In practice, as contrasted with high principle, there is no ethical audit on official behaviour. Literally nothing is prohibited absolutely. Undoubtedly, most governments prefer to be positioned over policy defending threats and actions that they know, or suspect strongly, will meet with widespread public approval. However, they know also that there is little, if anything, that is utterly beyond a reasonable effort at plausible justification. Even undoubted strategic failure (e.g. the BEF in Flanders, May 1940, or South Vietnam in spring 1975) proves to be a justificatory challenge concerning which governments not infrequently are able to attempt, at least, to find a mix of excuses. So many and so potentially significant do the influences upon policy outcomes tend to be that it will be highly unusual for senior officials to be left literally naked of any possibly plausible explanations for failure. It will be commonplace for popular journalists and other would-be opinion leaders to agree in moral terms over an evident recent failure of policy. In practice, though, there is hardly ever even a reasonable probability of a useful evaluation of official deeds and misdeeds conducted in moral terms. It is always important for a government to be able to mobilize political support for a policy course that lends itself to being recast in moral terms. Self-righteous anger, particularly if no noteworthy personal sacrifice is likely to be required as a consequence, is potent fuel for political consequences.

146   *Morality and its ethics*

Politics is a game played with long traditional rules, and is rewarded and punished also in well-established ways. The winners in politics are rewarded for their electoral (or other) success with the grant of executive authority, probably for a fixed duration. There is no ethical audit, either before or after their adoption of policies. The government of every country makes some decisions on policy and grand strategy it is likely to regret, but it is unlikely that politicians will find themselves utterly bereft of all semi plausible lines of possible justification for error. Undoubtedly, disastrous policies sometimes are chosen and followed for a while, but it is more usual for the political owners of such poor policy choices to have a self-excusatory list of explanations for failure. To many, if not most, politicians the critical issue is not who was right, but rather who lacks a plausible excuse for undeniable failure. When or if moral value is added to policy debate, virtually all hope of fair and balanced accounting will vanish promptly. There is probably nothing in statecraft and strategy completely beyond the reach of justification. I have claimed already that there is a persisting problem with respect to the morality of state policy and strategy, flowing from the substantive choices that political communities make over right and wrong and praiseworthy or blameworthy behaviour. As a general rule concerning political authority, what matters most is the identity of currently extant politicians. It will not much matter whether the moral order of a polity rests upon beliefs, perhaps simply professed beliefs, in some supernatural source of authority, or more tangibly in a coercive capability exercised by those politically in charge. Even an essentially coercive authority will acquire some limited moral credit as a source for obedience, simply as a result of prudent habits on the part of the public. Over time, this expedient obedience should acquire some moral credit, if for no greater reason than habit and expediency.

We humans are used to living by rules, with their precise content being less significant than their existence. Similarly, we all live our lives by rules great and small; our personal space is ordered by society and its regulations, many of which bear the possibility of negative sanction should we choose to disregard them. Our personal, social, and professional space(s) are crowded with regulations that typically threaten punishment for disobedience.

Political complications: not a moral tale

International politics is not a field of activity wherein virtue commonly is expressed in moral terms. Political and possibly strategic success usually is assessed easily enough, but such assessment does not usually include a notable moral element. It can be important, politically important that is (e.g. as for Britain over German misbehaviour towards neutral Belgium in 1914), for an adversary to be condemned as unmistakably guilty of a serious infraction that can be painted in moral terms for Western popular democracies; such alleged moral villainy usually has modest political virtue. Nonetheless, the professional policymakers and strategists who compose, develop, and act in international affairs usually are not confused about the relatively low relevance for high statecraft and strategy of ethical misbehaviour. What renders moralizing expressions of unhappiness with foreign misdeeds harmful is the damage those actions may cause to friendly interests. It can be difficult to weigh the virtue in moral condemnation when one is scarcely confused at all about the thoroughly amoral nature of the disagreeable actions in question. Russia's forcible restoration of authority over Crimea in 2014 was a plain challenge both to formal interstate agreements and to norms of good (enough) behaviour in the new Post-Cold War Europe. The territorial seizure by Moscow was, of course, vilified in moral terms (inter alia) by NATO, but the political and strategic truth was that Russia behaved as it wished to, for the reason that it was able to do so. Some make-weight moralizing assertions were uttered by NATO, but no one was confused about the political or strategic reality: Russia behaved as it did simply because it could. Potential deterrent effects were too weak to be effectively dissuasive. Moreover, Vladimir Putin's bold geostrategic seizure may well have been motivated as much, if not more, by domestic ambition to restore a sense of Russian pride, as by any calculation of probable strategic advantage. Needless to say, perhaps, when cast in ethical spotlight, the restoration of Russian authority over Crimea was a persuasive demonstration of executive will. Putin showed determination not to be bound by agreements with the West made when Russia was too weak to stand up for its national interests.

The episode of Russian demonstration of quasi-military muscle and political determination over Ukraine is a good example of the nature of international politics manifesting itself when circumstances are permissive for boldness. General arguments about maintaining a good international order in Europe, with the sovereignty of all polities somewhat locally guaranteed, was revealed to be vulnerable. That limitation meant 'unless a greater power is both motivated and able' to deny the legitimacy of the current geostrategic settlement (Bisley, 2012). Good, at least tolerable, international order needs protecting by someone (Howard, 2001). When an international order affronts the self-assessed dignity and vital interests of a great power, it will have to be defended sooner or later.

The principal concern of this text has been about the relationship between politics and strategy, but it is just possible that some readers might believe those two streams of thought and action function roughly in parallel and merit near equal respect and attention. Such a belief would be a serious error. The course of strategic history shows unmistakably that strategic decision typically resides where it should, in a position of practical authority behind political choice. To the possible moral discomfort of some readers, I need also to register the belief that ethical considerations play a distinctly subordinate role in argument over policy and strategy. We have it on the authority of Thucydides that 'fear, honor, and interest' comprise a useful summation of the policy motive in a polity (Thucydides, 1996: 43). Considerations of 'honour' are of course bound substantially by the moral values current in the polity of contemporary concern. Late fifth-century Athens was no stranger to moral contention, but it was an argument that means relatively little to us in the twenty-first century. The moral values of Ancient Athens and the ethical behaviour they required were very much the prisoner of public opinion in the *agora* (public meeting place). Then, as indeed in almost all contexts since, moral certainty has been equated with the superior apparent weight of public opinion, not with a divine source of practical advice. Because of the nature and the character of public debate, the search for feasible strategy tends not to resemble a quest after military truths, but rather to be akin to a hunt for the practicable. As often as not, probably less, the strategy that is found and selected in good part because of its compatibility with current interests will require severe amendment when the difficulties it probably neglected need to be faced seriously.

Timing

Timing is critically important for both politics and strategy. Unfortunately for the strategist and politician, however, unmistakeable evidence for good or bad timing is

148 *Morality and its ethics*

revealed only in the light that may be shed by its passage in the metaphor of the great stream mentioned here earlier. The policymaker and the strategist render themselves exceptionally vulnerable to the unanticipated and therefore the unexpected if they do not shine brightly in their abilities to guess imaginatively as to the enemy's future moves. Such anticipation is probably more likely to reflect guesswork than calculation resting upon empirical evidence. However, an adversarial system as in a context of war may require some imaginative leaps of faith that need the analyst to transcend in understanding what is possibly deducible from his best-guess evidence (about the future!). While belligerents seek knowledge of the 'where' and the 'how' of strategic menace, in addition they must also strive to answer the 'when' question, which can be no less vital. From William of Normandy in 1066 to Adolf Hitler in 1944, timing has proved critically important for strategic choice and its eventual political consequences. Strategists ought to know that there is never any guarantee that political and strategic timing will march in step as one through the course of history. A major complication for the strategist is the likelihood that the opposing belligerent may decide to attempt to delay the timing of an active intervention, and thereby possibly delay and frustrate what otherwise might have been a timely stroke. International politics quite often records military movements planned to convey timely warning of concern. It can become a problem rather than simply a complication if one belligerent decides that he has been morally challenged, in which context the political stakes will be augmented by a noteworthy boost. The insertion of moral content into international political crises is apt to encourage the subsequent commitment of military forces by way of forward deployment in-theatre. It is a general truth about international politics that when disputes are augmented with moral content they tend to become far more difficult to resolve. Whereas an interest, expressed in terms of people and geography, probably can be negotiated on the basis of some physical division if that is what is at stake. It is far more of a challenge to find a tolerable way in which to negotiate about and arguably perhaps divide a principle asserted in moral terms.

All politics have to be domestic to some degree

Politics as an activity is wondrously adaptable to its local circumstances. The professional politician need not be committed personally to any set of beliefs in particular. His commitment, rather more probably, supremely is to the pragmatic goal of winning, with the compromises advisable and necessary for that goal being met as they must as in the candidate's political competition; though certainly such a stance should enhance relative freedom of candidate choice and possible actions. Assuredly most polities do accommodate the usually strongly expressed opinion of some genuine conviction politicians. But, as a general rule, personal values, especially if they are made manifest in moral terms, tend to limit a candidate's appeal rather more than they can enhance it. Fascination with the stratosphere of politics, strategy, and security can lead to some neglect of the ubiquitous truth that all politics is, indeed has to be, to some noticeable degree local and rather immediate. Political authority and the power that can be realized thereby has to be nurtured and usually bought or at least rented, in terms that make sense to those asked to commit to a cause or, more often, to an interest. Far removed from the eighteenth-century ideas of Jean Jacques Rousseau, most people do not strive to comprehend the general interest, rather do they tend to endorse and possibly advocate a material idea of interest that assumes some physical form. Typically in practice

Morality and its ethics   149

the idea of interest is understood as being somewhat promissory to the person's net benefit. By far the most persuasive shorthand summary identifying people's motivations for political attitudes and behaviour was provided for all time by Thucydides with his timeless triadic summary of the subject in terms of 'fear, honor, and interest'. It is not always easy for the rulers in a popular democracy to ensure they have reached a robust decision balancing, for example, fear with honour, but these three themes continue to be substantively authoritative into the twenty-first century. In need of particular emphasis at this juncture is the high political relevance of what has been termed and understood as public mood (Schilling, Hammonds, and Snyder, 1962). An aggressive actor in world politics, one willing to take high risks in the hope of securing major political gain, is ever in danger of overplaying a policy hand that is, or should be, played only with an acute awareness of the risks he may be running. So complex may the domestic and international politics of a crisis prove to be, that in practice the course of events will escape predictability, let alone control. One of the reasons policymakers should not lose all interest in the investigation of political culture is that some apparently minor happening may be found only in real time, probably unexpectedly, to have an impressive politically mobilizing capability on the adversary. Strategists, and especially strategic theorists, can so isolate themselves from cultural contact and even dependency that they inadvertently neglect triggers for popular irritation and anger. The Thucydidean category of motivation we understand as honour (and dishonour) is particularly apt to mislead those who choose to push harder than is prudent in the context of an acute crisis. The general truth in this point holds that because all political power over human affairs ultimately is domestic in nature, necessarily it is always local. In short, there has to be a domestic reality to the acquisition and use of political power, always. Understanding of the politics of rivalry and perhaps even succession may be a challenge for foreign observers to untangle for advantage, but neglect of pertinent detail in this category of authority is apt to prove unaffordably expensive. Virtually no matter how concentrated political power may appear to be, there will always be a very particular story about its exercise. With respect to political power we are talking about institutions and individuals who will exercise authority in ways, and to ends, that are richly human, substantially regardless of the cultural rewards that particular societies choose to provide (Rosen, 2005).

Permissive context

Statesmen and strategists prefer to have reputations as politicians and officials whose word is reliable, unless, that is, they find themselves perilously exposed by yesterday's promises, and as a consequence potentially revealed as people whose words cannot be taken routinely at face value. In modern, which is to say nuclear, times at least, politicians and strategists have been extremely careful not to make contingent promises of strategic action for which they might just be held to account. It is necessary for the politics of international diplomacy to accommodate some ambiguity and even deliberate but distinctly functional deception. It has long been well appreciated that diplomacy has to value expediency over, perhaps in addition to, truth. After all, the practical purpose of much of diplomacy is to enable and possibly facilitate agreement across frontiers, not necessarily to reflect a completely honest mutual understanding of what is, and why that is the case. Quite often, the path to diplomatic success, tolerability at least, lies in the political ability to ride over and in effect ignore rather obvious examples of

150 *Morality and its ethics*

misbehaviour. Allegedly, at least, this is tolerated and even condoned in the interest of sustaining an international dialogue. I need to say that the record of Soviet, then Russian–US arms control endeavour over the course of nearly fifty years has amply fed my discomfort with an adversary who seems incapable of sustained behaviour that would even be close to overall assessment as beyond ethical reproach. That said, there is nonetheless a case to be made in favour of some tolerance of a modest level of suspect and possibly modestly proven misbehaviour. A trouble is that one can provide faulty education in this way, with Russian policymakers becoming seriously indifferent to the truth. It can be a general problem for policy and its diplomacy to know when to blow the whistle and expose what have to be understood as lies, as opposed to the taking of a tolerant view of state misbehaviour that contrasts negatively with our own. Because attitudes and practices differ markedly among societies and their cultures, it can be a demanding challenge to know when official misbehaviour probably means something significant, and most probably when it does not. Soviet and now Russian cheating on the terms of supposedly solemn arms control treaties is just one category of strategic malpractice that confuses experts in the West. Is the cheating deliberate and well known in Moscow, or is it simply the case of Russian carelessness over some details as usual? While there is something that can be said in praise of some tolerance of unfriendly Russian ways, also there is much to be said in praise of denying Russian officials even the possibility of their misunderstanding our tolerance. What must be potentially dangerous for international order, peace, and security would be for Russian officials to learn from our political tolerance that a professed determination to insist on the honest obedience to international agreements is an issue upon which we are less than serious.

Expediency

There is an important sense in which professional politicians are always arguing and claiming in what can best be characterized as an expedient mode. It is not necessarily the case that truth always falls early victim to what may be more expedient explanation and justification, but rather that it is ever likely to do so. It is a considerable problem both for politician-policymakers and for strategists that rarely, but still genuinely, it is necessary for some close approximation to the truth to be told to, and believed by, particular audiences. While it suffices if a foreign leader chooses to act and behave as if he believes our nuclear menaces, it would be more reassuring were we to believe he was deterred by the dangers we had articulated and specified in threats we had not been backward in articulating (Kahn, 1960). Although it is tempting to suggest that expediency should be considered a good enough guide for crisis-time behaviour, I am compelled to be dissatisfied with that judgement. Expedient decisions frequently are hasty ones, with their near immediate availability and general convenience being a good part of their appeal. The course of strategic history leads me to favour the view that expedient decisions are too often apt to be endorsed substantially because of their immediate availability. Frequently in strategic history, political and senior military decision-makers have found themselves in situations wherein time genuinely is short, and almost any one among several apparent action options appears good enough, certainly sufficiently timely, at least. This was just, though only just, true for British intervention in Norway in April 1940, though in that truly desperate case a prudential argument for very prompt British action soon was proven to have been grossly imprudent. Often it has been exceedingly difficult for an intervening great power to know reliably just how the local ally on the ground really has been faring. The prompt acquisition of reliable knowledge often has the consequence of promoting a somewhat unintended scope and scale of land-air commitment. Confident superior understanding concerning how an internal conflict has been developing is likely to characterize a few of the policymakers with major responsibility. It is probably a certainty that the political and military case for intervention will not be short of spokespeople. This was the case for South Vietnam in the early and mid-1960s. It is wise to remember that the general context for debates about intervention in a probable counterinsurgency (COIN) situation is almost always political, not military-analytical, let alone significantly cultural (Gentile, 2013). It is a significant truth about human beings convinced about the correctness of their policy proposals, that they are certain to be easy to convince that strategic and then political success must soon reward their efforts. Where a 'conviction politician', which is to say one moved seriously by his political tenets, based in good part on genuine (if possibly erroneous) moral beliefs, is convinced he is doing the right thing, normal standards of assay of belief no longer hold. That thought is troubling because it is not bothered unduly by issues of evidence. What is more, the politicians who endorse military action with enthusiasm are likely to be difficult to correct from their current belief, because that conviction will have become all too sincere. A Tony Blair and a George Bush will argue from a policy brief in which they believe or at least about which they have become convinced. Such a belief, for example over Saddam Hussein's weapons of mass destruction, may well be false, in a significant part because the key decision-maker permits himself to trust unwisely in the veracity of corrupted evidence. Officials both senior and junior can find themselves at serious risk of endorsing allegedly key evidential detail that rapidly becomes so much a part of the accepted folk wisdom of a government that it would be politically disloyal to dare to raise politically embarrassing criticism of it. In this situation it can be all but necessary, certainly personally expedient, to convince oneself that some arguments over arms control compliance really are relatively too unimportant to be worthy of a domestic and possibly an international row to risk exposing.

Political convenience of ambiguity

Uncertainty is a political reality that commonly overhangs argument about strategy and politics. Of course there are military deployments and actions by an already firmly established political adversary that it would be a challenge to misinterpret. However, relatively few acts, particularly those possibly hostile, truly are self-defining quite beyond the semi-plausible scope of misinterpretation as being benign. When politicians talk and perhaps even behave in a context of international crisis, it is quite common for them to believe genuinely in the high moral worth of their policy stance. They will believe not only that they are behaving prudently, if probably on the cautious side of the options considered, but also that this has been the right thing to do. This means that a crisis-time political leader and possibly his key senior military advisers are likely to believe their policy choices are notably right in ethical terms. Their preferences are very likely to have been pre-judged on moral criteria, a standard that is near certain to bias analysis. When a politician, and even a senior soldier, already is convinced genuinely as to the high moral rectitude of a favoured policy course, he is not likely to listen with sincere attention to views advanced in disagreement. In practice, moral conviction

152   *Morality and its ethics*

tends to foreclose upon balanced argument, because political leaders will then be morally strongly in need of support that slides from the ethical sphere all too easily into the political and the high moral. When a political leadership chooses to take the potentially high risk of war, the last thing it will need is any (disloyal) breaking of executive ranks in favour of the arguments advanced by troublesome and annoying critics.

Domestic approval or tolerance

Japanese political and strategic folly on a truly grand scale served well enough to solve Roosevelt's (and Churchill's) major problem of how to engage popular American interest in other people's rather obviously thus far non-American war. But, when the political and strategic stakes in a war are not self-evidently as engaging as was the near unarguable case in December 1941, it can be a fair-sized political challenge to compose a sufficiently impressive shortlist of vital national interests allegedly now at hazard (Gray, 2012: 185–9). I must correct a possible deficiency even at this very late juncture in my analysis. It may be essential for the interest of good enough Order in East–Central Europe today that Putin understands that Article V of the NATO Treaty of 1949 applies in the fullest terms to all NATO members. That treaty obligation and guarantee applies quite literally regardless of how those new members of the Alliance are located as a tier of relatively weak states along Russia's western border, from Bulgaria in the South to Estonia in the North. Article V of the treaty is the near magical guarantee that the Baltic and Black Sea members of NATO regard with what may be good enough reason as the true basis of their national security. Unsurprisingly, political and military leaders of this Eastern tier do not hesitate to define their security dependency on NATO in some moral terms. They are, of course, very concerned to behave with their defence roughly along the lines of being highly cooperative allies of the American superpower. Nonetheless, they cannot help but be alarmed by recent developments in the European balance of power as it likely pertains directly to their national security, both collectively and individually. In a political and moral context such as this, the close relationship between morality and its seemingly inevitable ethical precepts for NATO, and alliance military strategy, becomes unmistakable. This Eastern tier of NATO cannot argue hopefully for a military-strategy case for friendly superpower intervention on their behalf.

There were circumstances in superpower political and strategic relations during the Cold War when the most prudent policy seemed, at the time and even in long retrospect, to be that of certainty. This was the view taken by President Harry S. Truman, while it was close to being axiomatic for the administration of 5-star General Dwight D. Eisenhower from 1953 until 1962. Without appearing dismissive or truculent, Eisenhower weathered the storm occasioned by Nikita Khrushchev's nuclear tipped missile diplomacy. He succeeded in sounding and looking like a nuclear-age political leader who carried a proper weight of nuclear menace comfortably enough. Khrushchev's would-be missile diplomacy did not cut much ice with the 5-star general, who was in fairly early possession of aerial intelligence (the U-2) that appeared credibly to prove the missile menace was more bluff than actuality, albeit one that matured on his political watch at least. However, Russian nuclear missile threats did find politically notable public expression in Britain by the close of the 1950s. The campaign for Nuclear Disarmament attracted support from the middle ranks as well as the usually fairly politically active Left in Britain. By then a nuclear-armed polity itself, Britain seemed credibly to be a certain victim/participant in any war that became nuclear as a consequence of NATO's defence of Western Europe. During the Cold War decades (1946–89), the danger to Britain was believed to be so severe that the potential harm to the country in the event of a failure of deterrence, or even an accidental conflict that escalated beyond reliable central control, was widely believed to be morally roughly in balance with the risks.

Policymakers are not usually embarrassed for long by an apparent absence of telling evidence alleging hostile motivations stimulating foreign opposition to national goals. If that ethical soundness does not match the characteristics of our local behaviour, we will need to apply some appropriate political 'spin' in order to attempt to shift some hearts and minds. Financial persuasion is likely to prove beneficial for the net national interest in such situations. It may not succeed, but it would be a challenge to discover a region, let alone an individual polity wholly indifferent to the well targeted bribe. Political cultures vary by wide margins around the world, notwithstanding the exaggerated assessments that continue to be offered in description, if not always in praise of globalization (Porter, 2015). It is prudent never to forget that we humans do share fundamental physiological and psychological characteristics. The entire great stream of time of our relatively brief habitation of this planet should have provided us with evidence enough of the substantial commonalties that persist for reasons that hold authority far beyond the relatively superficial trappings of culture, noteworthy though those can be.

Conclusion: ethics and security

It would be a mistake to leave readers with the belief that I was dismissive of the relevance of moral principles and ethical guidance for strategy and politics. Whatever the private beliefs of policymakers and strategists, they know that their most attentive publics on the domestic scene are, or appear to be, convinced that right and wrong in thought and about behaviour in world politics is both entirely commonplace and readily detectable. Moreover, if unmistakeable evidence of wrongful behaviour surprisingly is not transparent to a swift, if nonetheless expert but still adequately revealing national glance, one can always retreat into the region of an expediently evidence-light realm of suspicious anticipation. Near nationwide attitudes of public approval or disapproval are not usually hard to encourage and inculcate. People everywhere have first-hand knowledge of thought and behaviour that culturally, though not invariably legally, is widely condemned as being corrosively anti-social. Throughout strategic history bad news about our neighbours on Planet Earth has not been especially difficult to manipulate as to its ill possibilities. The key concept, of course, is security. However, to be key in critically important respects does not mean to be easily detectable with attention to the detail of evidence.

Strategy and politics, the principal subjects here, may appear to be fundamental to the search for security, but that judgement is not as obviously the case as a rapid examination of apparent evidence could lead us to believe. The great sweeping concept of security suffers from a near, actually historically quite frequent, imprecision in meaning. This does not necessarily translate as a useless vagueness, but instead rather as a permanently unsettled argument about the meaning of security: personal, familial, tribal, national, international, and whatever else is found convenient for the orientation or of spinning debate.

154 *Morality and its ethics*

Moral principles and their ethical guidance are always fundamental and essential to the notion of living a good enough life as an individual, family member, and citizen. As I sought to explain early in this work, critically essential though the ambitious concept of security always must be, very commonly it cannot be the focus of argument resting on competing bodies of evidence. The evidence presented may fall seriously short of a standard in which we should place trust. If Aron was basically correct in his belief that prudence must be the primary standard to which we ought to hold our statesmen, one is soon brought to realize that this most vital task can hardly help but place demands for quality of supporting evidence that cannot be met (Aron, 1966: 285). We dare not be too trusting of the motives of Others because it is possible we will, as it were, wake up from our dream-like slumber only to rediscover that the Russian bear continues to aim to win foreign friends and gain influence by means of a characteristic hugging manoeuvre. The bad news for security that flows from the very nature of usually unavoidably competitive, though not necessarily belligerent, relations can hardly avoid driving we humans into playing the all too often fatal game of security. Elementary logic and even a fairly light acquaintance with strategic history tell us that suspicion is apt to precede a prudent anticipation. Also, the entire span of world history leads us to believe that whereas global empire thus far has been neither feasible nor as a direct consequence attractive, a seemingly endless replay of old bids for natural advantage do make some practical sense, given the strategic historical context of such behaviour.

With reference to behaviour, both personal and also very much wider, that we have long understood to be political, it has become near axiomatic to accept explanation that is somewhat 'economical with the truth'. This telling phrase was popularized by Alan Clark, a British politician, brilliant diarist, and poor military historian. Far from shocking an unduly credulous Britain, Clark instead gained popularity rather than notoriety for reason of this provision of an easy wit. Some foreign observers of the British scene may have been shocked at least a little, if that concept can survive being both oxymoronic and ironic, but generally it has been tolerated in Britain in good part because it has been felt to be sufficiently clever as to dare risk breaking ethical rules so obviously as to sound unavoidably both humorous and cynical. In this book I have denied myself the undoubted pleasure of cultural comparisons for the purpose of illustrating by example how morally principled ethics can and do differ between societies, even ones long as closely aligned as the American and the British. We continue to be divided by our common language and distinguishable by our somewhat distinctive abilities to manifest ethical surprise at the plain evidence of non-matching examples of allegedly unethical behaviour. To a British writer, such as this author, there is found to be all too much of a sober seriousness about many Americans that it can be a struggle to take quite at face value. Of course, the somewhat lighter touch that Britons bring to the table of strategy and politics may well largely be explicable, if not necessarily excusable, with heavy reference to the respective positions in world politics that the two countries have exchanged over the course of the past century.

Key points

1   An electorate expects its polity's foreign and military policies to be presented on some moral basis, even though public policy is not usually argued in ethical terms.
2   It is surprising how small is the role played by ethical considerations in public policy.

3   The demand and search for security has been permanent throughout all of strategic history.
4   Strategy presents itself as unique sets of challenges that usually require somewhat imaginative and unique solutions.
5   The moral context of a conflict is often not understood ahead of time, meaning that potentially intervening polities cannot really make ethical judgements about their possible behaviour.
6   Despite the body of laws and norms created over the course of the past century, political and strategic authorities are really beyond ethical guidance and moral discipline, if they so choose.
7   Considered both overall and in detail, strategic history is not a morality tale wherein ethical virtue can be expected to succeed because of its solid appeal to righteousness.
8   All politics ultimately are domestic somewhere.
9   Politicians and soldiers are attracted to expedient solutions to their practical problems; both groups, though soldiers to a lesser degree, can be expected to be rather economical with the truth! Especially when reliable truth is hard to find.

Further reading

Burleigh, M. (2010) *Moral Combat: A History of World War II*, London: Harper Press.

Coates, A. J. (1997) *The Ethics of War*, Manchester: Manchester University Press.

Coker, C. (2008) *Ethics and War in the 21st Century*, Abingdon: Routledge.

Fisher, D. (2011) *Morality and War: Can War be Just in the Twenty-First Century?* Oxford: Oxford University Press.

Gray, C. S. (2013) *Perspectives on Strategy*, Oxford: Oxford University Press, Ch. 2.

Guthrie, C. and Quinlan, M. (2007) *Just War: The Just War Tradition: Ethics in Modern Warfare*, London: Bloomsbury Publishing.

Kennedy, D. (2006) *War and Law*, Princeton, NJ: Princeton University Press.

McMahan, J. (2009) *Killing in War*, Oxford: Clarendon Press.

Shaw, M. N. (2008) *International Law*, 6th edn, Cambridge: Cambridge University Press.

Walzer, M. (1977) *Just and Unjust Wars: A Moral Argument with Historical Illustrations*, 3rd edn, New York: Basic Books.

Yoder, J. H. (2009) *Christian Attitudes to War, Peace, and Revolutions*, Grand Rapids, MI: Brazos Press.

11 Strategic future

Reader's guide: Vital five factors: politics; strategic theory; human nature; historical contexts; and surprises.

Introduction: an holistic understanding

It has been the central thesis of this book that relatively little of strategic historical significance has changed over time historically recorded. This is not to try and argue foolishly that material and ideational changes have been insignificant, but rather that when we examine them we should be impressed more by their modesty than their ability to recast a familiar context. In writing this book I was somewhat surprised to learn how modest change has been in matters of the highest importance. Probably, it is necessary to emphasize the fact that *Strategy and Politics* is not written as an aspiring work of history. The ambition here simply is to explain how and why strategy works as a rather unreliable servant of politics. Historical examples in this text are offered solely as potential aids for understanding, not in the hope of persuasion concerning yesterday's squabbles.

In order to attempt to make some sense of the arguments and examples deployed here, five large factors have been drafted into service: politics, strategic theory, human nature, context, and surprise. These factors, more accurately perhaps the clusters of ideas attached to each, have been chosen because they are all innocent of historically specific meaning. Each has been useful in providing vital guidance for progress in several chapters. Probably important above all else is acknowledgement that the passage of time happens at a steady rate and that it may have consequences for all aspects of human life and in all locales simultaneously.

The five organizing factors deployed and employed are: politics; strategic theory; human nature; context; and surprise. These are transhistorical ideas, not owned by any particular person or school of analysis.

Five concepts

1 Politics rules

Politics will not always rule to consistent good effect, but it ought always to provide guiding purpose. Lest the argument has been buried unduly in these chapters, the high importance of policy intention must be re-emphasized. The fundamental logic of strategy is indifferent to the prospects for policy success, but not for the feasibility of the objectives specified and sought. In practice, much that is feasible should not be pursued, reflecting as it will a poor choice of objectives. The idea most clearly in need of understanding is that of choice of values. Probably the key idea here is that of legitimate, indeed legitimating, authority. We can make no assumption that the public is always, or even only usually, correct in its policy endorsements. All that can be claimed is that to be accounted legitimate, executive authority must be seen and understood to have passed the local tests for legitimacy. There is never any guarantee that the authoritative political process will succeed in producing any outcome more impressive than that of a winner, wise or perhaps foolish.

From the wide range of historical experience we know that politicians and their policymaking are capable of pursuing folly in many guises, no matter how seemingly enlightened and prudent the policy impulse may have begun by being. The essential logic of strategy should serve to limit the range of political folly, but there can be no guarantee that that will be so. Unduly hasty reading of *On War* might mislead us into the error of believing that there is something almost magical about policymaking that provides direction in favour of feasibility and prudence, but unfortunately that is not the case. Political process, politicians, and political ambition are all eminently capable of misdirecting public policy. The logic of strategy expressed as 'ends, ways, and means', frequently is violated in quite abundant malpractice (Yarger, 2008). That logic can only provide basic logical structure, not judgement resting on assessments made non-metrically of quantities of key values. It is entirely appropriate for us to register clearly how ways and means should serve policy goals well enough, but we should never confuse logical with real-world pragmatic feasibility. For example, no sense can be made of a design in strategy unable to offer persuasive qualitative assessment of significant values. Even in that crucial regard it can be most important to understand that although quantity of military strength is always likely to be key, 'moral forces', particularly determination, can be yet more important (Clausewitz, 1976: 97).

It would be tempting to seek to argue that political process strives typically to rule prudently, certainly roughly in accordance with the known and suspected beliefs of the voting citizen. Unfortunately, however, no such assumption can be made. It is true that a bare logic of strategy relatively disinterested in policy substance will capture the essential categories of required logic, but that focus can offer nothing specifically helpful concerning the feasibility of political ambition. It is necessary to remember that political process is all and really only about winning or losing politically, not about the wisdom in the pursuit of particular policy goals.

2 Strategic theory

Many scholars appear uncomfortable with strategic theory. This is unfortunate because the prime function of theory is to simplify and clarify life for those who need to theorize (Clausewitz, 1976: 579). Here, as elsewhere in my writings, I have sought to distinguish as clearly as possible between strategy's general theory and strategy as a category of particular theories governing behaviour in particular military regards. Far from being complicated, let alone needlessly so, strategic theory has one dominant function: to explain that which otherwise in its absence is likely to be confused and confusing (Gray, 2013: 12–20). This book has striven to distinguish with maximum clarity between, on the one hand, the general theory of strategy, and on the other hand, theories that pertain carefully only to particular elements of military power.

158 *Strategic future*

The general theory of strategy is advanced to explain how and why military power can serve the political ends of state policy, whatever they may be. The theory has been identified and selected so as not to privilege particular military elements, regardless of the environment most suitable for their deployment and operation. Since I first chose the content of my preferred general theory of strategy, I have increased the dicta identified only very modestly, shifting from 21 such dicta only up to 23 (Gray, 2015b). In this book, as elsewhere also, I have found it important to be able to accommodate a very limited increase in numbers of dicta. Of most importance for the general theory of strategy has been an urgent need to cope with any and all varieties of military capability, regardless of their environmental specialism.

As a general rule, one would not anticipate much movement in the numbers or particular content of dicta in a general theory. By definition, it has been chosen selectively in supporting detail so as to be capable of leading readily in understanding to the whole body of strategic phenomena. It is both efficient and effective to make this critical distinction between the general and the particular. There are several different methods that can be employed to make the distinction, but the simple binary choice is my preference. The most obvious reason for drawing the general and particular distinction is in order not to confuse what changes with what does not. Tactical change is frequent, as soldiers and sailors adjust and adapt their weapons for better fit with tactical circumstances, while an operational level of alteration requires major changes in organization and leadership. As weaponry has changed, so also necessarily have tactics and operational design. Strategy and its desired effect, however, has not necessarily shifted in concert.

Always bearing in mind the overarching relative importance of strategy and its anticipated effect, strategic theory will be revisited to meet the apparent needs of new classes of weapons, such as nuclear and cyber. By and large, a competent general theory of strategy will be able to privilege intended effects and not be confused by particular technical shifts.

3 *Human nature*

In the study of strategy and politics it is all too easy, perhaps I should say convenient, to airbrush individual people out of what should be considered necessary appraisal. The relative strengths and weaknesses may almost fade out of sight when one is examining possible shifts in the balance of power with their probable meaning for International Order, for example. I need to insist that this work primarily is about the whole course of our strategic history, though certainly it is not designed to provide such in detail. By and large I have sought to skate around human particulars, in favour of pressing the case for functions and instrumentalities. This has been deliberate, but I admit that it can leave a text rather short of people, significant individuals in particular. Of course decisions are made and implemented by individuals as well as groups. Noteworthy violence has not been done to historical understanding by referring generally to politicians, policymakers, and strategists, but I admit to the possibility that some individuals may have vanished too thoroughly from ready view. The principal reasons for this economy in method simply have been both the necessity for economy in method, and a determination on my part not to be diverted by arguments keyed on individuals.

Whether such economy is or is not effective, it cannot be doubted that one pays a price in absent human detail that might aid understanding. Thucydides' triadic offering of the statesman's leading motivations – fear, honour, and interest – was exemplary in its clarity, and wholly indifferent to the technical or social detail of contemporary weaponry at the close of the fifth century BC (Thucydides, 1996: 43). Indeed, the more closely one thinks about warfare at the time of the great struggle between Athens and Sparta, the more one should be able to recognize the essential timelessness of that conflict (Gray, 2014c: 12). The source of that lasting condition was Thucydides' attention to the detail of human nature (Rosen, 2005). Once we have grasped and considered the stressful situations in which Greek politicians and strategists found themselves, we are enabled to appreciate that political and strategic, though not practical or operational thought and behaviour, have altered only to a modest degree over the course of millennia. This phenomenon of repeated experience is mainly a debt to our persisting, rather culture indifferent, human nature. As argued here earlier, it seems to this author that it makes more sense than not to identify and argue for a strategic, as well as a political common sense that is not disciplined by the constraints of particular periods with their confining limitations. While suitably respectful of historical subject expertise, I have also become concerned lest human nature and some of its leading characteristics all but disappear from view amidst the ever rich detail of time, place and circumstance. In those regards, there is need for more attention to be paid by historical scholars to the changes in culture of several kinds (e.g. moral, political, strategic), as contrasted somewhat to the more obvious shifts in circumstance.

4 Historical context

Strategy and Politics is a book written beyond the bounds of historical narrative, but certainly not at all indifferent to it. Unsurprisingly, the twentieth century served up ample evidence encouraging change of most varieties. Attitudes and opinions recorded cultural change in abundance, in some leading cases with regard to erstwhile hegemonic state leaders of International Order. Not unreasonably, a book such as this that has striven to be relaxed about the pertinence of historical context may appear to be unwisely relaxed also about the relevance of historical context for the meaning commonly assigned at the time to events that could lend themselves to a variety of interpretations. While I have not sought energetically to identify contextual differences for politics and strategy, I have nonetheless been alert to the possibility of major shifts in understanding and ascribed meanings.

I have found that at the admittedly high level employed in part by Thucydides and also by Clausewitz, there has been a somewhat surprising substantial continuity of human nature, and political and strategic experience, not much confounded by the contextual detail of the periods in question. To say this is not to claim that nothing of great moment altered. But it is to claim that a close reading of both the Athenian and the Prussian authors should not lead even the hasty reader far astray. Certainly it is true to argue that much, indeed probably most, of the meaning to events is provided by their historical placement. The challenge to our understanding, though, is to be able to determine how great a cause and consequence are attributable to a particular context. As a general rule, historical context yields the vital meaning to events. Bereft of context, we tend to have difficulty understanding what particular events may mean. Intelligence agencies always are poring over contextual detail in order to aid their interpretation of the implications of change. Relatively few potentially significant events prove to be all but self-interpreting, naked of contextual assistance as a vital aid to understanding. For

160   *Strategic future*

a contemporary example, make what we will of Vladimir Putin's foreign (and domestic) policy, that effort cannot sensibly be unravelled for comprehension if we fail to attempt to grasp the policy path pursued both for the past decade and in the 1990s before this recent period. The historical context for Putin's land grasp in Crimea is gross state failure under Gorbachev followed by a decade of economic and financial chaos.

A common challenge for the scholar is to decide just how attentive he needs to be to yesterday's events and their consequences. Indeed, it may aid our understanding more than a little if we are able to grasp the historical reality of the unique path of history as comprising truly a great stream of time (Neustadt and May, 1986). It can be expedient for scholars to visualize the past as flowing in a near continuous stream, but it is most important that we do not forget that today's, also yesterday's, events have to be the outcome of forces and developments in times past. It is a common dilemma for historians to be seriously uncertain, for excellent reasons, about where to begin their narratives in the stream of time. How far back should we go in order to be sufficiently sure that issues and trends still unresolved today did not change or corrupt a course of history that might have been attempted otherwise?

5 *Surprise*

Little, if anything, should be surprising about strategy and its politics, but in practice as well as sometimes in theory, surprises do happen. The rapidity of Germany's return to the slim ranks of great powers was a surprise to many in the early and mid-1930s, while the Russian Federation today gives some appearance of shaping its policy and strategy while its leader has been on steroids. This book devotes a chapter to the important topic of defence planning, because non-permissive lead times on advanced military equipment today have to mean that errors in those departments could not be corrected readily. It is an inconvenient and uncorrectable truth that reliable information about the future cannot be available from that future. It has to follow that our defence analysts and would-be futurists, no matter how supposedly expert, simply can do no better than with guesswork. That may be superior guesswork, but it cannot possibly be reckoned as reliable. It is for that reason I seek to insist upon historical understanding on the Michael Howard model, requiring empathetic study in width, depth and context (Howard, 1983: 215–17). Above all else, it should not rest upon particular predictions that would easily be falsified as a result of very few changes in key variables.

The strategic future is unknowable in what could well prove to be some vital detail, but nonetheless our politicians and officials are obliged to attempt to try and know what is reliably unknowable. The best, albeit distinctly imperfect, method known to this author is to seek a broad understanding of how politicians and functioning strategists typically have behaved in somewhat like contexts in the past (Gray, 2014a). Seriously to be avoided are efforts to 'pick a winner' among an array of political and strategy options that an adversary could be willing to test. Needless to say, perhaps, it is difficult to resist definitional discipline with respect to surprise. If an event or other development is defined as being surprising, it is not very enlightening to resist the logic in the common meaning of language and somehow convey the idea that the surprise in question was not really all that surprising after all. Rather than pursue that futile path, I prefer to suggest we attempt to understand the nature of the event at issue and strive to place it amidst other generically like happenings, comprehended functionally in terms that make strategic sense to us. What is to be avoided if at all possible is discrete choice of a favourite option or scenario. All too obviously no one adversary option is likely to emerge as the 'winner', meaning that we need broad, as opposed to narrow, coverage of unwelcome events (Gray, 2014b).

What we do know from the strategic history of all periods is that 'surprise happens' and that we cannot possibly insure ourselves strategically in all respects. That granted, we are obliged to try to be sufficiently correct so that we might adapt and adjust to unexpectedly shifting times and circumstances.

Conclusion: strategic history

It has been a fair sized challenge to write a book resting on the belief in the essentially unchanging nature of such basic factors as politics, human nature, and strategy. All the while I have recorded faith in the ability and general willingness of human beings to adhere to enduring functional behaviours. *Strategy and Politics* has trekked through much troublesome terrain, endeavouring to keep focus on the central relationship selected as organizing concepts for this venture. The relationship between strategy and politics is not in serious doubt, not in principle at least. However, strategic practice can prove a more testing matter, as strategists and their political masters sometimes have chosen to pursue an expedient military course that, they hope, will obviate the necessity for conflicted and therefore difficult strategic choice. However, above all else this book has sought to explain the reasons why politics always must be the master in the relationship. The undoubted fact that policy and its underlying politics is not always allowed the guiding role in strategy should be taken as a warning, not as advice. As a matter fundamental to its definition, war and its warfare must be about politics.

Key points

Politics must always rule over strategy.

Further reading

Gray, C. S. (2010a) *The Strategy Bridge: Theory for Practice*, Oxford: Oxford University Press.

Gray, C. S. (2014c) *Strategy and Defence Planning: Meeting the Challenge of Uncertainty*, Oxford: Oxford University Press.

Key terms

Atomic weapons   Weapons that derive their energy from the process of nuclear fission.

BEF   British Expeditionary Force.

CBO   The Combined Bomber Offensive conducted by the UK's RAF Bomber Command attacking Germany at night, and the US Army Air Forces attacking by day. Agreed at the Casablanca summit between Roosevelt and Churchill in January 1943.

C4ISTAR   Command, control, communications, computing, intelligence, surveillance, targeting and reconnaissance.

Clausewitz, Carl von (1780–1831)   Author of *On War* (1832), the most widely respected work on the theory of war ever written.

COIN   Counterinsurgency.

Collective security   The principle that an aggressor state should be opposed by the entire international community (all for one, and one for all!).

Combined-arms warfare   The theory that every military asset fulfils its potential when employed in combination with other assets (together we are stronger!).

Concert System   The occasional nineteenth-century practice of summit-level, or near-summit-level, meetings by great powers, where they would concert efforts to maintain or restore international order.

Containment   The fundamental concept underpinning US foreign policy towards the Soviet Union during the Cold War.

Coup d'oeil   An instantaneous, perhaps instinctive, grasp of a complex and confused military situation.

CT   Counter-terrorism.

Culture   The beliefs, values, attitudes, habits of mind and preferred practices of a community.

Détente   The relaxation of tensions; a term that was first popular in the 1970s.

EMS   Electromagnetic Spectrum.

Extended deterrence   The extending of protection by (generally) nuclear deterrence over distant friends and allies.

First-strike bonus   The predicted military benefit that should accrue to the belligerent who attacks first with nuclear weapons.

Fleet train   The at-sea logistic fleet provided to support the combat navy.

Geopolitics   The political meaning of geography.

Globalization   The process of ever-greater global interaction among states, communities and economies.

Grand strategy   The purposeful employment of all the instruments of power available to a security community.

Great Depression   Collapse of much of international commerce following the Wall Street Crash of 29 October 1929, and its consequences in sharply reduced economic activity and high unemployment.

Great War   A war involving all, or at least most, of the world's great powers.

Guerrilla warfare   A style of warfare waged by the weaker belligerent, favouring surprise and small-scale engagements.

Hybrid war   War waged in different styles, separately and in combination.

Hydrogen, or thermonuclear, weapons   Nuclear weapons that require the fusion of two isotopes of hydrogen. This is achieved by implosion effected by an atomic fission 'trigger'.

ICBM   Intercontinental ballistic missile (4,000-mile range or more).

Insurgency   A popular uprising, probably employing the tactics of guerrilla warfare, initially at least aiming to unseat the sitting government.

International community   The notional collectivity of all humankind, with the UN currently its rough approximation.

Irregular warfare   Warfare in which at least one belligerent is not a state with regular armed forces, and/or warfare conducted in a guerrilla style.

ISIS   Islamic State of Iraq and Syria.

Joint warfare   Warfare as a joint endeavour by two or more of the geographically specialized forces: army, navy, and air force (and now orbital-space and cyber as well).

Jomini, Baron Antoine Henri de (1779–1869)   The most influential military writer of the first half of the nineteenth century, especially with respect to strategy.

League of Nations   International organization established by the Versailles Treaty of 1919 for the purpose of keeping, or restoring, international order and peace.

Manoeuvre warfare   A style of combat dependent upon mobility; usually contrasted with attrition.

Military revolution (MR)   Great change in the contexts of warfare that cannot be resisted. Examples include the Industrial Revolution, the Nuclear Revolution and the Information Revolution.

Military-technical revolution (MTR)   A revolution in military affairs driven by technological change.

Mutual assured destruction (MAD)   A condition of mutual societal vulnerability to nuclear destruction.

Operations/operational art   The conduct of a campaign, requiring the employment of tactical engagements and other behaviour for their campaign-level effects.

Peer competitor   A country or coalition sufficiently powerful to be one's near equal.

Pre-emption/prevention   A strategy of pre-emption entails a commitment to strike first in the last resort. By contrast, a strategy of prevention entails a readiness to strike first in order to prevent the presumptive enemy from being ready to initiate hostilities on its terms.

Regular warfare   Open warfare between the uniformed armed forces of states.

Reparation   A bill for the recovery of costs suffered by the actions of the defeated belligerent in war. The bill may be augmented by a penalty amount (indemnity) intended to punish a defeated belligerent for its sins – just for losing.

Revolution in military affairs (RMA)   A radical change in the character of warfare.

164   *Key terms*

SALT (Strategic Arms Limitation Talks)   Soviet–American arms control process from 1969 to 1979. A SALT I package in 1972 included an interim agreement on offensive arms and the Anti-Ballistic Missile (ABM) Treaty. It led to a SALT II treaty in 1979, which was politically infeasible as the political context deteriorated sharply.

Schlieffen Plan   The German plan to defeat France in a six-week campaign. It was implemented as the Schlieffen–Moltke Plan (having been amended by Moltke the Younger, Schlieffen's successor) in August–September 1914: it failed.

Sea lines of communication   Imaginary lines at sea which mark the most important maritime routes.

Special Forces   Small elite units trained to undertake tasks beyond the scope of normal military competence.

Stability   A much-favoured quality in security politics, this refers to an absence of potentially dangerous change. Cold War strategic theory recognized crisis stability, deterrence stability and arms-race stability.

Strategic history   The history of the influence of the use, and threat of use, of politically motivated force.

Strategic moment   A particular short period assessed to be of extraordinary strategic importance and opportunity.

Strategy   The use made of force and the threat of force for the ends of policy as decided by politics. It is the bridge that connects politics and policy with military power.

Submarine-launched ballistic missiles (SLBMs)   Missiles deployed under the sea that are effectively invulnerable to detection.

Tactics   The use of armed forces in combat.

Terrorism   The use of violence to induce fear for political ends.

Total war   War waged with all the resources of belligerent societies.

Triad   The strategic forces triad comprises ICBMs, SLBMs, and manned bombers. Each 'leg' of the triad has distinctive tactical features.

Ungoverned space   Contemporary euphemism for 'bandit country', or territory that is not subject to effective governance.

War   Organized violence for political purposes.

Warfare   The waging of war; the fighting.

Weapons of mass destruction (WMD)   Nuclear, radiological, chemical, or biological weapons.

Bibliography

Arbella, A. (2008) *Soldiers of Reason: The RAND Corporation and the Rise of the American Empire*, Orlando, FL: Harcourt.

Aron, R. (1966) *Peace and War: A Theory of International Relations*, New York: Doubleday.

Bailey, J., Iron, R. and Strachan, H. (eds) (2013) *British Generals in Blair's Wars*, Farnham: Ashgate.

Barnett, R. W. (2009) *Navy Culture: Why the Navy Thinks Differently*, Annapolis, MD: Naval Institute Press.

Barrass, G. S. (2009) *The Great Cold War: A Journey Through the Hall of Mirrors*, Stanford, CA: Stanford University Press.

Baylis, J., Wirtz, J. and Gray, C. S. (eds) (2015) *Strategy in the Contemporary World: An Introduction to Strategic Studies*, 5th edn, Oxford: Oxford University Press.

Bisley, N. (2012) *Great Powers in the Changing International Order*, Boulder, CO: Lynne Rienner Publishers.

Black, J. (2009) *War: A Short History*, London: Continuum.

Black, J. (2012) *War and the Cultural Turn*, Cambridge: Polity Press.

Booth, K. (1979) *Strategy and Ethnocentrism*, London: Croom Helm.

Booth, K. (2007) *Theory of World Security*, Cambridge: Cambridge University Press.

Booth, K. and Wheeler, N. J. (2008) *The Security Dilemma: Fear, Cooperation and Trust in World Politics*, Basingstoke: Palgrave Macmillan.

Brodie, B. (1973) *War and Politics*, New York: Macmillan.

Bull, H. (1997) *The Anarchical Society: A Study of Order in World Politics*, New York: Columbia University Press.

Bungay, S. (2000) *The Most Dangerous Enemy: A History of the Battle of Britain*, London: Aurum Press.

Burleigh, M. (2010) *Moral Combat: A History of World War II*, London: Harper Press.

Churchill, W. (1938) *The World Crisis, 1911–1918*, London: Odhams Press.

Cimbala, S. (ed.) (2012) *Civil-Military Relations in Perspective: Strategy, Structure and Policy*, Farnham: Ashgate.

Clark, C. (2012) *The Sleepwalkers: How Europe Went to War in 1914*, London: Allen Lane.

Clausewitz, C. von (1976) *On War*, ed. and trans. Howard, M. and Paret, P., Princeton, NJ: Princeton University Press.

Coates, A. J. (1997) *The Ethics of War*, Manchester: Manchester University Press.

Cohen, E. A. (2002) *Supreme Command: Soldiers, Statesmen, and Leadership in Wartime*, New York: Free Press.

Coker, C. (2008) *Ethics and War in the 21st Century*, Abingdon: Routledge.

Creveld, M. van (2008) *The Culture of War*, New York: Ballantine Books.

Davis, P. K. (ed.) (1994) *New Challenges for Defense Planning: Rethinking How Much is Enough*, MR–4–RC, Santa Monica, CA: RAND.

166 *Bibliography*

Echevarria, A. J., II (2014) *Reconsidering the American Way of War: U.S. Military Practice from the Revolution to Afghanistan*, Washington, DC: Georgetown University Press.

Elliott, C. L. (2015) *High Command: British Military Leadership in the Iraq and Afghanistan Wars*, London: C. Hurst.

Enthoven, A. C. and Smith, K. W. (2005) *How Much Is Enough? Shaping the Defense Program, 1961–1969*, Santa Monica, CA: RAND.

Etzold, T. H. and Gaddis, J. L. (eds) (1978) *Containment: Documents on American Policy and Strategy, 1945–1950*, New York: Columbia University Press.

Farrell, T. (2005) *The Norms of War: Cultural Beliefs and Modern Conflict*, Boulder, CO: Lynne Rienner Publishers.

Finlan, A. (2008) *Special Forces, Strategy and the War on Terror*, Abingdon: Routledge.

Fisher, D. (2011) *Morality and War: Can War be Just in the Twenty-First Century?* Oxford: Oxford University Press.

France, J. (2011) *Perilous Glory: The Rise of Western Military Power*, New Haven, CT: Yale University Press.

Freedman, L. (2006) *The Transformation of Strategic Affairs*, Adelphi Paper 379, London: International Institute for Strategic Studies.

Freedman, L. (2013) *Strategy: A History*, Oxford: Oxford University Press.

French, D. (1990) *The British Way in Warfare, 1688–2000*, London: Unwin Hyman.

Frieser, K. H. (2005) *The Blitzkrieg Legend: The 1940 Campaign in the West*, Annapolis, MD: Naval Institute Press.

Fuller, W. C., Jr. (1992) *Strategy and Power in Russia, 1600–1914*, New York: Free Press.

Gaddis, J. L. (1982) *Strategies of Containment: A Critical Appraisal of Postwar American National Security Policy*, New York: Oxford University Press.

Gat, A. (2006) *War in Human Civilization*, Oxford: Oxford University Press.

Geertz, C. (1973) *The Interpretation of Culture*, New York: Basic Books.

Gentile, G. (2013) *Wrong Turn: America's Deadly Embrace of Counterinsurgency*, New York: The New Press.

Gooch, J. (1994) *The Plans of War: The General Staff and British Military Strategy c.1900–1916*, London: Routledge and Kegan Paul.

Gray, C. S. (1982) *Strategic Studies and Public Policy: The American Experience*, Lexington, KY: University Press of Kentucky.

Gray, C. S. (1992) *Why Arms Control Must Fail*, Ithaca, NY: Cornell University Press.

Gray, C. S. (1993) *Weapons Don't Make War: Policy, Strategy, and Military Technology*, Lawrence, KS: University Press of Kansas.

Gray, C. S. (1999) *Modern Strategy*, Oxford: Oxford University Press.

Gray, C. S. (2005) *Transformation and Strategic Surprise*, Carlisle, PA: Strategic Studies Institute, US Army War College.

Gray, C. S. (2007) *The Implications of Preemptive and Preventive War Doctrine*, Carlisle, PA: Strategic Studies Institute, US Army War College.

Gray, C. S. (2009) *Fighting Talk: Forty Maxims on War, Peace, and Strategy*, Westport, CT: Praeger Security International.

Gray, C. S. (2010a) *The Strategy Bridge: Theory for Practice*, Oxford: Oxford University Press.

Gray, C. S. (2010b) 'Strategic Thoughts for Defence Planners', *Survival*, 52: 159–178.

Gray, C. S. (2012) *War, Peace and International Relations: An Introduction to Strategic History*, 2nd edn. Abingdon: Routledge.

Gray, C. S. (2013) *Perspectives on Strategy*, Oxford: Oxford University Press.

Gray, C. S. (2014a) 'Strategy and Culture', in Mahnken, T. G. and Blumenthal, D. (eds) *Strategy in Asia: The Past, Present and Future of Regional Security*, Stanford, CA: Stanford University Press.

Gray, C. S. (2014b) 'Dowding and the British Strategy of Air Defense, 1936–1940', in Murray, W. and Sinnreich, R. H. (eds) *Successful Strategies: Triumphing in War and Peace from Antiquity to the Present*, Cambridge: Cambridge University Press.

Gray, C. S. (2014c) *Strategy and Defence Planning: Meeting the Challenge of Uncertainty*, Oxford: Oxford University Press.

Gray, C. S. (2015a) 'Nicholas John Spykman, the Balance of Power and International Order', *Journal of Strategic Studies*, June, http://www.tandfonline.com/doi/full/10.1080/01402390.2015. 1018412#abstract (accessed 13 July 2015).

Gray, C. S. (2015b) *The Future of Strategy*, Cambridge: Polity Press.

Great Britain, H. M. Government (October 2010) *Securing Britain in an Age of Uncertainty: The Strategic Defence and Security Review, Cm 7948*, London: HM Stationery Office. https://www. gov.uk/government/uploads/system/uploads/attachment_data/file/62482/strategic-defence-secur ity-review.pdf (accessed 13 July 2015).

Grygiel, J. (2013) 'Educating for National Security', *Orbis*, 57: 201–216.

Guthrie, C. and Quinlan, M. (2007) *Just War: The Just War Tradition: Ethics in Modern Warfare*, London: Bloomsbury Publishing.

Hamilton, R. F. and Herwig, H. H. (eds) (2010) *War Planning 1914*, Cambridge: Cambridge University Press.

Handel, M. I. (2001) *Masters of War: Classical Strategic Thought*, 3rd edn, London: Frank Cass.

Hanson, V. D. (2001) *Why the West Has Won: Carnage and Culture from Salamis to Vietnam*, London: Faber and Faber.

Hattendorf, J. B., Veenendaal, A. J., Jr. and Westerflier, R. van Hovell tot (eds) (2012) *Marlborough: Soldier and Diplomat*, Rotterdam: Karwansaray.

Hennessy, M. A. (1997) *Strategy in Vietnam: The Marines and Revolutionary Warfare in 1 Corps, 1965–1972*, Westport, CT: Praeger.

Herbig, K. L. (1986) 'Chance and Uncertainty in *On War*', in Handel, M. (ed.) *Clausewitz and Modern Strategy*, London: Frank Cass, pp. 95–116.

Herwig, H. H. (1980) *'Luxury' Fleet: The Imperial German Navy, 1888–1918*, London: George and Unwin.

Heuser, B. (2010) *The Evolution of Strategy: Thinking War from Antiquity to the Present*, Cambridge: Cambridge University Press.

Howard, M. (1983) *The Causes of Wars and Other Essays*, London: Counterpoint.

Howard, M. (1991) *The Lessons of History*, New Haven, CT: Yale University Press.

Howard, M. (2001) *The Invention of Peace and the Re-invention of War*, London: Profile Books.

Huntington, S. P. (1957) *The Soldier and the State: The Theory and the Politics of Civil–Military Relations*, Cambridge, MA: Harvard University Press.

Johnston, A. I. (1995) *Cultural Realism: Strategic Culture and Grand Strategy in Chinese History*, Ithaca, NY: Cornell University Press.

Johnson, J. L. (May 2013) *Assessing the Strategic Impact of Service Culture on Counterinsurgency Operations: Case: United States Marine Corps*, unpub. PhD diss, Reading: University of Reading.

Johnson, R. (2011) *The Afghan Way of War: Culture and Pragmatism: A Critical History*, London: C. Hurst.

Kahn, H. (1960) *On Thermonuclear War*, Princeton, NJ: Princeton University Press.

Kane, T. M. (2013) *Strategy: Key Thinkers: A Critical Engagement*, Cambridge: Polity Press.

Katzenstein, P. J. (ed.) (1996) *The Culture of National Security: Norms and Identity in World Politics*, New York: Columbia University Press.

Kelly, J. and Brennan, M. (2009) *Alien: How Operational Art Devoured Strategy*, Carlisle, PA: US Army War College.

Kennedy, D. (2006) *War and Law*, Princeton, NJ: Princeton University Press.

Kennedy, P. (ed.) (1979) *The War Plans of the Great Powers, 1880–1914*, London: George Allen and Unwin.

168 *Bibliography*

Kent, G. A. (2008) *Thinking about America's Defense: An Analytical Memoir*, Santa Monica, CA: RAND.

Kissinger, H. (2014) *World Order: Reflections on the Character of Nations and the Course of History*, London: Allen Lane.

Krepinevich, A. F., Jr. (2009) *7 Deadly Scenarios: A Military Futurist Explores War in the 21st Century*, New York: Bantam Books.

Krulak, C. (1999) 'The Strategic Corporal: Leadership in the Three-Block War', *Marines Magazine*, 28: 28–34.

Lasswell, H. D. (1936) *Politics: Who Gets What, When, How?* New York: Whittlesey House.

Lawrence, T. E. (1991) *Seven Pillars of Wisdom: A Triumph*, New York: Anchor Books.

Libicki, M. C. (2009) *Cyberdeterrence and Cyberwar*, Santa Monica, CA: RAND.

Luttwak, E. N. (2001) *Strategy: The Logic of War and Peace*, new edn, Cambridge, MA: Harvard University Press.

McChrystal, S. (2015) *My Share of the Task: A Memoir*, New York: Portfolio/Penguin.

McInnes, C. (2002) *Spectator-Sport War: The West and Contemporary Conflict*, Boulder, CO: Lynne Rienner Publishers.

Mackinder, H. J. (1962) *Democratic Ideals and Reality*, New York: W. W. Norton.

McMahan, J. (2009) *Killing in War*, Oxford: Clarendon Press.

Macmillan, M. (2001) *Peacemakers: The Paris Peace Conference of 1919 and Its Attempt to End War*, London: John Murray.

Mahnken, T. G. and Maiolo, J. A. (eds) (2014) *Strategic Studies: A Reader*, 2nd edn, Abingdon: Routledge.

Marx, K. and Engels, F. (1962) 'The Eighteenth Brumaire of Louis Napoleon', in Marx, K. and Engels, F. *Selected Works in Two Volumes*, Vol. 1, Moscow: Foreign Languages Publishing House.

Mawdsley, E. (2005) *Thunder in the East: The Nazi–Soviet War, 1941–1945*, London: Hodder Arnold.

Mearsheimer, J. J. (2014) *The Tragedy of Great Power Politics*, upd. edn. New York: W. W. Norton.

Murray, W. (2011) *Military Adaptation in War: With Fear of Change*, Cambridge: Cambridge University Press.

Murray, W. and Grimsley, M. (1994) 'Introduction: On Strategy', in Murray, W., Knox, M. and Bernstein, A. (eds), *The Making of Strategy: Rulers, States, and War*, Cambridge: Cambridge University Press.

Murray, W., Knox, M. and Bernstein, A. (eds) (1994) *The Making of Strategy: Rulers, States, and War*, Cambridge: Cambridge University Press.

Murray, W., Sinnreich, R. H. and Lacey, J. (eds) (2011) *The Shaping of Grand Strategy: Policy, Diplomacy, and War*, Cambridge: Cambridge University Press.

Murray, W. and Sinnreich, R. H. (eds) (2014) *Successful Strategies: Triumphing in War and Peace from Antiquity to the Present*, Cambridge: Cambridge University Press.

Neustadt, R. E. and May, E. R. (eds) (1986) *Thinking in Time: The Uses of History for Decision-Makers*, New York: Free Press.

Olsen, J. A. and van Creveld, M. (2011) *The Evolution of Operational Art: From Napoleon to the Present*, Oxford: Oxford University Press.

Otte, T. G. and Neilson, K. (eds) (2006) *Railways and International Politics: Paths of Empire, 1848–1945*, Abingdon: Routledge.

Paret, P. (ed.) (1986) *Makers of Modern Strategy: From Machiavelli to the Nuclear Age*, Princeton, NJ: Princeton University Press.

Pinker, S. (2011) *The Better Angels of Our Nature: The Decline of Violence in History and its Causes*, London: Allen Lane.

Porter, P. (2009) *Military Orientalism: Eastern War Through Western Eyes*, London: C. Hurst.

Porter, P. (2015) *The Global Village Myth: Distance, War and the Limits of Power*, London: C. Hurst.

Quade, E. S. and Boucher, W. I. (eds) (1964) *Analysis for Military Decisions: The RAND Lectures on Systems Analysis*, New York: RAND McNully.

Ricks, T. E. (2009) *The Gamble: General Petraeus and the Untold Story of the American Surge in Iraq, 2006–2008*, London: Penguin Books.

Rid, T. (2013) *Cyber War Will Not Take Place*, London: C. Hurst.

Rosen, S. P. (2005) *War and Human Nature*, Princeton, NJ: Princeton University Press.

Ryan, A. (2012) *On Politics: A History of Political Thought from Herodotus to the Present*, London: Allen Lane.

Schelling, T. (1960) *The Strategy of Conflict*, Cambridge, MA: Harvard University Press.

Schilling, W. R., Hammond, P.Y. and Snyder, G. H. (1962) *Strategy, Politics, and Defense Budgets*, New York: Columbia University Press.

Shaw, M. N. (2008) *International Law*, 6th edn, Cambridge: Cambridge University Press.

Simms, B. (2013) *Europe: The Struggle for Supremacy, 1453 to the Present*, London: Allen Lane.

Simpson, E. (2012) *War from the Ground Up: Twenty-First-Century Combat as Politics*, London: C. Hurst.

Smith, J.E. (2012) *Eisenhower in War and Peace*, New York: Random House.

Smith, M. L. R. (2014) 'Politics and Passion: The Neglected Mainspring of War', *Infinity Journal*, 4/2: 32–36.

Smith, R. (2005) *The Utility of Force: The Art of War in the Modern World*, London: Allen Lane.

Sondhaus, L. (2006) *Strategic Culture and Ways of War*, Abingdon: Routledge.

Spykman, N. J. (1938) 'Geography and Foreign Policy', *American Political Science Review*, 32(2): 213–236.

Spykman, N. J. ([1942] 2007) *America's Strategy in World Politics: The United States and the Balance of Power*, New Brunswick, NJ: Transaction.

Spykman, N.J. ([1944] 1969) *The Geography of the Peace*, Hamden, CT: Archon Books.

Stevenson, D. (2006) 'Strategic and Military Planning, 1871–1914', in Imlay, T. C. and Toft, D. (eds) *The Fog of Peace and War Planning: Military and Strategic Planning under Uncertainty*, Abingdon: Routledge, pp. 75–99.

Stoker, D. (2010) *The Grand Design: Strategy and the U.S. Civil War*, Oxford: Oxford University Press.

Stoker, D. (2014) *Clausewitz: His Life and Work*, Oxford: Oxford University Press.

Strachan, H. (2007) *Clausewitz's On War: A Biography*, New York: Atlantic Monthly Press.

Strachan, H. (2013) *The Direction of War: Contemporary Strategy in Historical Perspective*, Cambridge: Cambridge University Press.

Svechin, A. R. ([1927] 1992) *Strategy*, Minneapolis, MN: East View Information Services.

Taleb, N. N. (2007) *The Black Swan: The Impact of the Highly Improbable*, New York: Random House.

Thucydides (1996) *The Landmark Thucydides: A Comprehensive Guide to The Peloponnesian War*, ed. Strassler, R. B., trans. Crawley, R., rev. edn, New York: Free Press.

Till, C. (2009) *Seapower: A Guide to the Twenty-First Century*, Abingdon: Routledge.

Tzu, S. (1963) *The Art of War*, trans. Griffith, S. B., Oxford: Clarendon Press.

Vasquez, J. A. (2009) *The War Puzzle Revisited*, Cambridge: Cambridge University Press.

Walzer, M. (1977) *Just and Unjust Wars: A Moral Argument with Historical Illustrations*, 3rd edn, New York: Basic Books.

Williams, P. D. (ed.) (2013) *Security Studies: An Introduction*, 2nd edn, Abingdon: Routledge.

Winters, W. (1998) *Battling the Elements: Weather and Terrain in the Conduct of War*, Baltimore, MD: Johns Hopkins University Press.

170   Bibliography

Winton, H. R. (2011) 'An Imperfect Jewel: Military Theory and the Military Profession', *Journal of Strategic Studies*, 34: 853–897.

Yarger, H. R. (2008) *Strategy and the National Security Professional: Strategic Thinking and Strategy Formulation in the 21st Century*, Westport, CT: Praeger Security International.

Yoder, J. H. (2009) *Christian Attitudes to War, Peace, and Revolutions*, Grand Rapids, MI: Brazos Press.

Zabecki, D. T. (ed.) (2006) *Chief of Staff: The Principal Officers Behind History's Great Commanders*, 2 Vols. Annapolis, MD: Naval Institute Press.

Index

Act of Union (1707) 90
adaptability 75, 76–7
Afghanistan, British and American experiences in (2000s) 1, 4, 24, 37, 42, 43, 63, 69, 73, 86, 87, 103, 129; civil–military relations 112, 114, 115, 121, 122, 123, 124
air force 54, 64
Alaska 83
Alexander of Macedon 92
Alexander the Great 17
ambiguity, political convenience 151–2
American Civil War (1861–5) 38, 51, 70, 83, 87, 112, 121; Gettysburg battle (1863) 84, 86, 122
Anarchical Society, The (Bull) 30
Angles 90
Anti-Ballistic Missile (ABM) Treaty 163
armed forces 3, 11, 16, 59, 64, 115, 131, 143; history and geography 87, 90; power and passion 15, 16; and war 30, 40, 42; *see also* conflict; force; war
arms control 62, 73, 150, 151, 164; *see also* nuclear weapons; weapons
assumptions 2, 5, 6, 7, 8, 24, 115, 127; for Britain 71–4; defence planning 134, 135; political 55, 115, 135; politics, power and security 14, 16; strategy-making 64, 65, 69, 70, 71–4, 75, 77; theory for practice 54, 55, 58
asymmetry 30, 50, 87, 119
Athens, ancient 147, 159
atomic weapons 162
authority 18, 19

balance of power 12, 15, 27; military power 26
'bandit country' (ungoverned space) 163
Basra, Iraq 115–16
battle 37–41; *see also specific battles*
BEF (British Expeditionary Force) 123, 128, 162
Bethmann-Hollweg, Theobald von 103
Bismarck, Otto von 48
'Black Swan' events 76, 104, 137

blame 114–15, 117
'blowback' 115
Bolshevik Republic 88
Bonaparte, Napoleon 47, 51, 58, 77
Brezhnev, Leonid 87, 89
Britain: Afghanistan and Iraq, intervention in 1, 4, 24, 37, 42, 43, 69, 73, 103, 114, 115, 123, 129; Army 65, 114; and China 73; conscription 99; in eighteenth century 20; Empire 15, 16, 72, 82, 85, 93; and First World War 15, 25, 65, 133, 146; geography 90, 93; history 90–1; national security concept 55; political-military ineptitude 115–16; Royal Air Force 51; and Second World War 26, 33, 68, 91, 93, 99, 133, 150–1; statecraft and strategy 25; strategy-making 68, 71–5; War Studies 36
British Expeditionary Force (BEF) 123, 128, 162
Bull, Hedley 30

C4ISTAR 162
Caesar, Julius 17
cards, war as game of 27
CBO (Combined Bomber Offensive) 162
Central Europe 85, 152
chain of command 111–13
Chamberlain, Neville 33
charisma 68
Charter of United Nations 30
Chernenko, Konstantin 89
Chicago School 7
Chilcot, Sir John/Chilcot Enquiry 116
China 72–3, 76; Taiping Rebellion (1850–64) 38
Churchill, Sir John (Duke of Marlborough) 12, 17, 39, 91, 124
Churchill, Winston 2, 9, 13, 68, 152
circumstance 96, 98; as context 105; discipline of 101–7; *see also* culture
civilians, violence against 143
civil–military relations 111–25; chain of command 111–13; challenges for politicians

172 *Index*

and strategists 113–19; context of strategy 119–20; cooperation, competition and conflict 116, 117, 120–1; enduring structure 118–19; operational consumption of strategy 121–3; politics and human nature 118–19; prudence concept 113, 114, 115, 116, 117, 120, 121, 123; relations of power and blame 114–15, 117; and tribal loyalties 116–18; ubiquity challenge 114; unequal dialogue 120, 121; United States 115–16, 119, 121, 122; and war 23, 24, 45; *see also* military strategy

civil wars 38, 50; *see also* American Civil War (1861–5)

Clark, Alan 154

Clausewitz, Carl von 4, 6, 11, 24, 27, 41, 44, 57, 66, 70, 142, 159, 162; and defence planning 131, 132, 135, 136; on 'grammar' and 'logic' of war 40, 42, 46, 54, 132, 138; and moral forces 14, 15, 17, 18, 32; and theory for practice 60, 61; *On War* 7, 45, 47, 131, 157

climate of war 41

Cohen, Elliott A. 87, 111, 120, 136

COIN (counterinsurgency) 151, 162

Cold War (1946–90) 1, 2, 26, 27, 38, 72, 83, 91, 152; Post-Cold-War Europe 147; *see also* Soviet Union, former; superpowers; United States

collective security 162

Collins, Michael 27, 31

combined-arms warfare 162

Combined Bomber Offensive (CBO) 162

command and control 42, 59, 99

Commander in Chief of the armed forces, US President as 84

committee, strategy by 68

competence 5, 13, 34, 47, 54, 68, 86, 124; strategic 19, 24–5, 27, 45, 67, 113

conceptual construction, strategic theory as 52

Concert System 162

conflict vii, 4, 155, 159; accidental 153; armed 32, 38, 127, 132, 136, 137, 138; civil–military relations 114, 118, 119, 120; defence planning 128, 131, 132, 134–5; history and geography 87, 92; internal 151; land 58; nuclear 139; politics, power and security 11, 18, 20; protracted 40; strategy-making 66, 70; theory for practice 53, 54, 56, 59, 60; and war 32, 37, 42, 43, 48; *see also* armed forces; violence; war

conscription 99

containment 162

context: circumstance 105; civil–military relations 119–20; concept 79, 80; cultural 95–6, 108; historical 20–1, 159–60;

permissive 149–50; political 24–6; power of 79–80; strategy/strategy-making 69–71, 79, 119–20, 143; war 26, 40

counterinsurgency (COIN) 151, 162

counter-terrorism (CT) 162

coup d'oeil 162

Crimea 146–7, 160

Crusaders 136

CT (counter-terrorism) 162

Cuban Missile Crisis 89

cultural turn 101, 102

culture: American 100; boundaries, undefinable 103–4; and circumstance 96, 98; and common sense 101; concept 96, 97, 102, 107, 108; context 95–6, 108; debates 97; defined 162; domestic political pull of 98–9; evidence 96, 97–8, 104, 107, 109; existentiality and unavoidability 97; influence 98; and necessity 103; pervasiveness 98, 104–5; political 81, 144, 149, 153; and stereotyping 100–1; and strategy 95, 96, 97; uncertain evidence 103–4; uniformity in 117; unsettled argument 96–107

cyber power/cyber warfare 74

Danes 90

Dardanelles strait 2

Davis, Jefferson 51, 84

D-Day (Second World War) 13, 14, 69

defence planning 29, 70; difficulties 130–1; failure 134–7; function 126; future, unpredictability of 127–9; and politics 126–40; professional planners 130, 134–5; prudence concept 129, 131, 133, 134, 135, 139–40; uncertainty 126–7, 132, 133, 134, 135, 136, 137, 138

defence policy 70, 129

détente 162

deterrence 21, 74, 92, 99, 153; defence planning 128, 135; deterrent effect 137, 147; extended 162; nuclear 15, 62, 104

diplomacy 9, 60, 150; European 38; international 149; inter-state 39; missile 152; strategic 48

doctrine 7, 50, 51, 59

domestic law 30

Dowding, Sir Hugh 8, 50–1

drone strikes 142–3

Dumas, Alexander 58

E, W, M formula, strategy-making 66, 67

Eastern Europe 80–1, 85, 152

Echevarria, Antulio J. 106–7, 108

education 53, 59–61, 100

Eighteenth Brumaire of Louis Napoleon (Marx) 82

Eisenhower, General Dwight D. 13, 14, 44, 69, 152
Electromagnetic Spectrum (EMS) 162
electronic communications 26, 28
Elliott, Christopher 37
emotions 15, 16, 86
empathy 69, 101
empires: British 15, 16, 72, 82, 85, 93; French 16, 38; global 93, 154; Japanese 13, 92; maritime 92; Roman 7, 126; Russian 135, 137; Turkish 27, 38
EMS (Electromagnetic Spectrum) 162
ends, ways and means 11, 12, 24, 70
enemy, understanding 31–3
ethics, and security 153–4
Eurasia 72, 80, 82, 83, 88
European International Order 129
European Union (EU) 72, 99
European war 38, 39
evidence 2, 18, 29, 39, 45, 46, 48, 55, 62; absent 136, 139; culture 96, 97–8, 103–4, 104, 107, 109; empirical 44, 54, 64, 71, 81, 97–8, 99, 107, 127, 148; and future 136, 139, 148, 159; historical 7, 8, 44, 138, 145; and morality 145, 147–8, 151, 153, 154; reliable 144; sources 138; uncertain 103–4
expediency 150–1
expertise, tactical 58–9
extended deterrence 162

failure: defence planning 134–7; strategic 13, 86, 145
fanaticism 73
fear, motivation category (Thucydides) 3, 14, 15, 32, 42, 47, 48, 77, 147, 149, 159
fighting 18, 40, 58, 65, 86, 87, 112, 117, 132; fighting power 126, 129, 131, 140; see also war
first-strike bonus 162
First World War 1, 2, 6, 8, 26, 27, 38, 39, 103, 133, 146; Allies 128; Central Powers 2, 15, 128; history and geography 83, 85; politics, power and security 14, 25; and strategy-making 65, 70, 76; see also Second World War; war
fleet train 162
force 15, 23, 31, 131; see also violence, organized; war
forces: air force 54, 64; fighter 65; labour force 99; military 52, 66, 131, 133, 144; moral see moral forces; police force 30; see also armed forces
foreign behaviour 56
foreseeable future concept 71
France 33, 58, 72; Empire 16, 38
Freedman, Lawrence 12, 32
French Revolution 38
functional theory 52

Gallipoli Campaign (1915) 14
'Game of Thrones' 91
Gates, Robert 129
general strategic theory 7, 10, 74, 157–8; theory for practice 50, 51–4, 60, 63; and war 24, 44, 47; see also general theory; strategy; theory; theory and strategy
general theory 52, 53, 63; see also general strategic theory
genius 46–7; strategy-making 67–8, 69, 70
geography 20, 41, 52, 53, 54, 59, 109, 148; Britain 71, 72, 73, 90, 93; and history 79–94; international 81; physical 72, 79, 80, 81, 82, 83, 89–90, 91, 93, 107, 114; Poland 81; political 81, 91; psychological 104; Russia 80–1, 88, 90; strategic 82, 83, 92; United States 80, 82–3; see also history
geopolitics 162
Germany 33, 38, 39, 51, 81, 85, 120, 160; bombers 64–5; Soviet Operational-Manoeuvre Groups, North German plain 73; strategy-making 72, 74; see also Nazi Germany; Second World War
Gettysburg battle (1863), American Civil War 84, 86, 122
Gibraltar 90
global empire 93, 154
Global Village Myth, The (Porter) 8
Godwinsson, King Harold of Wessex 90, 124
'good enough' criterion/rule 1, 2, 3, 5, 62; defence planning 133, 135, 139; history and geography 86, 87; morality 150, 152, 154; politics, power and security 15, 16, 18, 21; strategy-making 64, 74, 77; and war 25, 31, 32, 43
Gorbachev, Mikhail 87, 89
governance process 67
'grammar' and 'logic' of war (Clausewitz) 40, 42, 46, 54, 132, 138
Grand Alliance 13, 69
grand strategy 3, 8, 56–7, 163; war 24, 34, 37
Grant, General Ulysses S. 112, 122
Great Britain see Britain
Great Depression 163
Great Patriotic War (1941–5) 88, 89
Great War see First World War
Grimsley, Mark 64
Grygiel, Jakub 136
Guderian, Heinz 134
guerrilla warfare 163
guilt 89

Harold, King 44
Hastings, Battle of (1066) 90
Hawaii 83
Hellenism 92

174 *Index*

Helmand Province, Afghanistan 114, 115, 124, 131
Herwig, Holger H. 87
Heydrich, Reinhardt 31
hierarchy 56, 67, 86, 87, 105, 116; of authority 37, 63; civil–military relations 120, 122; and war 33, 36–7
High Command 115
history: Britain 90–1; context, power of 79–80; evidence 7, 8, 44, 138, 145; and geography 79–94; learning from 25, 81, 103; political narrative 91–3; Russia 87–90; United States 83–7; *see also* strategic history
History of the Peloponnesian War (Thucydides) 4
Hitler, Adolf 16, 32, 33, 65, 68, 77, 86, 148; *see also* Nazi Germany
honour, motivation category (Thucydides) 14, 15, 32, 42, 47, 48, 77, 147, 149, 159
Howard, Michael 81, 82, 160
Huntington, Samuel P. 111, 115, 116
Hussein, Saddam 151
hybrid war 163
hydrogen (thermonuclear) weapons 163

ICBM (intercontinental ballistic missile) 163
imperialism 82, 85
Imperial Japan 60
incompetence in policy, strategy and tactics 25
Industrial Revolution 59
influence 15, 98, 108; and culture 104, 108
information technology (IT): globalized 28, 31; social media 56
insurgency 163
intelligence services 71
intention, and strategy 69
inter-categorical understanding 13, 24
interconnectivity of disciplines 11, 25, 36, 102
intercontinental ballistic missile (ICBM) 163
interest, motivation category (Thucydides) 14, 15, 32, 42, 47, 48, 77, 147, 149, 159
international community 26, 30, 103, 163
International Court of Justice 143
international crises 137, 145, 148
international law/order 30, 41, 129, 158, 159
Iraq, American and British experiences in (2000s) 1, 4, 24, 37, 42, 63, 69, 73, 86, 87, 103, 114, 129; civil–military relations 112, 115–16, 121, 122, 123
Irish Republican Army (IRA) 27
irregular war/warfare 27, 28, 30, 37, 142, 163
ISIS (Islamic State of Iraq and Syria) 30, 142, 163; *see also* Jihadists
Islamism 73, 76; *see also* ISIS (Islamic State of Iraq and Syria); Jihadists
IT *see* information technology (IT)

Japan 60, 69, 86; Empire 13, 92; Pearl Harbour attack (1941) 85, 92
Jihadists 30, 136
Johnston, Alastair Iain 97
joint warfare 54, 163
Jomini, Baron Antoine de 51, 163
Julius Caesar 17
Jutes 90

Kaiserschlacht 128
Kennedy, John F. 3, 121
Khrushchev, Nikita 87–8, 89, 152
Kosygin, Alexei 89
Kremlin, Russia 89, 96

labour force 99
Lasswell, Harold D. 3
Lawrence, T. E. 27
League of Nations 85, 163
Lee, Robert E. 17, 86, 122
Lenin, Vladimir 88
Leonidas, King of Sparta 50
Lettow-Vorbeck, Paul Emil von (Colonel) 27
limited war 41–3
Lincoln, Abraham 84, 112, 122
Louis XIV, King 15, 38
loyalties, tribal 116–18
Luftwaffe 51, 64, 73
Luttwak, Edward 8, 95

Mackinder, Sir Halford 83, 93
MacMillan, Harold 101
manoeuvre warfare 163
Marine Corps, US 115, 117
Marlborough, Duke of (Sir John Churchill) 12, 17, 39, 91, 124
Marx, Karl 82
Marxism–Leninism 88
material interest 15
McChrystal, General Stanley 3, 124
Meade, George 122
Mearsheimer, John J. 7
Medieval England 91
Meuse–Argonne Offensive (1918) 128
military behaviour vi, 3, 42, 50, 56, 67, 116, 119
military command 41–3
military forces 66, 131, 133, 144; theory for practice 52, 53; *see also* soldiers; war
military instruments 8, 25, 29, 31, 34; civil–military relations 117, 118
military means 6, 7–8, 13, 29, 53, 112; civil–military relations 115, 121; defence planning 127, 134; strategy-making 65, 66, 67, 77
military revolution (MR) 163

Index 175

military strategy 3, 13, 16, 71, 83; definitions 52–3; and function of theory 56–7; and war 24, 33, 37; *see also* strategy; strategy-making; war
military theory 27–8, 52, 111
Mongols 91
moral forces 6, 7, 32, 131, 144, 157; politics, power and security 10, 12, 14, 15, 16, 17, 18, 21
morality 141–55; ambiguity, political convenience 151–2; domestic approval or tolerance 152–3; ethically compliant behaviour 143; ethics and security 153–4; and evidence 145, 147–8, 151, 153, 154; expediency 150–1; moral forces *see* moral forces; moral standards and ethical guidance 142–4; permissive context 149–50; and political complications 146–7; principles 141, 154; prudence concept 150–1, 153, 154; and strategic history 141, 153; timing 147–8; values 144, 146
motivation categories (Thucydides) 3, 77; and morality 147, 149; politics, power and security 14, 15; strategic future 158–9; and war 32, 42, 47, 48
Munich Agreement (1938) 33
Murray, Williamson 64, 77, 133
mutual assured destruction (MAD) 163

Napoleonic Wars 58, 59; *see also* Bonaparte, Napoleon
national advantage 80
national security concept 55, 80, 97–8
NATO (North Atlantic Treaty Organization) 5, 33, 42, 62, 153; and culture 96, 99, 103; defence planning 129, 135, 137; history and geography 81, 85; and morality 145, 147; strategy-making 72, 74; Treaty of 1949 152
Nazi Germany 13, 16, 31, 41, 44, 60, 81; Great Patriotic War (1941–5) 88, 89; and strategy-making 64, 70; *see also* Hitler, Adolf; Luftwaffe; Second World War; Wehrmacht
necessity 103
net advantage and disadvantage, anticipatable 14
Nixon, Richard 88
Norman Conquest 90
North Atlantic Treaty Organization *see* NATO (North Atlantic Treaty Organization)
North Korea 2, 60
North Vietnamese Army (NVA) 60
nuclear deterrence 15, 62, 104
nuclear disarmament 73; campaign for 152–3

nuclear weapons 53, 88, 138, 152, 158, 162, 163; danger 142, 144; defence planning 137, 138; strategy-making 70, 73–4; and war 26, 27, 28, 29, 33, 47, 48; *see also* nuclear deterrence; nuclear disarmament; weapons

Obama, Barack 119, 124, 129
officer cadets 24
On War (Clausewitz) 7, 45, 47, 131, 157
operational command 18
operations/operational art 86, 163; strategy-making 65, 67, 70; theory for practice 51, 54, 58, 59, 61
organized violence *see* violence, organized

Panama Canal 83
particular general theory 53
passion 6, 14, 16
peace 6, 58, 70, 77, 114, 116; and war 23, 24, 29, 41; *see also* war
Peace of Westphalia (1648) 20–1
Pearl Harbour attack (1941) 85, 92
peer competitor 163
Peloponnesian War (431–404 BC) 25, 48, 86
Pershing, General John J. 'Blackjack' 85
Petraeus, General David 124
Pinker, S. 28, 127
Poland 81
policy 4, 15, 36, 67, 87, 146; defence 70, 129; and function of theory 55, 56; politics of 5–6; and strategy 57, 64, 84, 99–100; and war 25, 32, 34, 36, 37, 40, 42
policy ends 5, 11, 13, 15, 29, 62, 112, 144; *see also* policy
political assumptions 55, 115, 135
political culture 81, 144, 149, 153
political process 11, 12, 20, 56, 139; culture 98, 99; domestic 98; function of theory 55–6; power and passion 14–15, 16; security 18–19, 21; and strategy/strategy-making 23–4, 57, 65, 68, 71, 75; war 39, 42, 45, 46; *see also* politics
politics: concept 10, 36; and culture 102; and defence planning 126–40; domestic and external 29–31; domestic to a degree 148–9; and function of theory 55–6; game of 146; history and geography 91–3; and human nature 118–19; international 141–2, 148; military command for political control 41–3; and morality 146–7; of policy 5–6; political complications 146–7; political context 24–6; strategic future 156–7; and strategy *see* strategy and politics; and war 23–6, 33–4, 40, 43–7, 66; world political system 26, 82, 144, 149; *see also* policy; political process; strategy
Politik (Clausewitz) 4

176 *Index*

Porter, Patrick 8
power 14–16; balance of power 12, 15, 26, 27; circumstance 105; civil–military relations 114–15; concept 11, 14; of context 79–80; cyber power 74; and passion 6, 14, 16; power conversion challenge 67; unbalanced continental 72
power politics 29–30
pre-emption/prevention 163
preference, cultural 98
progress 59
prudence concept 2, 6, 8, 52, 95, 157; adaptability 76–7; civil–military relations 113, 114, 115, 116, 117, 120, 121, 123; defence planning 127, 129, 131, 133, 134, 135, 138, 139–40; history and geography 79, 81, 85, 90; morality 144, 145, 146, 149, 150–1, 152, 153, 154; politics, power and security 10, 12, 16, 18, 19, 20; strategy-making 64, 65, 67, 69, 71, 72, 73, 74, 75; and war 26, 32, 39, 40, 41, 42, 45, 46, 47
public mood 149
Putin, Vladimir 62, 89, 96, 99, 129, 135, 137, 145, 147, 152, 160

RAF (Royal Air Force) 51
Reagan, Ronald 3, 33
Red China 60
regular warfare 27, 163
reparation 163
resistance 31, 131
retreat 115
revenge, desire for 85
revolution 47, 60; nuclear 87–8
Revolution in Military Affairs (RMA) 47, 163
Romanov dynasty, Russia (1613–1917) 88
Rome/Roman Empire 7, 20, 91, 126
Rommel, Erwin 134
Roosevelt, F. D. 13, 152
Rousseau, Jean-Jacques 148
Royal Air Force (RAF) 51
Russia 72, 76, 99; and Crimea 146–7, 160; Empire 135, 137; geography 80–1, 88, 90; Great Patriotic War (1941–5) 88, 89; Kremlin 89, 96; morality issues 146–7, 150; Mother Russia 88, 89–90; post-Communist 89; purchase of Alaska by USA 83; and Second World War 98; strategic history 92–3; and Ukraine 40, 62, 147; *see also* Putin, Vladimir; Soviet Union, former

sailors 54
SALT (Strategic Arms Limitation Talks) 88, 163
Saxons 90
Schlieffen Plan 163
science 31

sea lines of communication 163
Second Indochina War *see* Vietnam War (1959–75)
Second World War 1, 2, 6, 15, 25, 32, 33, 38, 39, 58, 99; and Britain 26, 33, 68, 91, 93, 99, 150–1; D-Day (1944) 13, 14, 69; defence planning 133, 134; history and geography 81, 86; Pearl Harbour attack (1941) 85, 92; politics, power and security 13–14, 15; strategy-making 68, 69, 70, 112; *see also* First World War; Hitler, Adolf; Luftwaffe; Nazi Germany; war; Wehrmacht
security 16–21, 48; collective/community 127, 162; concept 17–18, 36, 55; and defence planning 133–4; dilemma 18; and ethics 153–4; and function of theory 54–5; global trade and finance 74; 'journey's end,' akin to 19; and morality 143, 144; national security concept 55, 80, 97–8; as product or commodity 10; uncertainty 17, 21; vagueness of concept 55
Security Council of United Nations 30
self-defence 30
Sherman, General William Tecumseh 112
SLBMs (submarine-launched ballistic missiles) 106, 163
Smith, M. L. R. 5, 14
Smith, Sir Rupert 93
Social Anthropology 101
social media 56
social science theory 111
SOF (Special Operations Forces) 122–3, 163
Soldier and the State, the (Huntington) 111
soldiers 67, 99, 121; and culture 100–1; defence planning 135–6; and theory for practice 50, 57, 58; and war 31, 33, 37, 41; *see also* war
South Korea 2
South Vietnam 151
Soviet Operational-Manoeuvre Groups, North German plain 73
Soviet Union, former 33, 43, 70, 72, 81, 83, 87–8, 150; *see also* Cold War; Russia
Special Operations Forces (SOF) 122–3, 163
Spykman, Nicholas John 79, 80, 82, 83, 114
stability 163
Stalin, Joseph 68, 70, 83, 85, 129; purges 88–9
Stamford Bridge, Battle of (1066) 90
state sovereignty 20–1
stereotyping 100–1
Stoker, Donald 83–4, 112
Strachan, Hew 36, 46
strategic advantage 41, 58, 147
strategic analysis 14, 66, 130; and culture 100, 102, 106
Strategic Arms Limitation Talks (SALT) 88, 163

strategic behaviour 30, 91, 130; and culture 102, 109; and war 35, 39
strategic choice 17, 20, 47, 62, 80, 113, 148, 161; and culture 100, 107; and theory for practice 55, 61, 62
strategic competence 19, 27, 45, 67, 113; challenges 24–5
strategic corporal 24
strategic effect 34, 39, 69, 70
strategic failure 13, 86, 145
strategic future: concepts 156–61; historical context 159–60; human nature 158–9; politics rules 156–7; surprise 160–1
strategic history 17, 83, 84, 91, 163; concept 51; context 20–1; and culture 102, 105; defence planning 126, 132–3; future 130; global 137; modern 54; and morality 141, 153, 158; and strategy-making 64, 65, 67, 68, 70, 74, 76; and theory for practice 51, 54, 60; and war 25, 27, 28, 32, 39, 47; *see also* history
strategic moment 163
strategic performance 1, 2, 25, 32, 51, 112
strategic practice vii, 87, 144, 161; civil–military relations 112, 113; politics, power and security 13, 19, 20; theory 53, 61; and war 24, 25, 27
strategic studies 15, 36, 37, 44
strategic ways 5, 6, 13, 29, 77, 121, 134; strategy-making 65, 66
strategy: as adversarial concept and practice 20, 48, 61, 142; as art 12, 31, 42, 61; concept 11, 113, 123, 143; context 69–71, 79, 119–20, 143; and culture 95, 96, 97; discipline of 112–13; function 43, 46, 52; and future *see* strategic future; general strategic theory *see* general strategic theory; grand *see* grand strategy; logic of 156–7; military *see* military strategy; and morality 144–6; no rules for 144–6; operational and strategic argument 24; operational consumption of 121–3; and policy 57, 64, 84, 99–100; and political process 23–4, 57; and politics *see* strategy and politics; practice of *see* strategic practice; in Second World War 112; security as purpose of 54–5; 'so what?' question 96, 97, 101, 122; and theory *see* theory and strategy; war and warfare 23–4, 36, 42; weakness 5, 119; *see also* politics; strategy-making
strategy and politics 11, 12, 50; and culture 95, 108; strategy-making 64, 68; temporal dimension 136; and timing 147–8; war 20, 23–4, 34, 37–8
strategy bridge 12, 57, 84, 88, 118
strategy-making 64–78, 80, 113, 127; assumptions 64, 65, 69, 70, 71–5, 77;

context of strategy 69–71; E, W, M formula 66, 67; genius 67–8, 69, 70; hierarchy 96; holistic understanding 64–5; military means 65, 66, 67, 77; operations 65, 67, 70; and personality 68; and political process 71, 75; as process 65–9; prudence concept 64, 65, 67, 69, 71, 72, 73, 74, 75, 76–7; strategic history 64, 65, 67, 68, 70, 74, 76; strategic ways 65, 66; strategy and politics 64, 68
submarine-launched ballistic missiles (SLBMs) 106, 163
Sudetenland, Czechoslovakia 15, 32, 33
superpower antagonism 27
superpowers 27, 72, 87, 152
Svechin, Alexandr 42, 112–13, 144
Syracuse, Athenian expedition to (Peloponnesian War) 25

tactical expediency 75
tactics 12, 37, 84, 163; and strategy/strategy-making 3, 67, 70; theory for practice 51, 57, 58–9, 60
Taiping Rebellion, China (1850–64) 38
Taliban 115
terrorism 163; *see also* fanaticism; ISIS (Islamic State of Iraq and Syria); Jihadists
theory 25, 33–4, 61; education, doctrine and training 59–61; function 54–9, 63; general and specific 52; guidance 61–3; Marxist 88; military 27–8, 52, 111; for practice 50–63; and strategy *see* theory and strategy
theory and strategy 27, 51, 85, 127; civil–military relations 111; functional theory of strategy 52; general theory of strategy *see* general strategic theory; logic in 12; strategic future 157–8; strategy puzzle, explaining 54–9
thermonuclear weapons 88, 163
Third Reich 13, 16
threat identification 12
Thucydides 17, 86; motivation categories 3, 14, 15, 32, 42, 47, 48, 77, 147, 149, 158–9; and war 25, 31, 42, 43, 47
timing issues 147–8
total war 163
trade, global 74
training manuals 59, 60
Treaty of Utrecht (1713) 39, 90
Treaty of Versailles (1919) 25, 85
triad, strategic forces 163
tribalism, in military 99; tribal loyalties 116–18
Truman, Harry S. 152
truth, strategic theory as 52
tsarism 72
Turkish Empire 27, 38
Turkish Empire, Arab Revolt (1917–18) 27

178   *Index*

Ukraine 40, 62, 129, 147
ultima ratio regis (final answer of king/
    sovereign) 116
uncertainty 4, 17, 21, 55, 64, 72, 119, 145, 151,
    160; and culture 107, 108; defence planning
    126–7, 132, 133, 134, 135, 136, 137, 138;
    evidence 103–4; politics, power and security
    10, 16, 17, 18, 21; and war 32, 41
unequal dialogue 120, 121, 136
ungoverned space 163
United Kingdom *see* Britain
United Nations 30
United States 26, 72, 128; Afghanistan and
    Iraq, intervention in 1, 4, 24, 37, 42, 43, 63,
    69, 86, 87, 103, 112, 114, 121, 122, 123,
    129; American Civil War (1861–5) 38, 51,
    70, 83, 84, 86, 87, 112, 121; Army Rangers
    117; civil–military relations 115–16, 119,
    121, 122; Commander in Chief of the
    armed forces, US President as 84; and
    culture 81, 99, 100; and defence 47, 128;
    geography 80, 82–3; Marine Corps 115,
    117; national security concept 55, 80; Pearl
    Harbour attack (1941) 85, 92; and Vietnam
    War 4, 32, 43, 62, 86, 87, 103, 105, 112,
    115, 122, 123, 129, 151; War of
    Independence 83; White House 84, 121,
    122; *see also* Cold War

Venn diagrams 13, 14
Vietcong 32, 60
Vietnam War (1959–75) 4, 32, 43, 62, 86, 87,
    129, 151; civil–military relations 112, 115,
    122, 123; and culture 103, 105
violence: against civilians 143; organized 23,
    41, 47–8 *see also* war

Waffen SS 98
war 15, 23–49; adversarial nature of 31, 42,
    46, 65, 66, 148; aims 34; battle 37–41; civil
    wars 38, 50; concept 40; context 26, 40;
    continuity in nature with change in
    character 47–8; defence planning 137–8;
    definition 164; domestic and foreign policy
    29–31; as a duel 40, 46; enemy,
    understanding 31–3; episodic antagonism
    28; European 38, 39; 'grammar' and 'logic'
    of (Clausewitz) 40, 42, 46, 54, 132, 138;

hierarchy 36–7; inter-state 28, 29, 38;
    irregular 27, 28; laws of 30; limited 41–3;
    major 37–8; military command for political
    control 41–3; motives 23, 38, 41; and peace
    23, 24, 29, 41, 70; and policy 32, 34, 36, 37,
    40, 42; and politics/political process 23–6,
    33–4, 39, 40, 42, 43–7, 66; and prudence
    concept 39, 40, 41, 42, 45, 46, 47; separate
    worlds of strategy and politics 34–5; small
    wars 37; and strategic history 25, 27, 28, 32,
    39, 47; strategy and politics 20, 23–4, 34,
    37–8; strategy-making 70; varieties of 43–7;
    vs. warfare 40–1; war-like, coercive
    behaviour 40, 45–6; *see also* civil–military
    relations; conflict; defence planning;
    fighting; soldiers; violence, organized; war;
    warfare
warfare 24, 34, 37, 39, 42, 43, 47, 50, 66;
    consequences 30–1; cyber warfare 74;
    defence planning 132, 137; irregular 28, 30,
    37, 142, 163; joint 54, 163; regular 27, 163;
    vs. war 40–1; *see also* war
War of Independence, United States 83
War of Spanish Succession (1701–14) 12, 39,
    72, 91
War Studies (Britain) 36
Waterloo, Battle of (1815) 39
weapons: cyber weapons 74, 158; of mass
    destruction 38, 151, 164; nuclear *see* nuclear
    weapons; quantity 129–30; thermonuclear
    88, 163
Wehrmacht 14, 70, 120, 134; *see also* Nazi
    Germany; Second World War
Wellington, Duke of (Arthur Wellesley) 53,
    58, 91
Wilhelm II, Kaiser 76, 87
William the Conqueror 43–4
Wilson, Woodrow 85
Winton, Harold 52
WMD (weapons of mass destruction) 38,
    151, 164
world political system 26, 82, 144, 149
world wars 26, 38; *see also* First World War;
    Second World War

youth radicalization, Islamism 73

Zhukov, Georgy 89